ISBN
157076046 2

MORE CROSS-TRAINING

Also by Jane Savoie

Cross-Train Your Horse:
Simple Dressage for Every Horse, Every Sport

That Winning Feeling!
Program Your Mind for Peak Performance

That Winning Feeling! Audios
Tape 1: *Choose Your Future*
Tape 2: *Learning Relaxation and Imaging Skills*

The Half Halt–Demystified! Videos
Tape 1: *Learning the Half Halt*
Tape 2: *Putting Your Horse on the Bit*

MORE CROSS-TRAINING

BOOK TWO

Build a Better Performance Horse with Dressage

JANE SAVOIE

PHOTOGRAPHS RHETT B. SAVOIE
DRAWINGS SUSAN E. HARRIS AND PATRICIA PEYMAN NAEGELI

Foreword by Anne Kursinski

Trafalgar Square Publishing
North Pomfret, Vermont

First published in 1998 by
Trafalgar Square Publishing
North Pomfret, Vermont 05053

Susan Harris' drawings reprinted with permission of Macmillan General Reference, from *Horse Gaits, Balance and Movement* by Susan E. Harris. A Howell Book House publication. Copyright © 1993 by Susan E. Harris.

Library of Congress Cataloging-in-Publication Data

Savoie, Jane.
        More cross-training ; build a better performance horse with dressage /
Jane Savoie : photographs, Rhett Savoie : drawings, Susan Harris and Patty Naegeli.
                    p.   cm.
        Includes bibliographical references and index.
        ISBN: 1-57076-090-X
        1. Dressage.   2. Horses—Training   I. Title
SF309.5.S4   1998
798.2'3—dc21   98-27214
                                                               CIP

Cover and book design by Carrie Fradkin, C Design
Typeface: Poppl-Pontifex and Tiepolo

Printed in Hong Kong

10 9 8 7 6 5 4 3 2 1

Dedication

To my family who has given me unconditional love through thick and thin

Rhett Savoie

David and Lorraine Kaplan

Jack and Rhoda Cimino

Linda Drukman

Table of Contents

Acknowledgements   *ix*
Foreword by Anne Kursinski   *xi*
Author's Note   *xiii*

STAGE THREE: THE PROFESSIONALS' SECRET   *1*

CHAPTER ONE
   The Half-Halt   *3*

CHAPTER TWO
   Connection   *27*

STAGE FOUR: FANCY STUFF!   *53*

CHAPTER THREE
   Float Like a Butterfly—Self-carriage   *55*

CHAPTER FOUR
   Coiling the Spring—The Collected Gaits   *71*

CHAPTER FIVE
   Going Sideways to Develop Collection   *85*

CHAPTER SIX
   More Lateral Movements   *115*

CHAPTER SEVEN
   Shifting into Second Gear—
   The Medium and Extended Gaits   *135*

CHAPTER EIGHT

Flying Changes   *155*

CHAPTER NINE

Typical Problems Solved by Using "Fancy Stuff"   *177*

CHAPTER TEN

Putting it All Together: How to Organize
a Logical, Systematic, Daily Work Session   *199*

Afterword   *223*
Glossary   *225*
Suggested Reading   *231*
Index   *233*
Illustration Credits   *238*

Acknowledgements

A project like these two books is rarely done alone and this one is no exception. It's my distinct pleasure to thank all of the talented people who helped me with their time, effort, skill, and support.

To the gifted riders and gracious owners who generously allowed themselves and their horses to be photographed showing both the "do's" and the "don'ts:"

Michele Bump
Carole Ann Cahill
Lynda Cameron
Jamie Cripps
Deborah Dean-Smith
Amy Foss
Christopher Hickey
Ruth Hogan-Poulsen
Gerri Jenkyn
Renate Kundrun
Claire Talbot
Kelly Weiss

To my husband, Rhett Savoie, for his skill behind the camera and his unfailing patience during this massive project. Rhett, you can finally walk through the living room again without having to tiptoe through the wall-to-wall carpet of manuscript pages, photographs, and illustrations.

To my publisher, Caroline Robbins, who sweated shoulder to shoulder with me for six years over the creation of these books. During that time she worked tirelessly as my editor, conscience, supporter, and most importantly, my friend. I could always count on her to be the voice of reason when I couldn't see things clearly.

To Martha Cook of Trafalgar Square Publishing for her many contributions to this project. She wears many hats and they all fit comfortably. Thank you, Martha, for all your efforts but especially for your special ability of always making me feel that I was your most important project even when you were buried in something else.

To Lynn Palm Pittion-Rossillon and Anne Kursinski for agreeing to write forewords for Book One and Book Two, respectively. I consider it a great honor as I have tremendous admiration for both the skill and training philosophies of these two women.

To the following trainers who I have had the very great privilege of working with:

Linda Jaskiel-Brown, for introducing me to the joy of dressage

Robert Dover, my "brother", for being the major influence in my education by teaching me the priniciples as well as the art of dressage

Cindy Sydnor, whose elegance I constantly strive to emulate and whose teaching style set the pattern for my own

Pam Goodrich, for helping me to think creatively

The late Herbert Rehbein, for his pure genius on a horse

Sue Blinks, for inspiring me with her loving approach to training. She's a shining example that excellence and kindness do, in fact, go hand in hand.

To Susan Harris, for generously allowing us to use her brilliant drawings from her book *Horse Gaits, Balance and Movement.*

To Patty Naegeli, whose lighthearted illustrations not only educate but also remind us that riding is supposed to be fun.

To my dear friend Ann Kitchel, who graciously allowed me to take over her arena at Huntington Farm during the photo shoots.

To all my friends who supported and commiserated with me through each "final" rewrite. I love you all.

Foreword

I am delighted to write a foreword to Jane Savoie's excellent second book on cross-training with dressage—*More Cross-Training: Build A Better Performance Horse With Dressage.* Although I'm a hunter and jumper rider and coach, not a dressage specialist, her philosophy and teaching methods are very similar to my own.

I use dressage daily when riding my horses both young and old. I honestly don't know of any better way to communicate and become "one" with them. Dressage is the basic language—words, sentences and paragraphs—that I use constantly to encourage my horses to become physically stronger, lighter in self-carriage, supple, obedient, and more beautiful and pleasurable to ride.

Everything I do when jumping, I practice before on the flat—lengthening, shortening, turning left and right with a minimum amount of effort. (As I say in all my teaching clinics: "If you can't ride the horse forward, backward, and turn in both directions on the flat, you will not be able to do so over fences.") I don't often jump my horses between shows—and my experienced horses *only* at shows—because I keep them fit and "elastic" with dressage work, starting them in a "long and low" frame, then building up to collection.

In the 1970's, I rode jumpers for Jimmy Williams at The Flintridge Riding Club in Southern California who believed strongly in training his horses and riders with dressage. I was fortunate to be there when he arranged for Hilda Gurney (1976 US Dressage Team Olympic Bronze Medalist) to come to the riding club weekly to teach me, and the other riders, the progressive steps of dressage training.

I loved riding dressage and kept at it—even showing some nice moving ex-jumpers in competition to see if they could be dressage horses. We were quite successful and sold several horses that way after we realized they were not going to have a career "over fences." Hilda helped me with my Junior Hunter Champion, Heirloom. We trained him to Grand Prix Level dressage. It was a tremendous feeling to be able to do piaffe, passage, and tempi changes with him—and then see him win in the hunter ring too!

My greatest achievement, however was Eros—a five-year old Thoroughbred who was high headed, hollow-backed and a bit wild in temperament—who, four years later, went on to win a silver medal in the show jumping competition at the Olympic Games in Atlanta in 1996. He became a pleasure and a joy to ride on the flat, and his jumping became "softer," and more "round," on course. I owe it all to the systematic training using classical dressage techniques.

Since I've been competing internationally, I have watched and learned from some of the top show jumping riders in the world—riders like Hugo Simon and Nelson Pessoa. The flat work they do is all about suppling their horses, having them truly on the aids, from tremendous collection to a racing gallop and back again.

Both Jane's first book, *Cross-Train Your Horse: Simple Dressage for Every Horse, Every Sport* and Book Two, *More Cross-Training*, are full of wonderful ideas and training techniques for riders at all levels. Enjoy!

ANNE KURSINSKI
Member of the United States Show
Jumping Team since 1978.
Silver medalist at 1996
Olympic Games in Atlanta.

Author's Note

Hello again! I'm so glad all of you "cross-trainers" have enjoyed your first taste of classical training and are excited about staying with me to see what comes next.

Let's take a moment to look back at what we covered in **Book One**, *Cross-Train Your Horse: Simple Dressage for Every Horse, Every Sport*. Was it a surprise to you to find out that you didn't necessarily have to ride a Warmblood or wear a top hat and shadbelly coat in order to "do dressage?" The results of my survey of experts from all riding disciplines showed a unanimous agreement that dressage is for every horse and every rider. After all, who *doesn't* enjoy riding a horse who is calm, willing, and obedient?

Training in Book One started with a discussion of longeing—both its role in your horse's education and in helping you develop an independent seat so you can become a more effective trainer. The "meat" of the first book focused on your horse's work under saddle. It was there that I introduced the first two of my four stages of training. Stage One was what I call *Dressage 101*. As with any good introductory course, its discussion of **the Basics** laid a solid foundation from which you could branch off into any discipline.

Stage Two delved into the nuts and bolts of training—all the transitions, figures, and movements you'd want to do with your horse to have a responsive partner who is fun to ride.

Some riders are perfectly content to stop at the end of Stage Two. (I had hoped, however, that some would be curious enough to take a look at what can be built on such a solid foundation— and if you are reading this second book, it seems that is the case!).

After all, at this point, you should have a happy, responsive horse who knows quite a lot: he understands about going forward and being straight; he accepts a contact with your hands so you can communicate with him through the reins; he moves in a regular rhythm and a steady tempo in all three paces; he can do transitions, circles and turns, back up, lengthen his stride, and go sideways. You've also learned how to use all these movements to solve some simple training problems.

Now that you've stayed with me, here's what is in store for you in this book. Stage Three is particularly exciting because it lets you in on "the professionals' secret." This secret is the **half-halt**. With it, you'll soon be able to put your horse "on the bit," which will add a whole new dimension to your training; it will enhance everything you already know how to do by making both you and your horse more physically comfortable. Once he is on the bit, your horse's back will feel springy and easier to sit on, he'll move more fluidly, and this "connection" from his back end to his front end will set up both of you for even greater things.

Knowing how to give a half-halt and put your horse on the bit will make it easy for you to go on to Stage Four—*Fancy Stuff!*. This final stage addresses the issue of self-carriage, which is the ultimate goal of dressage. Self-carriage enables you to bring back, to the *ridden* horse, the beauty of movement he has when he's at liberty. Your half-halt allows you to rebalance him so that his forehand is lighter and freer, thus making his movement just as expressive as he is when out cavorting in his field.

The information in Stage Four brings you through the work that is required in dressage tests at Third Level in the United States and Medium Level in the United Kingdom This includes collected, medium and extended gaits, advanced lateral movements, and flying changes. I stop there in this book, because that's all you'll really need to know to incorporate classical training into your regular program. You won't have to do canter pirouettes, piaffe, and passage in order to effectively cross-train with dressage.

I'm sure you're eager to begin, but before we get started, I want to mention a few "housekeeping" notes that will help you get the most from this book.

In Book One, I told you that you didn't need a real dressage arena to cross-train. This is also true of the work in this book. It can be done anywhere—on the trail, in a field, paddock, or in a ring. However, I do encourage you to try to school in the space defined by a regulation-sized dressage arena with letters placed at the right spots (see Chapter Ten).

This will be particularly important when we get to advanced lateral movements, because riding accurately to specific points insures that you develop your horse equally on both sides of his body.

Dressage tests and figures are officially described in metric measurements, so in order to get you into "dressage mode," in this book I'll use meters instead of feet when discussing school figures, distances, and dimension.

I want to mention that nearly all the movements and exercises are done with the horse going to the left. I say "nearly," because toward the end of this book there are some exceptions.

Are you ready? I hope I've whetted your appetite for what lies ahead. Tighten your girths and fasten your chin straps! Whether you wear breeches or chaps, ride Quarter Horses, warmbloods, or Arabians, I invite you to continue with me on what I hope will be an intriguing journey into classical training.

J.S.

STAGE THREE

THE PROFESSIONALS' SECRET

D o you ever wonder why you struggle with movements and transitions that professional riders seem to do effortlessly? Are you puzzled by the fact that your trainer's horse can be persuaded to march by large rocks, farm equipment, umbrellas, and all manner of scary objects, while your horse is overwhelmed by his flight instinct?

Well, here in Stage Three, you're about to discover the secret of professional trainers. This is an exciting point in the education of both you and your horse. In fact, if I were told that I could only teach you one concept to help you train your horse successfully, I would choose the information you're about to learn in this stage.

Here's what professionals know that you don't. They know the formula for "putting their horses on the aids" (their horses react instantly and obediently to invisible signals); this secret is a versatile aid called the **half-halt**.

In Chapter One, I will dissect the half-halt into manageable pieces and put it back together for you in an understandable, user-friendly way. I'll even give you tips on what to do if your horse just doesn't seem to be getting it.

Then, in Chapter Two, I'll show you how to use the half-halt to **connect** your horse—also known as **putting him on the bit**. You'll love this part, because when a horse is **"on the bit,"** not only is he more comfortable to ride but it's also a lot easier for you to communicate with each other. This is the beginning of your being able to reach a whole new level of working together happily.

The pure joy and expressive movement of a horse at play.

CHAPTER ONE

The Half-Halt

W hat, you may well ask, is a half-halt? How can I possibly do a half-halt? And why would I want to anyway?

Well, like Robert Dover, I too feel that the half-halt is the most essential tool in riding. Learning how to give a half-halt not only allows you to take charge of your horse's body and mind whenever you need to, but it also enables you to proceed further in the development of your horse as an athlete.

The word "half-halt" itself often creates confusion. The term is something of a misnomer because the half-halt really has nothing to do with *halts* at all. In fact (as Olympic dressage rider Lendon Gray suggests), it might help you to call it a "half-go" since every half-halt should contain the feeling of *adding* power from the horse's hind legs up to your hand. But more about that later.

Think of the half-halt as an *aid*. You could call it a "bringing-to-attention" aid. It will help you rebalance your horse, mentally or physically, whenever you need to. Think of this aid in the same way that you use your outside leg behind the girth as an aid to signal your horse to canter, or you close both legs near the girth as an aid to ask your horse to do a transition from the walk to the trot.

One major difference, however, is that you use the half-halt as an aid far more often. You use it every time your horse needs a reminder to pay attention to you, either because he's distracted by his surroundings or because you want to warn him that you are about to ask for a new movement. You give a half-halt to rebalance him every time he's heavy on the forehand, leaning the wrong way around corners, yanking at the reins, sticking his head up in the air, feeling stiff in his body, or is otherwise resistant and uncomfortable to ride.

"The half-halt is the most important concept in all of riding, because it calls the horse to a perfect state of balance, harmony and attention."

Robert Dover,
Three-time Olympic
and World Equestrian
Games bronze medalist
in dressage

1.1

Trying to train a horse to be more athletic without a half-halt is like trying to nail a board to a wall without a hammer. Impossible! You don't have all your tools.

As an instructor I often meet riders who blame themselves when they have a hard time controlling their horses. They think the fault is theirs because they're not properly coordinated or talented enough to ride and train as effectively as a professional does. Well, if they haven't learned how to give a half-halt, they're right!

After all, imagine someone giving you a board and some nails—but no hammer—and asking you to nail that board to a wall. It would be quite a task for you to put the board up. Well, trying to train a horse to be more athletic without the half-halt as an aid is like trying to nail a board to a wall without a hammer. It's pretty difficult because you don't have all your *tools* (fig. 1.1).

So I tell my students not to be so hard on themselves. I remind them, "You're not born knowing how to give a half-halt and your horse wasn't born knowing how to respond to one!" But with what you've been taught up to this point in **Book One**, you're ready to learn. I'll teach you in a clear-cut, step-by-step approach. Then it will be up to you to train your horse.

PREPARING TO GIVE A HALF-HALT

It's essential that you know how to give a half-halt because when you ride your horse you are always dealing with the issue of *balance*. Since your horse was not "designed" to carry weight on his back, he often loses his balance with a rider on top. The half-halt is the key—the *aid* that you use—to restore lost balance (fig. 1.2).

As we begin Stage Three, the half-halt is simply used to *regain* lost balance. Later on in Stage Four (Chapter Three), I'll describe how more advanced riders give half-halts to *maintain* balance, by using them while preparing for new movements and exercises.

In Book One, *Cross-Train Your Horse: Simple Dressage For Every Horse, Every Sport,* I laid the groundwork for a half-halt; I told you about riding your horse forward and straight, in a regular rhythm, with an inviting contact. This groundwork must be established before you can give a successful half-halt. In other words, you can execute a half-halt only when you have the following prerequisites:

Horse

1. **Forward**—not only over the ground but also *"thinking"* forward.
2. **Straight**—with the hind feet following the tracks of the front feet and the spine overlapping the line of travel.
3. **Rhythm**—steady and regular.

1.2
Since a horse is not designed to carry weight on his back, he can easily lose his balance like this horse does in a canter-to-trot transition.

Rider

Contact with the horse's mouth is inviting and sympathetic because it is firm, consistent, elastic, symmetrical and with a straight line from the bit to the hand to the elbow.

If you lose any of these qualities while giving the half-halt aid, stop what you're doing and re-establish whichever prerequisite is lacking. Only then can you try again to give the aid. For instance, if you give a half-halt and the horse stops *thinking* forward, you'll need to go through the process of putting him in front of the leg again before continuing to use half-halts to correct any of your horse's resistances.

The Aids for a Half-Halt

Let's break down the half-halt—or if you prefer, the "half-go"—into it's parts. The half-halt itself is the combination of the driving aids (both legs and seat), the outside rein, and the bending aids (both legs and the inside rein), maintained for about three seconds.

During those three seconds, close both legs and push with your seat as if asking for that 100% wholeheartedly forward response that you practiced when you put the horse in front of the leg (see Chapter Six in Book One). This is the "go" part of your half-go. But, rather than allowing the horse to go more forward as you did then, receive and contain this energy almost immediately by closing your outside hand in a fist. This becomes the **rein of opposition.** Make sure you *feel* the energy surge forward into the rein just before you actually close this outside hand.

By using your driving aids a fraction of a second before you use your rein aids, you ride your horse from *back to front.* This is your goal no matter what type of riding you do, because it's the only way

1.3

When giving a half-halt, think about inflating a balloon. Your driving aids blow it up, and closing your outside hand in a fist puts the knot at the end. If you close your hand before you drive your horse forward, you'll tie the knot before you inflate the balloon. If you use your driving aids without closing your fist, you let the air whoosh out of the balloon. In both cases, your half-halt doesn't work.

you can honestly **connect** your horse and make him more athletic and obedient. If you're preoccupied with creating an artificial "head-set" by fiddling with your hands, you'll be riding your horse from *front to back*, and you'll never truly be in charge. Remember, she who controls the hind legs–the "engine"–controls the horse. Always ride from *back to front* by directing the power from the hind legs forward into your hands.

To the naked eye, it will appear that you use all of these aids simultaneously. However, freeze-frame photography should show you using your driving aids first, then closing your outside hand, and finally, if necessary, vibrating your inside rein to keep the horse straight. (Remember, "straight" means straight on a line and bent along the arc on a curve.)

It is absolutely necessary for you to send your horse forward with your driving aids a fraction of a second before you close your outside hand. If you close your outside hand before you use your driving aids (or even exactly at the same time, for that matter), it's like picking up the telephone before it rings–no one is there!

To help you imagine this concept, think about a balloon. Your driving aids blow up the balloon, and closing your outside hand in a fist puts the knot at the end of it to keep it full of air. So, to give a good half-halt, use your seat and legs first, and then close your outside hand just as you'd inflate a balloon first and then tie the knot (fig. 1.3).

The Aids for a Half-Halt (on a circle to the left)

Seat: Stretch up and use your seat in a driving way as if pushing the back of the saddle toward the front of the saddle. Be sure to stay sitting in a vertical position when you push with your seat. Leaning behind the vertical can cause the horse to stiffen or hollow his back, and his head and neck will probably go up in the air as well.

Legs: close your legs steadily as if squeezing toothpaste out of a tube.

Outside rein (right rein): close your hand in a fist.

Inside rein (left rein): vibrate, if necessary, to keep the horse's neck straight.

The aids are applied *almost simultaneously,* but basically they should be thought of in this order:

Driving aids first to create energy;

Outside rein second to contain energy;

Inside rein third, if necessary, to keep the neck straight.

Apply these aids for about three seconds by increasing the pressure of your legs and reins so that it is slightly more than the maintenance pressure you have when your legs are softly draped around your horse's sides and your hands have a firm but gentle feel of his mouth. After you give the half-halt, *relax.* This relaxing—the finish of the aid—is as important as the aid itself because it is the horse's reward. When you relax, let your legs rest lightly on your horse's sides again, keep correct contact with his mouth, and continue riding your circle.

For simplicity's sake, when first learning the half-halt, try it without the push from your seat. Just use your legs for the driving aids. Later, when you get comfortable with the timing and coordination of the half-halt, you can add the push with your seat toward the end of the three-second count as part of your driving aids.

You may have noticed that I said (when I laid out the aids above) that using the inside rein is optional. Since three seconds is a long time to keep your outside hand closed in a fist, some horses might bend their necks to the outside. (This usually happens going in one direction more than the other—when the horse's soft side is on the outside.) If this does happen, the horse obviously isn't straight anymore. He needs to be straight in order for your half-halt to be effective.

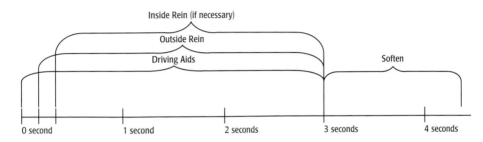

Half-Halt Timeline

1.4 to 1.6
Keeping the Neck Straight
During the Half-Halt

1.4

Amy Foss and Special Effects are going to the left with his soft side on the inside. Since Special Effects' neck stays straight in front of his body as Amy sends him forward through her outside hand during the half-halt, she doesn't need to use any inside rein. Her driving aids and outside rein are doing the job perfectly.

To prevent the horse from bending his neck to the outside, give a few soft squeezes on the inside rein at the same time that your outside hand is closed. Use of this inside rein is optional because its use depends on whether or not your horse bends to the outside.

If you're not sure how much inside rein to use or whether to use it at all, just apply a half-halt without it. Close your two legs and outside hand for three seconds and watch your horse's neck while you're doing it. If his neck stays straight, you don't need to use any inside rein when giving the half-halt. If the neck bends a bit to the outside, you need a little inside rein. If it bends a lot to the outside, you'll need even more inside rein during the next half-halt.

To sum up, the degree to which your horse's neck bends to the outside tells you how much inside rein to use in order to keep him straight (figs. 1.4 to 1.6).

1.5

When Amy combines her driving aids and outside rein during this half-halt going to the right with his stiff side on the inside, Special Effects' neck bends slightly to the outside. The bend in his neck tells her she'll need to use a little inside rein next time she gives a half-halt in this direction in order to keep his neck straight. This is what generally happens when the horse's soft side is on the outside.

1.6

In this case during the half-halt, his neck bends a lot to the outside. During the next half-halt, Amy needs to use an even greater influence of the inside rein to counteract the action of her closed outside hand.

If you find the previous explanation of the half-halt at all confusing, trying thinking about it this way instead. The half-halt is a marriage of the driving aids, the bending aids, and the outside rein. The outside rein is very important because it opposes too much speed from the driving aids, and too much bend from the bending aids.

In other words, if you applied the driving aids (seat and both legs) and bending aids (inside rein and both legs) to their extreme without adding the outside rein, your horse would run very fast on a very small circle. But the outside hand says, "You're not allowed to speed up or bend to a greater degree than you already have. Instead you must yield to the outside hand and because you're being driven, you'll bend your hind legs more."

When all three aids are correctly combined, the horse maintains his original speed and stays straight as he steps more forward under his body. He yields in front—flexing "in" (longitudinally as opposed to laterally) at the poll—to the closed outside hand, and he bends the joints of the hind legs to a greater degree. This changes his balance and **frame**, or silhouette, so that it looks more **round**. In the next chapter, you'll see that this change of balance and the resulting round frame is called "**connection**" or "**on the bit**". This is what you're looking for (figs. 1.8 to 1.11).

Robert Dover has a saying to help his students absorb the relationship between the driving and restraining aids during a half-halt. He says that if your horse slows down, you have too much "halt" (outside rein) and not enough "half" (driving aids). Alternatively, if your horse speeds up when you give a half-halt, you have too much "half," and not enough "halt."

Many riders are surprised when I tell them that the half-halt lasts for three seconds, because they have been taught that it only lasts for a moment. I tell you to do this for three seconds because I want you to use it to bend the joints of the hind legs for two to three steps.

I'm not saying that there won't be times when you give a shorter or a longer half-halt. In fact, once your horse has learned to respond correctly to the half-halt, you might apply the aid for only one second. On the other hand, if you're struggling to maintain a round frame during a transition, you can sustain it for four or five seconds. (I'll delve into variations of the half-halt at the end of this chapter.)

But, it's helpful for you as you're learning, to think of the half-halt as lasting for the amount of time it takes to inhale and exhale—about three seconds for most people. When you breathe in, you tighten your stomach and the small of your back, and the breath is like a wave that travels up your stomach into your chest. As you breathe out, your shoulders go back and down and the wave goes down your back into your seat. At the same time, close your legs. As the horse begins to move forward, you'll feel this surge of energy come into the rein. At this moment, close your outside hand in a fist. Then you can relax all the aids and proceed forward in a new state of balance and attention (fig. 1.7).

Your first task will be to teach your horse the half-halt while riding in

1.7
Using a half-halt to improve balance

a) *This horse is not in good balance. His hind legs are out behind his body and his weight is on his forehand.*

b) *As his rider gives the half-halt, the horse bends the joints of the hind legs, steps more underneath his body, and yields in front so that he comes into a better balance.*

1.8 to 1.11
The Half-Halt Sequence

1.8
This is the frame and balance that Woody adopts on his own. His hind legs are out behind his body, lazily pushing him along. His back is so hollow and low that I feel like I'm sitting in a depression. His neck is raised and stiff, and he is not flexing in at the poll.

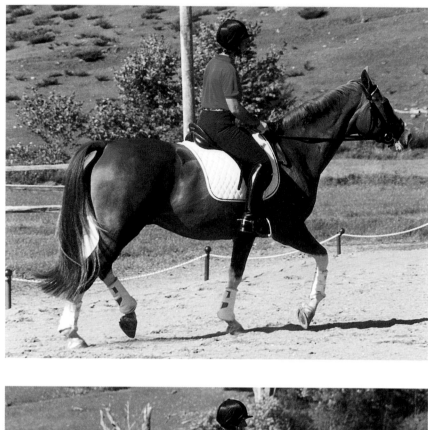

1.9
I'm starting to give a half-halt and as I use my driving aids to send him through the outside rein, the shape of his topline begins to change.

1.10

I continue to drive him through the outside rein. (Note that the contact with my outside hand is more firm than it is with my inside hand.) His hind legs are coming more underneath his body and they begin to carry rather than push.

1.11

As I finish the half-halt, Woody looks like a more compact package from tail to poll. I'd still like to see more of a "bloom" through the base of his neck just in front of his withers, and a greater degree of relaxation of the muscles on the underside of his neck, but I'm satisfied with the amount his balance has changed with my first half-halt. I'll soften the aids now and follow up with another half-halt to improve his balance even further.

1.12 to 1.15
Common Mistakes
During the Half-Halt

1.12
During this half-halt, Amy has used too much inside rein, and has also allowed her outside hand to move forward. As a result, Special Effects bends his neck too much to the inside.

each of the three paces. Start on a circle, since the curve of the circle helps the horse step through that outside rein. Usually the horse begins to understand and change his balance and frame during the very first session, although it often takes several sessions before his response is more or less confirmed.

Once you can execute a half-halt in all three paces on a curved line, follow the track of the ring and do the same thing on a straight line. If you run into difficulties, go back to the circle and review the half-halt there.

In Chapter Two, I'll explain other situations during which you can use this same half-halt to improve or maintain your horse's balance and frame. For now this is where you should start; teach your horse to respond to the half-halt during all three paces on circles and straight lines.

1.13
Here, Special Effects bends his neck to the outside of the circle because Amy isn't using enough inside rein in order to keep him straight.

COMMON MISTAKES

Since most of us work without an instructor much of the time, it's helpful to be able to recognize our mistakes by evaluating the feedback we get from our horses. By noticing what the horse does when we give a half-halt, we can improve and refine the use of this aid.

The following are the most common mistakes riders make when learning how to coordinate the "parts" of the half-halt.

1. Too much bend of the neck to the inside during the half-halt. This happens when you've used too much inside rein or not enough outside rein (fig. 1.12).

2. Too much bend of the neck to the outside. In this case you need to vibrate your inside rein more (fig. 1.13).

1.12 to 1.15
Common Mistakes
During the Half-Halt con't.

1.14
Because Amy is pulling backward on the reins during this half-halt, her horse shortens and raises his neck. Never use your arms during a half-halt. Instead, keep your hands in correct riding position in front of your body and send your horse forward with your driving aids until he meets your hands.

3. Horse shortens his neck during the half-halt (fig. 1.14). He's telling you that you've brought your arms backward while you're giving the aid. Your arms must never be drawn backward while giving a half-halt, or doing anything else for that matter. To help you avoid bringing your arms back, picture your hands in the correct position and imagine that there's an invisible shield or wall directly behind them, making it impossible for you to bring your hands closer to your body. Instead of bringing your arms back, send your horse forward with your legs, and when he *arrives* at your outside hand, close it in a fist.

4. Your horse becomes crooked by swinging his hindquarters in or out. You've probably either used unequal pressure from your legs, or your legs are not placed correctly on your horse's sides. Remember that when riding straight lines your legs should be side by side and when riding curved lines your inside leg is on the girth while your outside leg is behind the girth (fig. 1.15).

Here's a different view of Amy and Special Effects as they trot on a circle to the left. Because of the angle of the photo, you can see that during this half-halt, he has swung his hindquarters to the right and is no longer bent to the left along the arc of the circle. This can happen either because Amy has pressed harder with her left leg than with her right leg or because her left leg is placed too far behind the girth, causing her horse to yield away from it.

5. Your horse's tempo changes either faster or slower during the half halt. If you fail to "match" your driving aids with the closure of your outside hand in a fist, the horse's speed will change. By "match" I mean you should use these aids not only at the same time but to the same degree as well.

    a. If your horse goes faster, keep the same leg aids but close your outside hand more firmly.

    b. If he slows down, you've probably used more influence of outside hand than driving aids. If you feel that you didn't use too much outside hand, then your horse might have fallen behind your leg. If this is the case, interrupt riding the half-halt and go through the process of putting him in front of your leg again. Once he is solidly going forward, you can resume giving the half-halt.

6. Forgetting to relax or soften after three seconds. This causes the horse to stiffen against the aids. Even if you feel that you're not getting the desired result from your half-halt because your horse is resisting, relax after three seconds. Wait for a few seconds, then try again.

• *Helpful Hints* •

USING LENGTHENINGS TO EXPLAIN THE HALF-HALT TO YOUR HORSE

If you're having trouble teaching the half-halt to your horse, first check your prerequisites for the half-halt (page 4) and then go through the list of common rider mistakes (page 15 to 18). If that all seems fine to you but your horse still doesn't seem to understand what you're asking for, here are some additional ideas you can use to explain it to him.

First, let's talk about the uneducated horse and what he thinks he has to do when you give a half-halt. During the half-halt, your driving aids create energy and your outside rein contains that energy within the horse's body. The green horse says, "Now, wait a minute! How can you ask me to stop and go at the same time?" Since many horses tend to be lazy, if given this dilemma they opt to pay attention to the outside hand and stop or slow down rather than decide to go forward from your legs *through* that closed outside hand (fig. 1. 16).

In this case I add extra "go" to my "half-go" by using the momentum of a lengthening to give the horse the idea that he must go forward "through" the closed outside hand. But before I tell you how to do this, let me take a moment to describe this sensation of stepping through the hand. When a horse isn't stepping through the hand, he feels as if he's jammed up against it. You feel the kind of resistance or blockage you'd feel if you were trying to drive your car with the emergency brake on. However, when he steps through the hand, the contact feels rubbery and soft, the energy feels like it can flow from the hind legs through the horse's body into your hand and back to the hind legs in an uninterrupted cycle, a bit like a flywheel that continues to turn by itself because it doesn't meet any resistance. Not only can you feel when your horse steps through your hand, but you can see it as well. As your horse steps through your hand, you'll notice that his neck changes shape. It gets longer, rounder, and often lower.

1.16

During a half-halt, your legs and seat create energy while your outside rein contains that energy within the horse. The green horse says "Now, wait a minute! How can you ask me to stop and go at the same time?" You need to teach him to go forward through your closed outside hand, and the instant he does, stop giving the aid and reward him.

To use lengthenings as a way to explain to my horse how the driving aids and restraining aids can be combined, I start on a circle where I know my outside rein has to be more definite because of the bend. Then I ask for a lengthening, and when we're really "motoring" along, I close my outside hand in a fist for three seconds while maintaining the lengthening. While doing this, my inside rein is doing its usual job of keeping the horse straight—that is, I vibrate it just enough, together with my leg aids, to produce the bend needed on a circle.

If my horse doesn't become rounder, which I'm able to see by checking to see if he lowers and stretches his neck, as well as rounding it, I soften my outside hand for a moment and ask again. When the power of the lengthening carries him forward through my closed outside fist and he becomes rounder, I immediately praise generously.

Once my horse understands, I alternate between closing my outside hand when I've got a good lengthening, and applying my driving aids and closing my outside hand (a normal half-halt) while in a normal working gait. In both cases my legs close in the same way to create energy. By riding my horse from back to front in this way, I explain that every half-halt contains the feeling of a lengthening.

USING LEG-YIELDING TO EXPLAIN THE HALF-HALT

You can also use a leg-yielding exercise to teach an uneducated horse the concept of going forward through a closed outside hand. Turn onto a line that divides your ring in half lengthwise, then leg-yield over to the track that goes around the outside of the ring. Start by asking your horse to do a leg-yield from the middle of the arena over to the left, away from your right leg. (Eventually you will be doing the exercise in both directions.)

As the horse crosses over with his right hind leg, that leg not only goes sideways, but it also goes more forward toward your outside (left) hand. At some point during this leg-yield, close your outside hand in a fist for about three seconds in the same way that you do during a half-halt. The sideways and forward action of the right hind leg as well as the momentum of the body traveling to the left will help drive the horse through that closed outside hand.

As soon as you see that the horse has stepped through your outside hand because he has lowered, lengthened, and rounded his neck, praise him. In this way he has a chance to feel how to carry his body and your weight in a new position. Once he understands the concept of going forward through your outside hand during the use of the leg-yield, go back to riding the half-halt while on a straight line. By alternating this leg-

1.17 to 1.19
Using Leg Yielding to Explain the Half-Halt

1.17
Deb Dean-Smith is leg-yielding Monique from the center of the arena over to the long side. Even though Monique's back isn't visible in this photo, you can assume that it is dropped and she is stiffening against Deb's hand because her head and neck are up in the air.

yielding exercise with the usual half-halt aid, you're explaining that in both cases you're asking him to do the same thing—step through the outside rein in order to change his balance and frame (figs. 1.17 to 1.19).

USING LEG-YIELDING
TO IMPROVE THE HALF-HALT

I've used leg-yielding not only with green horses but also with stiff or tight horses who are taking short steps. I often tell my students that the neck is a barometer of what the hind legs are doing. You can read the neck to see if the hind legs are coming under the body if you think of the length of neck and stride as being proportional. If the neck is three feet long, the hind legs are taking a three-foot-long stride.

1.18

As they leg-yield over toward the track and Monique steps forward and sideways with her right hind leg into Deb's left hand, she begins to relax and lower her neck.

1.19

Monique has now stepped through Deb's hand and softly yields to it as she lowers, lengthens and rounds her neck and flexes in her poll and jaw. The picture would be perfect if her ears were level.

The other day I was helping a friend with her Grand Prix dressage horse. This horse has a lot of education, so when his rider picked up the reins, this fellow cooperatively raised and arched his neck. But the neck was very short, which told us that the hind legs weren't really coming forward. I told her to half-halt and push the hind legs further under, but the horse continued to take short, quick steps. As it turned out, he had been worked very hard two days before and then had been given a day off. His muscles were stiff and tight.

We used leg-yielding as a gentle stretching and loosening exercise. In human terms we asked him to touch his toes, but allowed him to reach them gradually by asking him to first touch his knees, and when that was easy, touch his calves, and when that was easy, touch his ankles. In equine terms, we first leg-yielded in the walk from the centerline to the long side. When that was easy, we asked for progressively steeper leg-yields. The next step was relatively gentle leg-yields from one corner of the ring to the opposite corner. When that was easy, we went from the corner to midway down the long side and back to the far corner that was on the same side as the one we started from. When that was also easy, we zig-zagged back and forth across the arena three times. All of this was done in the walk with long, slow, sweeping steps.

Finally, she straightened him and asked him to come on the bit with a half-halt. Thanks to the stretching of the muscles during the leg-yields, the range of motion of the hind legs was markedly increased, and it was easier for him to take longer strides. As the hind legs reached further under the body, the neck got proportionately longer. Unlike the young horse who didn't understand the concept of the half-halt asking him to come on the bit, this horse couldn't respond to the half-halt because of his short, tight muscles.

USING "INCREASING HALF-HALTS" FOR ACCEPTANCE OF THE OUTSIDE HAND

When you first introduce the half-halt to your horse, he may stiffen against your hand when he feels you use your outside rein. If this happens repeatedly, give an "increasing half-halt." Start with a light half-halt, but gradually increase the pressure of all the aids over the course of the three seconds. (If you need "more leg," you can tap your horse with a whip at the same time that you are using your legs and hands to the maximum.)

Now here's the important part: while you're doing this, watch your horse's neck very carefully. The moment it becomes even slightly longer, relax all of your aids. By lengthening his neck, your horse is telling you that he's starting to step through your outside hand. He should be instantly rewarded for this both by softening all of the aids and by praising him (figs. 1.20 and 1.21).

1.20 and 1.21
Using "Increasing Half-Halts"

1.20

I'm cantering on a circle to the right here. Even after several half-halts, Woody continues to stiffen against my outside rein rather than step through it. His neck is tense, short and high. Notice how the muscles on the underside of his neck are bulging rather than soft and relaxed. Also, because he is coming against my hand rather than yielding to it, he tilts his head. So I start an increasing half-halt and as I do, I keep a close eye on his neck to detect even the slightest change in its shape.

Then start again with a light half-halt, only increasing the pressure if necessary. Always start with a light half-halt rather than immediately going to a strong one, so that you give your horse the option to respond to a more subtle aid. You always want to ride using the most refined aids possible. It's not much fun for either you or your horse to ride from strength.

By way of explaining the half-halt to your horse, increasing its intensity says the following: "This is the half-halt, and it's not going away. In fact, it will become increasingly more insistent until you begin to step through my outside hand. However, the instant you begin to step through my hand, the aid will be finished and you'll be rewarded."

In this way your horse learns that when he arrives at your closed outside hand, he should soften and yield to the action of the rein. He learns

1.20 and 1.21
Using "Increasing Half-Halts" con't.

1.21
His shape is starting to change as his neck becomes slightly longer, lower, and rounder. Also, note that as he steps through my outside rein, his ears become more level. It isn't a perfect response, but the subtle changes I see and feel are my signal to immediately stop giving the half-halt and soften as his reward. Judging by the amount that his frame has changed with this increasing half-halt, I will probably be able to give a normal half-halt next time to get him to step completely through the rein.

that he has other options besides jamming up against your hand. He needs to view the hand as a barrier, but it's a penetrable barrier. He can step through it and come into a different balance and rounder frame (fig. 1.22).

Remember, your horse doesn't know about the half-halt. It's your job to teach him. If you're having difficulties, take a moment to evaluate what could be going wrong. Ask yourself some questions. Is he forward, straight, and in a good working gait? Is my contact correct? Did I use too much inside rein? Did I need to have more influence of the inside rein? Did I remember to soften after three seconds?

Through patient repetition and rewarding any effort on his part, your horse will begin to understand the half-halt better. Then you will have an incredible tool that you can use to sort out all sorts of mental and physical "imbalances." You'll be able to give your horse a "call to attention" as well as make him better balanced and, therefore, more comfortable to ride.

The "Different" Half-Halts

Here's some final food for thought on this subject of the half-halt. Do you remember when I said that the half-halt is the most essential tool in riding? Well, now we're going to take that statement to another level. At the more advanced stage of training, I want you to realize that everything you create in the horse is the result of subtle variations of the half-halt.

Over the course of the next few chapters, I'll describe several versions of this basic three-second half-halt that can be used to help you deal with all sorts of training issues. Since the half-halts are given in a slightly different way, I've assigned different names to each half-halt depending on its purpose. These are labels that I have created so that my students and I are sure we're talking about the same thing.

Here's what's in store for you. I know you'll be excited about this preview of coming attractions because you'll see how the half-halt will become the solution to many of your training woes.

In the next chapter, I discuss how the basic three-second half-halt you've just learned can be used to connect your horse or, as we say in the dressage world, put him "on the bit." I call it the **connecting half-halt**.

In Chapter Four, you'll learn how to improve self-carriage with a **collecting half-halt**. This half-halt is of greater intensity and is done with shorter reins than the "connecting" half-halt. Also, once your horse reacts correctly to the aid, you'll find that it can be as brief as one second instead of the standard three seconds.

In Chapter Nine, you'll discover how **preparatory half-halts** can engage and ready your horse for a transition. These half-halts are applied more quickly than the basic three-second half-halt. They are done in the rhythm of the gait you're in and are timed so that they are given when the hind leg you want to engage is on the ground. Generally, this is the inside hind leg for a downward transition and the outside hind leg for a canter depart.

Also in Chapter Nine, I'll show you how you can apply a **reversed half-halt** to ask your horse to take an even contact with both of your

1.22

As your horse goes forward through your outside hand (at last!), he becomes more beautiful as his balance improves, and his frame becomes more "round."

hands. The elements of this half-halt are exactly the same as the "connecting" half-halt, but you simply switch the action of your inside and outside hands.

In that chapter, I'll also describe how you can blend the basic half-halt into the aids for all the transitions, movements, and exercises that you do with your horse so you can maintain good balance each time you start something new. In this case your half-halt might end up lasting as long as five or six seconds.

KEY POINTS

🐎 A half-halt enables you to restore your horse's physical and mental balance.

🐎 There is no "halt" in a half-halt. Think of it as a "half-go."

🐎 Before you give a half-halt, your horse must be forward, straight, moving in a regular rhythm, and you must offer him an inviting contact.

🐎 The half-halt is the marriage of the driving aids, the outside rein, and the bending aids, maintained for about three seconds.

CHAPTER TWO

Connection

I n the last chapter I discussed the half-halt in a general way and taught you *how* to give this most useful aid. I also mentioned that you can use this tool to restore both *physical* and *mental* balance to your horse.

Now that you know how to do a half-halt I'm going to show you exactly how you can use the half-halt to improve one of the common physical "imbalances." The balance issue I'm going to discuss is the feeling that your horse is in two parts—the back and the front. The half-halt is used to create a bridge between these two. This is called **connection**, or in "dressage speak," **putting your horse "on the bit."**

My first reason for teaching my own students to give a half-halt is so that they can "connect" their horses. It's a priority, because I know how uncomfortable it is for me to ride a horse that's not connected, and I figure if it's uncomfortable for me, it can't be much fun for my horse. Often riders who normally bounce around in the trot and canter are surprised to discover how much easier it is to sit closely to their horses in these paces when their horses are connected.

In addition to pure comfort for both horse and rider, it's advantageous to connect your horse because he becomes more graceful and more athletic as a result of carrying himself predominantly with his topline muscles. It's exciting to start with an animal that has average movement and make him more beautiful by developing his potential as an athlete.

"When training is correct the horse always becomes more beautiful... never less so," said Alois Podhajsky, late head of the Spanish Riding School in Vienna. When your horse is connected, his back serves as the bridge between his hind legs and his front legs. As I said earlier, your horse's power, his "engine," is in the hindquarters. He needs to be connected over his back so that the energy can travel from his hind legs over his back, through his neck, and be received by your hands (fig. 2.1).

> **"Going on the bit makes any horse move better, but it's particularly important for the endurance horse so he can move in the most efficient way possible."**
>
> Becky Hart,
> World Champion
> endurance rider

2.1

Your horse's engine is in his hindquarters, which is why you must ride him from back to front. His "horsepower" comes from behind!

In this book, I am going to limit my references to **"connection"** to the phrases, **"on the bit"** and **"round frame."** Since there are lots of other terms that riders use to describe connection, I want to mention them here to avoid any confusion later. They include: **"throughness," "through his neck," "through the back," "over the back," "roundness," "round outline, shape, or frame," "packaged,"** or **"moving from the hind legs into the hands."** They can all be used synonymously with "connection," "on the bit" and "round frame." After all, a rose by any other name...!

WHAT DOES CONNECTION LOOK LIKE?

"Connection," "on the bit," "round frame": let's try to get a handle on what, to many novice dressage riders, is an elusive concept.

These terms have a physical as well as a mental connotation. Physically, when a horse is connected, his frame becomes round because his hind legs come more forward under his body with every stride as they step toward the rider's hand (fig. 2.2). This power from behind is received by the rider's hand and the result is a round shape. His back looks convex and his neck is arched. The round shape is desirable because physically it makes him more comfortable to ride and more athletic.

Mentally, a connected horse becomes more submissive and obedient because his attention is on you, and his body is more balanced so he can react to your commands.

Keep in mind that when you're trying to decide if a horse is truly on the bit, it's not enough to just look at his neck. An arched neck can be deceiving to the uneducated onlooker. Always look at the whole horse—particularly the entire topline from the hindquarters to the poll—before you make up your mind about whether or not a horse is truly round. Here's what to look for:

First, for the sake of comparison let's look at a horse that's *not* on the bit (fig. 2.3). His hind legs aren't stepping well under his body, his back looks braced and tight rather than swinging elastically, his neck is stiffly held out in front of him for balance, and his nose is poked forward. This horse can't work on the bit, because his rigid or "frozen" back doesn't function as the bridge that enables energy to be transmitted between the hindquarters and the forehand. The power coming from the hindquarters hits a roadblock and dissipates. Horses that carry themselves like this

2.2

Ruth Poulsen and Mastermind show the "round" shape of a horse that is connected. Mastermind's convex back and arched neck are the result when his hind legs come well under his body and he steps toward Ruth's hand.

2.3

When he is not "on the bit," Mastermind's hind legs don't step well underneath his body, his back looks braced, his neck is held stiffly out in front of him, and his nose is poked forward.

This photo shows Moxie connected and in horizontal balance. An imaginary line drawn from the top of her croup to her withers is basically parallel to the ground. She carries about 60% of her weight on her forehand and 40% of her weight on her hindquarters.

can be very useful and still do lots of things, but they can't be truly athletic in this frame.

Second, look at a horse that *is* on the bit (fig. 2.4). This horse shows the desirable round shape of a connected horse. Starting from back to front, which we should always do in riding because the horse's power comes from the rear, this is what a connected horse looks like:

His hind legs reach well underneath his body.

His back muscles look relaxed so his back appears raised, round, and loose rather than dropped, concave, and rigid.

His neck is long and gently arched as he stretches towards the bit.

His poll is the highest point of his neck.

His nose is slightly (about five degrees) in front of an imaginary vertical line drawn from his forehead to the ground.

This horse is also in "horizontal balance." If you look at the height of the horse's withers compared to the top of his croup, you'll notice that they are about the same—basically level. Also notice that a line drawn from the withers to the croup is parallel to the ground line. Hence the expression "horizontal balance."

2.5

Woody is also on the bit, but his shape looks quite different from Moxie's in photo 2.4. This is because he is in a more advanced state of balance. Rather than traveling on the forehand in horizontal balance as Moxie does, he shows greater self-carriage. This means that he carries a larger portion of his weight on his hindquarters (maybe 10 per cent more), and an imaginary line drawn from his croup to his withers ascends rather than looking like it's parallel to the ground.

2.6

Don't be fooled into thinking a horse is on the bit in a more advanced state of balance just because his head and neck are raised and arched. Be sure to look at the whole picture. When you compare Woody's shape to the way it is in photo 2.5, you can see that his back now looks low and concave, and his shoulders have dropped so that he no longer has an "uphill" look from croup to withers. I could help him improve his shape if my lower leg were more underneath me rather than being too far forward.

2.7

Even though Moxie might look like she's in a round frame, she is not on the bit. She is "overbent" (or "overflexed"). Her hind legs don't step well under her body, there is a "dip" in front of her withers, her neck is short, her poll is low, her face is behind the vertical, and she has dropped the contact with the outside rein. In order to get her into this very incorrect frame, Deb has had to "saw" left and right on the bit by alternately squeezing and releasing on the reins. As are result, Moxie simply flexes in the jaw. In this frame, Deb has little control over her engine—Moxie's hind legs.

This horizontal balance is what you'll be asking of your horse as you start out. When you go on to Stage Four, the roundness of the horse's body will stay the same as it is here, but his balance will change when you ask for self-carriage. When the balance changes, his croup lowers, and as a result, his withers are correspondingly higher. The line running from his croup to his withers ascends rather than being parallel to the ground as it is in horizontal balance (figs. 2.5 to 2.8).

2.8
Different stages of balance
with horse on the bit.

a) *This horse is on the bit in*
horizontal balance. He engages
his hind legs, raises his back
and flexes his hip joints,
lumbosacral joint, and poll.

b) *This horse is also on the bit,*
but he's in self-carriage. He can
hold his balance even when the
rider surrenders the reins.

WHAT DOES CONNECTION FEEL LIKE?

It's often very difficult for riders to try to create something they haven't felt before. If you ride some leg-yields, you can get the feeling of what you're working toward with your half-halt. Close your outside hand in a fist while your horse is going sideways, and he should come into a rounder frame. This is the connection and feeling you're aiming toward—without having to go sideways to get it.

When he's connected, your horse should feel compact, comfortable, and controllable rather than a jumble of disconnected parts!

WHO BENEFITS FROM CONNECTION?

An endurance rider from Nevada quickly put me in my place when I innocently asked if riders in her discipline had any interest in riding their horses on the bit. She spoke to me as if I were a child: "Jane, think about it. Isn't your horse less fatigued if he works for an hour in the ring "on the bit" rather than in a hollow frame? Well, our horses need to go for miles and miles as efficiently as possible." I gave her an enlightened nod as I slunk off in embarrassment about my ignorance of her sport.

I was surprised again when I found out from hunter seat riders who were attending my dressage clinics that the requirements for them in competition have changed considerably. In the past it was acceptable for their horses to move with their backs down, their heads and necks up and their noses poked out. Now the judges have decreed that even hunters carry themselves in a round frame, and you need to ride in this way if you want to win.

Many pleasure riders—even those who just like to go out for a hack—have also joined the ranks of those who like to have their horses on the bit. It's certainly more comfortable to sit on a round, springy back that cushions you like a shock absorber than to be jarred by a hollow, stiff one. Plus, see that scary rock over there? The one that your horse is convinced is going to jump out and grab his leg any second? If your horse is "on the bit," it's going to be a lot easier to get him to go by it calmly and willingly.

A case in point is the story of Cellulosa. Cellulosa was a gift from a local sculptor who thought it might be amusing to place this very large, unique work of art at the entrance to the dressage area where I train in Florida. He appeared one day to stand sentry by our ring and his presence created quite a stir—particularly with the young horses (fig. 2.9)

The day Cellulosa arrived, a friend of mine was hacking Eastwood, my nine-year-old Dutch Warmblood. Woody didn't want any part of this strange creature (can you blame him?). He wheeled and spun away obviously thinking it was much safer to head back to the barn. Fortunately, my friend warned me about the trouble I might have, so the next day

2.9
Woody after he'd conquered his fear of the "demon" Cellulosa! Photo: Mandy Lorraine

2.10

Anne Kursinski riding Eros— silver medalists in Atlanta in 1996—demonstrate the importance of connection over the back. His athleticism is apparent in the suppleness, power, and confidence with which he does his job. Photo: Mary Phelps.

instead of just wandering by Cellulosa on a loose rein to do my warm up, I put Woody on the bit early on and kept him there until we were safely past without incident. While on the bit, Woody's attention was focused on me, and he marched right by.

How about jumpers and combined-training horses who go over fences? They need to be agile enough to cope with the tricky distances and turns created by clever course designers. The horse that's on the bit is ready to use his body like an accordion. He can compress and extend it, and turn handily as well. Your signals can travel to him without interruption. Because he's connected and his back is round, there's no broken circuit that stops the message from getting through (fig. 2.10).

The driving horse also benefits from being on the bit. When he moves in a round frame with a relaxed back and his head down, he is on the bit without *leaning* on it. He can only do this when his hind legs step well underneath his body (just as they need to do in riding), so that he doesn't use the bit as a "fifth leg." This balance is essential so that the driver can safely control both the horse and the carriage (fig. 2.11).

And, of course, working on the bit when schooling a horse in dressage techniques is essential. Consider the movements and exercises. They are not supposed to be an end in themselves, but are meant to be a means to an end—to develop one or more athletic qualities in your horse.

For instance, school figures such as circles and serpentines increase your horse's **flexibility**: his ability to smoothly bend left and right. Transitions create **suppleness**: his capacity to smoothly lengthen and shorten his body and stride. Lateral work promotes **self-carriage**: the shifting of the center of gravity toward his hind legs, which results in a lightening and freeing of his forehand. All these gymnastic exercises aren't effective as far as promoting your horse's athleticism unless they are done on the bit.

It's true that a horse can do all of these exercises either "off the bit" or not correctly on the bit. And,

2.11
Heike Bean's lovely pair of carriage horses work steadily on the bit, enabling them to turn and adjust speed quickly in all the phases of combined-driving competition. Photo: Ronni Nienstedt.

you might actually seem to manage to get pretty far with his training. But, somewhere along the line, you're going to get stuck. And the only way to sort out the problems will be to go back to **the Basics** and then put your horse solidly on the bit. It's a hard lesson to learn, but as our experts pointed out in Book One, shortcuts take more time in the long run. It's always better to build a good foundation from the beginning than to have to go back to the Basics later on and fill in the gaps.

HOW TO CONNECT YOUR HORSE (PUT HIM ON THE BIT)

At clinics, I'll often run into a rider who thinks that if she sits quietly and in harmony with her horse, the horse will become connected all by himself. Of course, it doesn't happen. What she needs to understand is that since a horse isn't "designed" to be ridden, it's normal for him to stiffen and drop his back when he feels weight on it. And when he feels contact with his mouth, he braces his neck and uses it as a balancing rod in much the same way as we use a bannister for balance when we go down a flight of stairs. Unless we show the horse that it'll be easier for him to carry a rider by putting him on the bit, it's probably not going to occur to him to adopt this round frame on his own.

You connect your horse (put him on the bit) with the same half-halt that you learned in the last chapter. But before you do a half-halt to connect your horse, take a moment to check your prerequisites for the half-halt. Is your horse going forward, straight, and in a good rhythm? Is your contact firm, consistent, elastic and symmetrical? Remember, that at this point, we don't concern ourselves with whether or not he's round. While working on these four prerequisites, your horse can carry himself any way he chooses, even if his back is hollow and his head and neck are up.

If you're primarily preoccupied with getting your horse's head down at all costs before you have your prerequisites solidly confirmed, you might end up "hand-riding"—most likely sawing left and right on his mouth. Or during a half-halt, you might vibrate the outside rein in the same way as you do on the inside rein, rather than just closing your outside hand in a fist.

You might then think that you've made your horse round because his neck is arched and his face is in. But if you were to see a photo or video, you'd notice that his neck is short and his face is on or behind the vertical rather than being slightly in front of it. If this is what you see, you've probably flexed him in the jaw rather than connecting him from back to front. This is a dead end street. Your horse might look like he's in good balance, but if you hand-ride and focus on the jaw, you won't have much influence over the rest of his body. The roundness you have is a useless kind of round because you have no control over his hindquarters and his back can't comfortably cope with your weight. To make your horse truly round, you need to ride his *whole* body from back to front.

Once you've checked your prerequisites for the half-halt and they are all in order, give a half-halt to put your horse on the bit. As I described in the last chapter when you do a half-halt, you combine your driving aids, your bending aids, and your outside rein.

Apply the aids for three seconds and then relax them. The half-halt connects your horse because when your driving aids send his hind legs under his body and he steps "through" your outside rein, his back becomes round, much as a bow bends when it is tightly strung.

With each half-halt, be sure to reward him if his frame gets even slightly rounder. In this way, you'll encourage him to repeat and improve his response the next time. It's not going to be perfect in the beginning. But by rewarding each effort, you'll improve your horse's spirit of cooperation and his understanding of the use of the half-halt for connecting and putting him on the bit.

TESTING THE "CORRECTNESS" OF THE FRAME

Unless you work with a trainer on a regular basis, you can be quite easily misled into thinking your horse is on the bit when, in fact, this is not necessarily the case. As I mentioned above, a horse's body can mimic a correct round frame, but this round shape can just be in his neck rather than encompassing his entire body. Occasionally horses adopt this position on their own, although we usually see this when riders forget to use their driving aids and resort to "hand-riding" as I described earlier. Often, when a horse is hand-ridden, we also see some slack in the reins because the horse is *behind* the bit (rather than *on* it), and not seeking a contact from the rider's strong or overly busy hands.

Another subtlety you'll discover when attempting to work your horse on the bit is that connection is not necessarily an all or nothing thing. There are many stages and degrees of connection that fall along the spectrum from totally *off* the bit to completely *on* the bit.

On several occasions, a new student at a clinic I'm teaching will tell me that she doesn't have any problem riding her horse on the bit, but she's having a problem with a particular movement. I can take one look at the horse's muscling and know whether this is an animal that's been worked consistently on the bit or whether the rider has been fooled into thinking that her horse is on the bit. When a horse has been worked on the bit for an extended period of time the muscles of his topline (the muscles over the top of his croup, back, and crest of his neck) develop. In particular, the beginning of the crest in his neck is heavily muscled rather than looking weak and concave, with a dip right in front of the withers. If I get on a horse with a correctly muscled neck, his neck looks widest at the base by my hands and tapers up to the narrowest point just behind his ears. If the widest point of his neck is at his poll or somewhere in the middle of his neck, I know that this horse has not been properly ridden "through his neck" for any length of time (fig. 2.12).

I tell you this not to worry you, but so that you realize that it's easy to be misled, and it's essential to have some way to determine the correctness as well as the degree of connection. The following are some tests that will give you confidence that the round frame you've created is the result of riding the horse honestly from back to front. These tests can give you some peace of mind that you're on the right track.

Pick up the trot, close both legs, and ask for a lengthening for a few strides. Feel the thrust of the horse coming from behind when you close

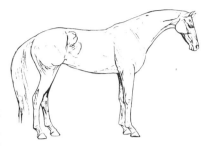

a) Good muscle developed from being ridden on the bit

b) A weak, underdeveloped topline. Notice, in particular, the concave look of the muscles at the base of the neck, the back, and top of the croup.

2.12
Working on the bit develops a strong topline

2.13

Woody's nice round shape indicates that he's given a good response to my connecting half-halt.

2.13 to 2.17 Test of the Half-Halt

your legs. Do this several times. Then give a half-halt and ask yourself the following question. If I hadn't closed my outside hand in a fist, would he have done as powerful a lengthening as the ones he has just been doing? If the answer is yes, you're riding your horse from back to front. If you don't feel the lengthening inside the half-halt, the round frame you think you've achieved might be the result of riding your horse from front to back—flexing him in the jaw and pulling his head in toward his chest.

The second test is to do a half-halt, then at the end of three seconds, open the fingers of both hands. Be sure not to straighten your arms to offer the reins to the horse, but let him take the reins from you only as much as he chooses. If he "chews" the reins from your hands by seeking the contact forward and down to the ground, your half-halt has connected him one hundred percent. If he stretches down somewhat, the half-halt has gone through a little. If he sticks his head straight up, he is not connected at all (figs. 2.13 to 2.17).

2.14

In order to check that he is honestly on the bit, I'll open my fingers to see if he'll "chew" the reins out of my hands. Since there is an elastic connection from his hind legs stretching over his back into my hands, he simply follows the natural progression of this connection as my reins get longer—and that is to go forward and down with his head and neck.

2.13 to 2.17
Test of the Half-Halt con't.

2.15

As I allow the reins to get even longer, he continues to seek the contact forward and down to the ground.

2.13 to 2.17 Test of the Half-Halt con't.

2.16

Here, I've given another half-halt, but when I slip the reins, Woody only stretches a little. He also looks flatter over his topline than he did in photo 2.15. This kind of response tells me my half-halt was only partially successful and that I didn't have a truly solid connection from back to front.

2.17

When I slip my reins after this half-halt, Woody sticks his head and neck straight up in the air—a clear sign that my half-halt didn't do its job of connecting him at all.

As I canter down the long side, I give a half-halt and then test the connection through my outside rein by softening my inside hand forward. I know that I have a firm connection because Woody's neck stays straight even without the influence of my inside rein.

2.18 and 2.19 Another Test of the Half-Halt

For the third test, give a three-second half-halt. After you think your horse has come into a round frame as the result of this half-halt, test by keeping your outside elbow bent by your side while putting slack in the inside rein by extending your inside hand forward toward your horse's mouth. (This is called a one-handed überstreichen). If your horse stays straight in his neck for a couple of strides, he's stepping from behind into your outside rein and your half-halt has gone through one hundred percent. The amount his neck immediately bends to the outside, making that outside rein loose, is the degree that he's not connected (figs. 2.18 and 2.19).

Now you have not only learned how to give a half-halt, but you know how to use that half-halt to put your horse on the bit. This round shape is a prerequisite for the next logical step in your horse's training—self-carriage.

2.19
*Here my half-halt
has not solidly
connected Woody
through the outside
rein. As I soften my
inside hand forward,
he drops the
connection with my
outside hand and
bends his neck
towards the rail.*

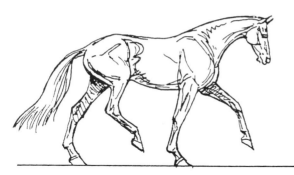

a) Generally, it's beneficial to ride a horse "deep" if he's the type that moves with a "closed" hind leg that steps well under his body.

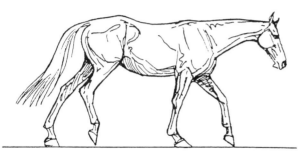

b) If, by nature, he moves with an "open" hind leg that trails out behind his body, riding him deep won't improve his balance and "throughness."

2.20 Closed and open hind legs

You'll discover in the next chapter that your horse must be correctly connected before he can be asked to carry himself, and that the same half-halt that you used to connect your horse in this chapter can now be used to promote self-carriage.

DEEP FRAME

Dressage riders often work their horses on the bit in a frame that is called **"deep."** When a horse is deep, he has the shape of an upside-down triangle. The hind legs come under the body, the back is raised, the neck is long, the poll is low, and the nose can be ever so slightly behind the vertical, but it must have the look and feel of seeking the bit.

This is a good frame to put your horse in at the beginning and end of your workout as a warm-up and cool-down. It allows the horse to stretch, loosen, and round the muscles of the topline. Working in a deep frame can relax a tense horse because as his muscles loosen he becomes more calm.

It's also a good frame to return to if you're having trouble maintaining a connection over your horse's back when teaching a new exercise. For example, if you start a leg-yield and your horse drops his back and comes above the bit, put him deep for your next effort. This position will teach him to do the movement using his whole body rather than dropping his back and shuffling along stiffly.

When riding your horse deep, it's important that you keep his hind legs coming forward under his body. It's not going to do him any good to stretch his neck long and low if his hind legs are trailing out behind and he feels like he's somersaulting forward, out of balance (fig. 2.20). If your horse tends to want to go with an "open" hind leg that trails out behind his body, you might not let him go as "deep" as the horse that tends to have a "closed" hind leg that steps well under his body (figs. 2.21 and 2.22).

2.21

Ruth is working Mastermind fairly "deep" in the trot. His hind leg steps well under his body, his back is raised, and his neck is long. Note that although his poll is low and his face is slightly behind the vertical, he definitely looks as though he's stretching toward the bit and seeking a contact with her hand.

2.22
Here Mastermind is being ridden slightly "deep" in the canter. This is a good example of a "closed" hind leg that reaches well under the body and a very round, convex-looking topline, from tail to poll.

If you ask your horse to go in a deep frame but then you drop the contact and let the reins get too loose as I've done here, you'll lose the connection from his hind legs into your hands. His back will be low and flat instead of round and convex.

It's just as important not to let your horse poke his nose too far forward and allow the reins to get loose. If you do, you'll lose the connection from the hind legs into your hands and his back will be flat instead of round (fig. 2.23).

Once you know how to give a half-halt, it's very simple to put your horse deep. Give a half-halt for three seconds and then open your fingers and allow your horse to "chew the reins out of your hands."

Remember that the length of the reins determines the length of your horse's neck. So, after you give the half-halt to connect your horse, open your fingers slightly and allow him to go forward and down with his head and neck. How deep he goes will depend on how much rein you let him have.

_2.24_

At first glance, these two horses might look the same because both have a low poll and their noses are behind the vertical. But when you look at the whole picture, you can see that the shape of their toplines and the way they use their hind legs is totally different.

"DEEP" IS NOT THE SAME AS "BEHIND THE BIT"

When a horse is in a deep frame, his poll is not the highest point and his nose may be slightly behind the vertical. This often confuses people because they see these two things and assume that the horse must be behind the bit.

Remember that it's *never* acceptable to ride a horse behind the bit because it indicates that the horse is being ridden from *front to back*. Being ridden from front to back means that the rider has forgotten to use her legs and is using her hands incorrectly. She does this either by using her hands too strongly or by sawing on the horse's mouth by alternately squeezing and releasing on the reins.

I tell people to be sure to look at the whole picture before they make a judgment about whether or not the horse is behind the bit. The horse that is deep and the horse that is behind the bit look similar because in both cases the poll is low and the nose is behind the vertical. The horse that is deep however, has his hind legs coming under the body, a round back, a long neck, and takes a contact with the rider's hand. The horse that is behind the bit on the other hand, doesn't come under his body with the hind legs, has a hollow back, a short neck, usually a dip in front of the withers, and avoids the contact with the rider's hand. It's a very serious fault to ride your horse behind the bit, but it's acceptable, even desirable, to ride a horse deep at times (fig. 2.24).

KEY POINTS

🐎 Working a horse connected (on the bit) makes him more athletic in his movement and more comfortable to ride.

🐎 The round shape of a horse that is on the bit must be created from back to front by driving the hind legs up to receiving hands.

🐎 When on the bit, the horse's hind legs reach well forward under his body, his back is relaxed, his neck is long and gracefully arched, his poll is the highest point of his neck, and his nose is slightly in front of the vertical.

🐎 The half-halt is the aid that you use to put your horse on the bit.

🐎 Be sure to test the correctness of the round shape. Is it truly created from back to front or are you "hand-riding" your horse into an artificial "head-set"?

🐎 There is a world of difference between riding a horse deep and riding him behind the bit. Working a horse in a deep frame is correct and often desirable. Working behind the bit is never correct because there isn't any connection from back to front.

STAGE FOUR

FANCY STUFF!

Once you understand the half-halt and can use it to put your horse on the bit, you're ready for Stage Four. Fancy Stuff! includes all the aids, movements, and exercises that will help your horse "dance like Baryshnikov" rather than plodding along like an elephant! In this first chapter of Stage Four, I'll talk about the development of self-carriage—a quality of balance that benefits horses in many disciplines.

In Chapters Four and Seven, I'll discuss how self-carriage enables your horse to work in this new and improved balance. Up until this point in his education, your horse has only been asked to show a working gait and a lengthening of that working gait. With the addition of self-carriage, you'll be able to produce three more "gears" in each pace—the **collected, medium,** and **extended gaits.**

In Chapters Five and Six, I'll explain how the more advanced lateral movements are done and how they're used, not only as an end in themselves, but as a *means to an end*—self-carriage.

Once your horse is in self-carriage, you'll find that it's easy for him to learn flying changes in the canter: the process of introducing these changes is explained in Chapter Eight. In Chapter Nine, I'll show you how you can use the new tools in your bag of tricks to resolve some old training problems. And finally, in Chapter Ten, I'll give you some examples of how to organize your work so that you school your horse in a systematic, logical way.

CHAPTER THREE

Float Like a Butterfly: Self-Carriage

To one extent or another, most riders in all riding disciplines can benefit from having their horses in self-carriage—that is, lighter on the forehand, with their center of gravity further back toward their hind legs.

A trail horse isn't much fun when he's plowing along so much on his forehand that your arms ache at the finish of your ride, while a jumper needs to be rocked back onto his hind legs to successfully negotiate fences (fig. 3.1).

An endurance horse needs to push himself up hills with his hindquarters rather than pull himself up with his shoulders, and as he goes down hills he also needs to support himself with his hindquarters well underneath his body so that he doesn't pound his front end into the ground (fig. 3.2).

Reining and cutting horses require a lot of strength from their hindquarters and a light forehand in order to spin and accelerate (fig. 3.3).

In competitive dressage, with all other things being equal, the horse who shows more self-carriage wins. For instance, if two different horses both perform a half-pass with good quality—that is, the half-pass is done in a regular rhythm with good bend and correct alignment of the body—the horse whose center of gravity or balance is more toward the hind legs so that he carries himself, rather than being heavy on the forehand, will get the higher score.

The fact is, in any equestrian sport, the horse who is balanced further back toward his hindquarters has an advantage over the one traveling on his forehand, simply because he moves with greater athletic ability (figs. 3.4 and 3.5).

3.1 a and b

Mara DePuy riding Hopper in the show jumping phase of the Three-Day-Event competition at the 1996 Olympic Games in Atlanta. Mara rocks her horse back on his hind legs so he can take off over this fence. Photo: Brant Gamma

3.2

This endurance horse at a ride in Colorado is pushing himself up the hill with his powerful hindquarters. Photo: Nancy Loving

Scott McCutcheon performing a spin with his reining horse. See the work being done by his engaged hind legs. Photo: Courtesy of the American Paint Horse Association.

3.4

Piaffe: the ultimate display of self-carriage.

3.5

A Western horse working in self-carriage.

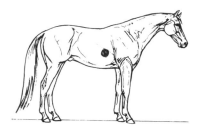

3.6

The location of a horse's center of gravity when he is standing still is more toward his front legs.

3.7

A horse starts off with approximately 60% of his weight on his forehand and 40% behind. Once he begins to carry himself this becomes more equal, and eventually, when he is more advanced, he will carry more weight behind than he does in front.

WHAT IS SELF-CARRIAGE?

You'll often hear various terms that imply or refer to self-carriage. They include: loading the hind legs, shifting the center of gravity toward the hind legs, lighter in your hands, elevating the forehand, "up" in front, gathered together, **packaged,** well-engaged behind, lowering and engaging the quarters, and **collection.**

But whatever it's called, let's try to clear up some of the confusion associated with the term. To many riders, it's merely a shortening of the horse's body with the head and neck raised and arched. To some extent this is true, but it's much more than that. In fact, you can shorten a horse without having him in self-carriage at all. This can be done (but please don't do it!) by riding him from **front to back**—cranking his head and neck into a "head-set" without activating and engaging his hindquarters.

A more important component of self-carriage than the mere shortening of the frame is the position of the horse's center of gravity. This changes according to the stage of training and the degree that the horse can carry himself. That is, the more the horse is in self-carriage, the more the center of gravity has been shifted toward his hindquarters. My students have found it helpful when I describe self-carriage as a "loading of the hind legs." This loading occurs when the horse engages his hindquarters by bending the joints of his hind legs. Because the horse is engaging and lowering his hindquarters, his entire forehand raises and becomes lighter and freer.

The main tool that you use to change his balance in this way and produce self-carriage is a half-halt. (I told you the half-halt would be useful!) In addition, exercises such as doing small circles and transitions, as well as backing up, also help your horse learn to carry himself. I'll get into these in the next chapter. You can also do a variety of lateral exercises to create self-carriage, which I'll discuss in Chapters Five and Six.

The challenge in developing self-carriage stems from the fact that all horses are built with their center of gravity more toward their front legs. This is because horses are shaped like a table with a head and neck stuck onto one end. If your horse didn't have a head and neck, his weight could be evenly distributed over the four legs of the table. But since his head and neck can weigh as much as 250 pounds, it's inevitable that his center of gravity is more toward his front legs (fig. 3.6).

No wonder your horse likes to "lie" in your hands! It's normal for him to have more weight on his forehand. Fortunately, he's born with the raw material that can be developed and strengthened so he can be trained to carry more weight on his hind legs and take the load off his front end.

To get the idea of loading the hind legs, pretend your horse is standing on two scales that can independently distinguish how much weight is

3.8 and 3.9

These two photos show Galen on the bit. Her hind legs are active and stepping well under her body. Her back is round, her neck is long and gracefully arched, and she takes a solid but pleasant contact with Deb's hand. The difference here is simply one of balance. In the first photo, she's being warmed up in a deep frame and her balance or center of gravity is more toward the forehand. In the second photo, Deb asks for more self-carriage by shifting Galen's balance or center of gravity more toward the hind legs.

on his front legs and how much is on his hind legs. In nature, the horse has about 60% of his weight on his front legs and 40% on his hind legs. As he begins the process of developing self-carriage, the weight proportion changes. Although initially he still has more weight on his front legs, it's less so than before. Then, as his training continues and he carries himself more, he will have equal weight on his front and hind legs. Eventually, when he's more advanced, he will show more weight on the rear scale than the front scale (fig. 3.7).

CONNECTION IS NOT SELF-CARRIAGE

Many riders confuse the idea of the horse being connected with being in self-carriage, or as it is often called, being "**collected**". For instance, I'll be teaching a clinic and a first-time participant walks her horse into the lesson on a loose rein and then asks me if she should "collect" her horse as she starts warming up at the trot. At this point I realize that this rider is using connection and collection synonymously.

Yes, I do want that horse *connected* as he starts to work, but the difference is that the connected horse's center of gravity can be very much toward the forehand because he's being worked long and low so he can stretch and warm-up his muscles correctly. It's not until he's properly

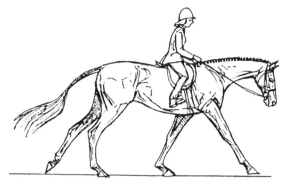

3.10

A horse in "horizontal balance" where withers and hindquarters are the same height, and the horse's topline is parallel to the ground.

3.11

Self-carriage: this horse "appears" shorter from poll to rail than 3.10.

3.12

When ridden from "front to back," the horse looks cranked into a stiff and constricted outline. Because he's being hand-ridden, he shows a low poll, short neck, hollow back, high croup, and his hind legs can't come under his body.

warmed up that his rider should think about starting to shift his balance toward his hind legs and asking him to carry himself. Your horse can be connected without being in self-carriage, and this should be the case during a warm-up, anyway. However, he must always first be connected and properly warmed up before you ask him to carry himself and become *collected* (figs. 3.8 and 3.9).

WHAT DOES SELF-CARRIAGE LOOK LIKE?

As I've mentioned earlier, most horses in a natural state are, in "horizontal balance," where the withers and croup are basically the same height, and the horse's topline is parallel to the ground. Most hunters or training-level dressage horses show this horizontal balance, and although these horses might be well balanced for their jobs, they are not collected (fig. 3.10). Depending on his level of training, a collected horse in self-carriage will *appear* shorter from poll to tail than a horse in a working gait, and the top of his withers will be relatively higher than the highest point of his croup. (See fig. 3.11). This elevation in front includes the entire forehand (not just the head and neck, but the withers, too) and it is the result of engagement—the bending of the joints of the hind legs and the subsequent lowering of the hindquarters (fig. 2.8b).

Don't be fooled into thinking a horse is in self-carriage just because his frame looks short. You can easily shorten a horse's neck by cranking him in with tight reins. But this is just the front-to-back riding I've talked about before, and merely simulates a collected frame while the horse is not being ridden from his hind legs forward into the bridle.

I've seen many riders who mistakenly think they're on the road to self-carriage because they've shortened their horse's frame in this way. Be sure to look at the whole picture. It's not enough that the horse's outline is short. If you're compressing him from front to back by cranking him into a "head-set," you'll notice that he probably also has a low poll, short neck, low withers, hollow back, high croup and he looks tense and stiff. And if the frame, physique, and movement don't become more beautiful during training, then it's a sure sign you're not on the right road (fig. 3.12).

Looking at the horse's entire silhouette will insure that you're also not deluded by seeing a high, arched neck. A rider can easily raise her horse's head and neck higher by lifting her hands in an attempt to elevate the forehand (please don't do this either!) But, when she does this, the horse's withers will remain low—the opposite of what happens with a collected horse. So always compare the height of a horse's withers to the height of his hindquarters before you decide whether he's really in self-carriage or just hauled in from front to back. When he's properly collected and in self-carriage, a horse has the uphill look of a speedboat in the water, or of an airplane taking off.

Another clue as to whether or not a horse has been correctly collected is to examine his way of going. Sometimes a rider thinks her horse is in self-carriage because his frame is shorter than normal and he covers less ground with each stride. However, if she's cranked him together by riding him from front to back, his movement has to suffer; he'll merely shuffle along stiffly. On the other hand, there's a lightness and gaiety in the paces of the horse in self-carriage. He looks animated and bounces over the ground expressively, much like the horse in freedom who gets the wind under his tail on a crisp autumn morning. Keep in mind that as you begin to ask for self-carriage, your horse may only be able to hold this new shape and balance for moments. It'll take time before he's strong enough to maintain it for long periods (figs. 3.13 to 3.17).

To sum up the qualities that you'll see with a horse in self-carriage: he has engaged hindquarters, a round back, withers that are higher than the top of his croup, a long, gracefully arched neck with the poll the highest point, his nose approaches the vertical, and he moves with buoyancy and expression.

WHAT DOES SELF-CARRIAGE FEEL LIKE?

The dilemma is the same here that it was when you were first starting to connect your horse or put him on the bit. Specifically, how do you create something you haven't felt before? Remember how I told you to learn the feeling of connection by doing leg-yields? Well, you can do the same sort of experimentation to learn the feeling of self-carriage. In this case, you'll have a chance to experience this new balance by doing some transitions.

For instance, to get the feeling of self-carriage in the trot, do several tran-

3.13

Note that Woody's hind
legs are stepping well
under his body, his croup
is low, and the elevation
of his front end includes
his entire forehand, not
just his head and neck.
He has the uphill look of
an airplane taking off.

3.14

Compare Woody's
balance in this picture to
the previous one. If you
were only to look at his
arched and raised neck
and head, you might at
first glance think he's in
self-carriage. But here
you can see that his hind
legs are pushing
backward and that his
withers have sunk down
so much that they are
lower than the top of his
croup.

3.15 and 3.16

In these two photos I'm pulling Woody into a shortened frame. His neck might be raised and arched, but I'm cranking it into this position. This can only have a paralyzing effect on his movement. The first photo shows a short, tight stride in the canter and, the second shows constricted movement in the trot. Note also, how the front toe flips up—a sure sign that he's being restricted.

<u>3.17</u>
The movement of a horse in self-carriage should resemble the lightness and gaiety of a horse at play. This is Woody in his favorite field at home at Huntington Farm, in South Strafford, Vermont.

sitions from the trot to the halt and immediately back to the trot again. Make sure your horse does the transitions clearly and distinctly, without any dribbly walk steps in between. Each time you step into the halt, in your mind's eye picture him lowering his hindquarters in the same way that a dog lowers his haunches to sit down.

After several transitions, just ride some sitting trot and see if his balance feels any different. Does your horse feel like he's carrying more weight on his hind legs and less on his front legs? Does he feel more "up" in front and lighter in your hands?

To get the feeling of self-carriage in the canter, go through the same process with several quick transitions from the canter to the walk and immediately back to the canter again. Then, just ride the canter and see if your horse's balance has changed.

One difference that you should feel after these transitions is that the contact with your horse's mouth will be much lighter. The transitions enable your horse to carry himself by creating a shift in the center of gravity more toward the hindquarters. As a result, he doesn't have to lean heavily on the reins for support.

A word of caution here, though. You should only work toward this lightness *when you're ready to start developing self-carriage*. Prior to that, when you're schooling your horse in the working gaits, the contact should be quite firm because you always want to feel the hind legs "stepping into your hands." (See Chapter One). Lightness during early stages of training in dressage *would not* indicate self-carriage. It would only be the result of a lack of connection, or even contact. And remember, *connection is a prerequisite to self-carriage* (fig. 3.18). Please review Chapters One and Two is you have any questions about this.

When a horse is in self-carriage, he should feel like he's organized into a compact package, rather than strung out with his hind legs out behind his body, just pushing his mass along. With a horse that is in self-carriage in the collected gaits, any change of movement, speed, direction, or length of stride, would be possible without further preparation from one step to the next.

For example, a horse that's in collected walk could be in collected canter or even piaffe in the very next stride (if he's been previously trained how to do that movement). As you get started you'll be working at collecting the trot, but you should still have the feeling that while in the collected trot you could easily move to collected canter or to an extended trot or to a halt by the very next step. But I'm getting ahead of myself! More on this when I discuss

3.18

This hunter might feel light in the hand, but the "lightness" is from lack of contact, not because the horse is in any sort of self-carriage.

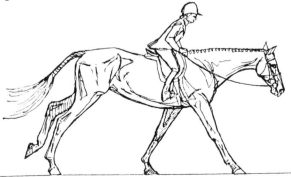

the collected gaits in the next chapter. The point here is to give you a feeling for what self-carriage will feel like.

WHEN DO YOU ASK FOR SELF-CARRIAGE?

You might ask, "When is my horse ready to start developing self-carriage?" It's difficult to designate a particular time, because not every horse will react in the same way to the demands of carrying himself. But I don't want you to think of self-carriage as something that you suddenly ask for one day. Developing it is a continuous process.

Once your horse understands and becomes confirmed in all of the work in my Stages One through Three, you can begin asking your horse to carry himself. A good indication of when to start is if your horse has satisfied all the prerequisites to self-carriage discussed in the first three stages, with harmony and understanding:

In all three paces, he needs to move freely forward with regular steps and be straight (Stage One, **Book One**); do a good lengthening (Stage Two, Book One); and produce a reliable half-halt (Stage Three). If this is not the case, your horse isn't ready, and all your efforts will be doomed to failure. So, spend more time working on **the Basics** before you begin to ask for self-carriage.

If your horse has met all the prerequisites, you'll start to ask him to carry himself for short periods every working day. Bear in mind that asking for self-carriage is like asking your horse suddenly to do deep knee bends. Think of how difficult it would be for you to do five hundred deep knee bends! By the time you got to one hundred your muscles would be screaming and you'd insist that you couldn't possibly do one more. You would need to build your strength gradually and so does your horse. Be sure to give him frequent rest periods and be satisfied with asking for a little bit at a time (fig. 3.19).

If you're a competitive dressage rider, your horse is first asked to show self-carriage in the collected and medium gaits at the Second Level tests. However, remember that proceeding through the levels in dressage competition is a gradual, progressive development of self-carriage.

At the lowest level (Training Level) the horse's balance is **horizontal** and his center of gravity is toward the forehand.

At the next level (First Level) the horse's balance is somewhat shifted toward his hindquarters, and although he is still

3.19

Suddenly asking your horse for self-carriage is the same as expecting yourself to do five hundred deep-knee bends without building up to it. By the time you get to one hundred, (or, maybe just fifteen or twenty), your muscles feel like a quivering mass of jelly.

somewhat on the forehand, he's less on the forehand than the Training Level horse. Therefore, he's carrying himself more than he was at the previous level.

The Second Level tests ask for collected and medium gaits. So, the Second Level horse has his center of gravity even more toward his hindquarters, and he's less on the forehand than the First Level horse. Understand that this self-carriage at Second Level doesn't spring out of thin air. Your horse should be gradually and systematically working toward this goal throughout the prior levels.

TIMETABLE

If you have a horse that isn't strong enough yet because he hasn't been in a program that systematically develops his strength over time, he might become bewildered or even angry when you ask him to carry himself.

Or, you might have a horse that doesn't have the conformation to make it easy for him to carry himself. For example, a Thoroughbred with straight hind legs can find it difficult to bring them into position for self-carriage. Look at this type of horse while he's standing still and you'll notice that the angles made by the joints of his hind leg are more open (less acute) than, let's say, certain Warmblood breeds. As a result, it's more difficult for this Thoroughbred type to engage his hind legs and take more weight on his hindquarters.

Consider a Quarter Horse whose croup is usually higher than his withers. This conformation throws his center of gravity even more toward his forehand, and it will be harder for this fellow to shift his center of gravity toward his hind legs.

That's not to say that the horse who is built like one of these can't be taught to carry himself. However, the whole process will take more time than with a horse who is better built to do the job. You need to systematically develop an animal so that he is able to engage his hind legs. Then he can bear more weight behind and can produce the uphill balance of the horse in self-carriage.

Okay. You're a patient person. You're willing to take that time. But what's reasonable? *Don't think in terms of days or months.* Think in terms of years. If your horse has been started under saddle and you work on the schedule that I've outlined, I would expect it to take you *two to three years* to teach him to truly carry himself (figs. 3.20 to 3.22).

Remember that each horse is an individual. Horses that are bred specifically for dressage often are asked to carry themselves within a year or so after real training begins, but this is not going to be the case for most of the readers of this book! So, whether it takes two years or six years, the end result should be a more beautiful animal who goes with ease and grace and without any discomfort or confusion.

3.20 to 3.22
Systematically Working
toward Self-Carriage

3.20
This photo shows Mastermind in a balance appropriate for a horse just starting out at my Stage Two (Book One). He is relaxed, moving forward with regularity and accepting the contact, but his balance is toward the forehand. However, from these basic building blocks of relaxation, rhythm, and stretching toward the bit, he has a solid foundation from which he can learn to shift his balance toward his hindquarters.

3.21
In this picture Mastermind is on the bit—appropriate for my Stage Three—and his balance is less on his forehand.

3.22
Here he carries himself even more than he did in the previous photo. Ruth asks for the balance of a collected trot as discussed in my Stage Four by activating and energizing his hindquarters to a greater degree. This systematic development of self-carriage has taken place gradually over a two-year period.

KEY POINTS

🐎 The center of gravity of a horse in self-carriage is more toward his hindquarters rather than toward his forehand as it is in his natural state. This change in balance allows him to move more athletically.

🐎 A horse must first be connected before he can be asked to carry himself.

🐎 When a horse is in self-carriage his hindquarters are lower and as a result, his entire forehand including the withers is raised.

🐎 When a horse is in self-carriage, it feels like any change in movement is possible from one step to the next.

🐎 Working in self-carriage takes a lot of the horse's strength—strength that needs to be developed gradually and systematically.

CHAPTER FOUR

Coiling the Spring: The Collected Gaits

a) Collected walk

Now that you understand what self-carriage is, how it feels, and why it's desirable, we can begin developing the collected gaits. In order to help you understand what collected gaits are, I can't do better than quote the descriptions from the rule book of the American Horse Shows Association (AHSA):

The Collected Walk
"In the collected walk, the horse remains 'on the bit', moves resolutely forward, with his neck raised and arched, and showing clear self-carriage. The head approaches the vertical position and a light contact with the mouth is maintained. The hind legs are engaged with good hock action. The pace remains regular, marching and vigorous. Each step covers less ground and is higher and more active than the steps of the medium walk because all the joints bend more markedly (figs. 4.1a and 4.2)."

b) Collected trot

The Collected Trot
"In the collected trot, the horse remains 'on the bit'. He moves forward with his neck raised and arched and his nose approaching the vertical. The hocks are well-engaged maintaining an energetic impulsion thus enabling the shoulders to move with greater ease in any direction. The horse's steps are shorter than in any of the other trots, but he is lighter and more mobile (figs. 4.1b and 4.3)."

The Collected Canter
"In the collected canter, the horse remains 'on the bit'. He moves forward with his neck raised and arched and his nose approaching the vertical.

c) Collected canter

4.1 Collected gaits

4.2 to 4.4 Collected Gaits

4.2

In collected walk, Woody marches forward with his neck raised and arched, and showing clear self-carriage.

This canter is marked by the lightness of the forehand and the engagement of the hindquarters. Therefore, it is characterized by supple, free, and mobile shoulders and very active quarters. The horse's strides are shorter than at the other canters but he is lighter and more mobile (figs. 4.1c and 4.4)."

Notice in these descriptions that a common feature of the collected gaits is that the horse covers less ground with each step. However, even though the steps are shorter, the horse should still expend the same amount of energy, (looking at it another way, he should use the same amount of calories per stride), or even more than he did in the working gaits to produce each stride. The shorter strides should feel like they are *bubbling* over with energy.

<u>4.3</u>
In collected trot, Woody's steps are shorter than in any of the other trots, but the hocks are well-engaged so that he moves with greater lightness.

<u>4.4</u>
In collected canter, Woody springs buoyantly over the ground. Because he's in self-carriage, he feels light and easily maneuverable.

4.5

Special Effects' walk has been shortened, but it is not collected. He shuffles along with short, restricted steps rather than with shortened steps that make a higher arc off the ground. Also, his neck is short, and there is a big bulge underneath it—a sure sign that Amy is trying to pull him into collected walk rather than riding him from back to front by driving his hind legs forward into her hands.

To do this, he'll have to lift each leg higher. By higher, I mean that if you're watching from the ground, you'll see that the legs make more of an up-and-down arc instead of taking long strides forward over the ground. If he only shortens the stride and the legs don't make a higher arc, he expends less energy. The result is a stride that is simply short—not collected. He'll just shuffle along over the ground with short, flat strides rather than short, engaged strides (fig. 4.5).

In other words, if it normally takes a horse in his working gaits four strides to go completely through a corner, in the collected gaits, he might take six or seven shorter, higher, more engaged strides in the same tempo to make it through that same corner.

But before we get started, keep in mind that in order to collect your horse, he first must be relaxed, forward, straight, and regular in his rhythm (the prerequisites for the half-halt). You must then offer an inviting contact so that you can connect him with a half-halt.

Once again, it all comes down to the Basics. This is the foundation that all quality work is built upon. If you need to review how to connect your horse with a half-halt, refer back to Chapter Two.

In this chapter, we'll look at how the same half-halt that you used to connect your horse, plus the movements you already know, like transitions, school figures, and the rein back can now be used to collect the gaits.

Later on, in Chapters Five and Six, we'll look at some new lateral exercises, such as shoulder-in, haunches-in, half-pass, and turn on the haunches. You'll see that these movements aren't necessarily an end in themselves. They can be used as a means to an end, which is to develop the collected gaits.

USING THE HALF-HALT
AS THE AID TO COLLECT THE GAITS

Now that you've *connected* your horse with a half-halt, let's use that very same half-halt to produce self-carriage so you can collect the gaits. This **collecting half-halt** also combines the driving aids, the bending aids and the outside rein, but its purpose is now different; it adjusts balance and shifts the center of gravity toward the hindquarters rather than simply connecting the "engine" to the front end. You'll find that all the elements of the **connecting half-halt** (driving aids, bending aids, closed outside hand) are present, but the emphasis changes in the *collecting* half-halt.

To review, the *connecting* half-halt is the marriage of three sets of aids: the seat and legs drive the horse forward, both legs and inside rein bend the horse, and the closed outside hand **(rein of opposition)** prevents him from going too much forward and from bending too much. Combining these aids should last about three seconds, and then you should relax by softening all of the aids. Later, as your horse becomes more highly schooled, you'll find that the half-halt can become more refined and often is as brief as a momentary closure of seat, legs, and hands.

But what, you might ask, is the difference between using the *connecting* half-halt to simply put your horse on the bit as we did in Chapter Two and giving a half-halt to *collect* the gaits? In one sense it's a "bigger" half-halt than you use to put your horse on the bit. When I say "bigger," however, I'm not necessarily referring to the strength of the aid. Rather, the horse's effort to **engage** should be "bigger." You ask for greater **engagement** with your *collecting* half-halt by driving the horse's hind legs further under his body so that he carries his own weight (and yours) completely, rather than using your hands as a fifth leg to help him out.

In a "collecting" half-halt, your outside rein shuts a door in front of your horse. He has to bend the joints of his hind legs, lower his hindquarters, and "sit down" behind, thus carrying more weight with his hind legs.

You'll also be influencing your horse differently with your outside rein. Before when you were simply putting your horse on the bit, you used your outside rein as the *connecting* rein. Now I want you to think of it as the *collecting* rein. When you use your outside rein, imagine it is shutting a door in front of your horse. When your horse yields to the outside hand, which is closed in a fist, he bends the joints of his hind legs, lowers his hindquarters by "sitting down behind," and, therefore, changes his balance by carrying more weight on his hind legs (fig. 4.6).

Also, with each *collecting* half-halt, you'll need to shorten your reins a bit. This adjustment of rein length is important because the length of your reins determines how long your horse's frame is. When you apply a *collecting* half-halt, you'll be shifting your horse's center of gravity more toward his hind legs. However, if your reins remain the same length as they were prior to the half-halt, your horse's balance will slide back toward his forehand after the half-halt.

Understand that in an effort to go back down on his forehand, your horse will try to pull the reins through your fingers. Keep your hands firmly closed around the reins. Once your horse realizes that this route of escape from self-carriage is closed, he'll learn to find his balance between the new, shorter boundaries of your legs and hands.

How to Ride the Collecting Half-Halt

Here's how to begin to turn your *connecting* half-halt into a *collecting* half-halt. Start off in the sitting trot. Ask your horse to do a lengthening so that when you close your legs, you both get a sense of thrust and power coming from his "engine." Then, when you bring your horse back from the lengthening to teach him a collected trot, do so with a *collecting* half-halt. This half-halt should have the same powerful feeling from behind *that the lengthening just did.*

You should always feel the vigor and thrust of lengthenings when asking for any half-halt and even more so for a *collecting* half-halt. When giving this *collecting* half-halt, apply the same amount of legs and seat that you would to ask for a powerful lengthening. When the energy you create with your driving aids meets your closed outside hand, your horse should hold the energy within himself (rather than feeding it out in a lengthening) and the result is a more collected trot (figs. 4.7 to 4.10).

While maintaining your horse's rhythm and tempo, close your legs and at the same time, brace your back and drive with your seat so that you feel as if you're pushing the back of the saddle toward the front of the saddle. Use your seat by pushing it along in a sweeping motion (not straight down into the saddle) in order to drive your horse's hind legs further underneath his body, bend the joints of his hind legs, and create greater engagement.

With each transition from the lengthening back to the collected trot, ask within that half-halt for a greater degree of self-carriage. Do this by shortening your reins a couple of inches and then by applying your aids more strongly than you do just to put him on the bit. Depending on how he feels to you, this may mean making the whole half-halt stronger, or it may mean emphasizing the driving aids more than the outside rein.

Always be sure to use your driving aids. If you forget to do this, your closed outside hand just "subtracts" energy. As a result, your horse might brace against your hand, stiffen his back, and lose his hind legs out behind his body (fig. 4.11). Or, he might stop coming well forward with his hind legs and lose the rhythm and tempo he had in the lengthening. Always think of every *collecting* half-halt as the *addition* of impulsion and engagement, not merely the *subtraction* of forward motion.

Maintaining Rhythm and Tempo During the Collecting Half-Halt

As I've mentioned before, because the term "half-halt" contains the word "halt," many people mistakenly think that a half-halt has something to do with stopping or slowing their horses down. Also, when you give a half-halt to collect the walk, trot or canter, the horse *seems* slower. This is because the steps are shorter, taking you more time to cover the same

4.7 to 4.10
Collecting Half-Halt Sequence

4.7
This pleasantly round shape is the result of the connecting half-halt I've given Woody while he's in the working trot. Notice, however, that his frame is long and his balance is somewhat on his forehand.

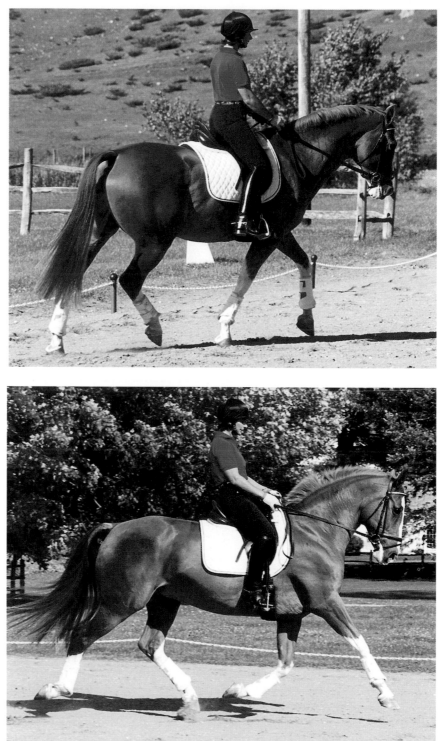

4.8
My goal is to collect the trot by shifting his center of gravity more toward his hind legs. So to turn my connecting half-halt into a collecting half-halt, I start by asking for a powerful lengthening in the trot.

4.9

As I bring him back from the lengthening, I keep using my seat and legs as if I'm still asking for the longer strides. I close my legs, drive with my seat as if I'm pushing the back of the saddle toward the front of the saddle, but I let this power meet a more restraining hand so that the energy stays within his body rather than being fed out in a lengthening.

Since Woody is being driven by my seat and legs while I close my outside (left) hand, he bends the joints of his hind legs, lowers his hindquarters, and, therefore, changes his balance.

4.10

As a result of the collecting half-halt, Woody's balance is quite a bit different than it was in photo 4.7. He's a shorter and rounder "package," his hind legs are more active, and he carries considerably more weight on his hindquarters than he did before.

4.11

Here I've neglected to use my driving aids to send Woody forward to meet my hand during the half-halt. Instead, I've only used my hands. As a result, he has braced against them, stiffened his back, and his hind legs are pushing out behind his body.

amount of ground that you covered with the longer strides of the working gait.

However, you should never slow down your horse's tempo or subtract the effort from his hind legs when you want to develop self-carriage and collect the gaits. If you do, you'll only get short steps without self-carriage. Using your hands too much results in short, unengaged steps. You need to drive your horse up to your hand so that he engages his hind legs and takes shorter, *higher*, more active steps. Think about *driving* him into a collected gait rather than *pulling* him into a slower one.

Keep in mind that the tendency of many horses is to slow down because at this stage they lack the physical strength to maintain their tempo (their rhythm may stay regular but the tempo slows down) when they're asked to show collected gaits. So always remember to maintain an even rhythm and a constant, unchanging tempo before, during, and after you give a half-halt. This rhythm and tempo must remain the same whether you're in the process of giving the half-halt or just riding the collected, medium, or extended gaits.

Remember the waltz that I described when we were discussing rhythm in the working gaits (Book One, Chapter Seven)? A waltz rhythm is always the same—a three-beat dance. But the tempo of the waltz can change depending on whether the music is played faster or slower. When giving a half-halt to create self-carriage and collect the paces, the "music" should always be played at the same speed.

More often than not when you're first teaching your horse to collect his trot, not only will he try to slow down but he might also lose the connection over his back. He does a disconnected trot, in dressage jargon, sometimes known as a "swimmy" or "passage-y" trot; his hind legs go backward, his front legs go forward, and his back sinks out from underneath you with every stride.

To correct this, keep in mind that horses almost always quicken their tempo when asked to lengthen, so if your horse wants to slow down when starting to learn to collect, you can use the lengthening to bring him back up to "normal" speed. Help him maintain his tempo by practicing some lengthenings to build thrust and energy. Keep this feeling of the quickness of a lengthening when you go to collect again. To check that the tempo stays the same, count out loud as you go from the lengthening to the collected gait.

USING SCHOOL FIGURES
TO DEVELOP COLLECTED GAITS
In Book One, we looked at how to ride circles and turns. Now you can use these movements, also known as school figures, to develop the collected trot and canter. As long as they're done correctly, smaller circles produce greater engagement of the hind legs and, therefore, create a more marked shift of balance toward the hindquarters.

What I mean by correctly is that your horse doesn't evade the difficulty of the smaller figure by swinging his hindquarters out or pressing his barrel against your inside leg instead of softly bending around it. As long as your horse stays bent along the arc of the curve and his spine conforms exactly to the line he's on, tighter school figures demand that he carry himself and collect the gait he's in. So a 15-meter circle collects the trot and canter more than a 20-meter circle, and a 10-meter circle collects the gaits more than a 15-meter circle.

USING TRANSITIONS TO HELP COLLECTED GAITS
Doing frequent transitions from pace to pace also promotes self-carriage and the development of the collected gaits. Skipping a pace, such as doing a transition from the canter to the walk and back to the canter again (also known as a **simple change of lead**), or from the trot to the halt and back to the trot again, intensifies the collecting effect of a transition.

When you start to do these more advanced transitions that skip a pace, all sorts of things can go wrong. For example, when you try to go from the canter to the walk, your horse will probably fall on his forehand and end up doing the transition through a couple of steps of the trot. The same thing will most likely happen when you first attempt to go from the trot to the halt. Your horse will lose his balance and shuffle through a few steps of walk. Keep in mind that in order for these transitions to be effective, they have to be done clearly and distinctly. Therefore, as you blend a half-halt into any downward transition, think about driving the hind legs further under your horse's body toward a more restraining hand (see Combining Aids to Improve Balance on page 193 for help in how to do this).

One other thing to think about when you do a transition from the canter to the walk is that in order for your horse to negotiate this transition in good balance, he needs to be covering ground in the canter no faster than the speed of the walk. If you ask for the transition from a normal canter during which your horse covers ground faster than he does at a walk, he has no option but to shift his balance onto his front legs.

To avoid this balance shift, think about cantering with shorter and shorter (but active) strides until your horse is covering ground in the canter at the same speed he'll be traveling when he walks. As you're cantering, half-halt and bring him more onto the spot for two or three strides before you actually "still" your seat and ask for the walk. This way he'll be able to softly step into the walk in the same balance he had during the last step of canter.

If you're still struggling with this canter-to-walk transition, pretend that you're actually asking for a transition to the halt. Then at the last moment soften your hands and allow your horse to walk on instead of coming to a complete stop. By the same token, if your horse walks into the halt during transitions from the trot to the halt, you can do the same sort of exercise: step into the halt and immediately back up without pausing. Do this several times and then just imagine that you're going to ask for a transition from the trot to the rein back, but allow your horse to halt instead.

Another thing that can go wrong when you start these more sophisticated transitions is that after doing the downward transition, your horse feels "**behind your leg**" for the subsequent upward transition. If you find yourself wanting to squeeze hard with your legs in order to do the upward transition, it means that you'll have to put your horse **in front of your leg** again as I described in Book One (Chapter Six). (You see, even at the more advanced levels your work often boils down to going back to Basics!) Your horse must feel electric and "hot off your leg" in order for the upward transitions to contribute to the process of developing collected gaits.

Now let's get started using these more advanced transitions to increase self-carriage. First, ride around in the collected trot or canter and evaluate your horse's balance before the transitions. Where is his center of gravity? How much weight is on the forehand? How heavy is the contact in your hands?

Then do either trot-halt-trot transitions or canter-walk-canter transitions. Do only about five strides in each before you do the next transition.

After doing several transitions, take a moment to reevaluate your horse's balance. As you trot or canter around, ask yourself if your horse feels less on the forehand, is carrying more weight behind, and is lighter in your hands. If he does, the frequent transitions have done their job.

BACKING UP TO IMPROVE ENGAGEMENT

Backing up can also be used to promote the collected gaits by getting the horse's hind legs further underneath his body. I've seen students markedly improve their horses' self-carriage by doing a rein back and then asking for an immediate transition to the trot or the canter. Go forward for only a few strides so your horse can feel his new balance, and then halt before the self-carriage degenerates. Then repeat the whole exercise. Only trot or canter a few strides at a time so that your horse has a chance to feel his ability to shift his center of gravity toward his hind legs.

KEY POINTS

- In the collected gaits, a horse's steps are shorter, higher, and more active than they are in the working gaits.

- By modifying your *connecting* half-halt slightly, you can turn it into a *collecting* half-halt.

- Always think of "*driving*" your horse forward into a collected gait.

- When you give a *collecting* half-halt, the rhythm and tempo of the pace should stay the same as it was before the half-halt.

CHAPTER FIVE

Going Sideways:
Lateral Movements to Develop Collection

I gave you an introduction to lateral movements—**work on two tracks**—in **Book One** (Chapter Ten), and I'd like to do a quick review here to refresh your memory.

All lateral work is not an end in itself. Instead, it is used as a means to an end: to warm up, loosen, and supple your horse's muscles as well as teach him to be obedient to your leg when it is placed behind the girth. In this chapter and the next, where I go into more advanced lateral movements, you'll see that the "end" also includes developing your horse's strength and his ability to carry himself more than would be possible if he were limited to **work on a single track**.

You don't decide to go sideways just because you're bored with going in a straight line and you'd like to do something different. Although, making your training fun and interesting is a side benefit that is as important for you as it is for your horse.

There are many mental as well as physical benefits gained by introducing lateral work. Besides keeping your work interesting, lateral movements increase your horse's obedience to the aids as he reponds to new combinations of your seat, legs, and hands. Physically, lateral work makes your horse more athletic in any number of ways.

For instance, in Book One (Chapter Ten), you learned how leg-yields, which are done in the working gaits, help to make a horse supple and loose so that he can move more freely. As a result, he can carry himself with more harmony and lightness. You also discovered that every horse is crooked to one degree or another; you learned how to use shoulder-fore to make your horse straight—one of the fundamental rules of classical training.

Now in this chapter and the next, you'll discover many additional benefits to doing lateral work. The more advanced lateral movements, which are ridden in the collected gaits, supple all parts of the horse's body and increase the elasticity of the "**bridge**" connecting his hindquarters through his back to his front end. They enable the horse to become more graceful in his movement as his gaits become more balanced, harmonious, and expressive. They increase the engagement of the hindquarters and, therefore, contribute even more to self-carriage, which you've already begun to develop in the collected gaits.

A lateral movement means that your horse goes forward and sideways at the same time. There are two categories of lateral movements, and the major difference between these two groups can be summed up in one word—bend.

The first category—lateral movements without bend—includes leg-yielding and turn on the forehand. I described these in detail in Book One (Chapter Ten). The turn on the forehand is an exercise in obedience to the leg. Leg-yielding is a useful warm-up exercise; it allows the horse to loosen, supple, and stretch his muscles.

The second group, the focus of this chapter and Chapter Six, has exercises that require bend and are, consequently, more demanding. This second group includes shoulder-fore, shoulder-in, haunches-in, haunches-out, and half-pass. I discussed shoulder-fore in Book One (Chapter Ten), but I'll review it and deal with the rest of the lateral movements with bend here. I'm also going to introduce the turn on the haunches as part of your two-track education.

Since bending is a requirement of the second category of lateral movements, I want to take a moment to review the concepts of "**inside**" and "**outside**". In many riding situations, "inside" and "outside" refer to the placement of your horse's body in relation to the arena: the "inside" of your horse's body refers to his side that is closest to the center of the arena, and the "outside" refers to his side that is closest to the rail. This is *not* the case in dressage. Instead, "inside" and "outside" are always determined by the direction toward which the horse's body is bent or flexed: if your horse is looking to the right and bent around your right leg, then his right side is his "inside", regardless of whether he's traveling around the arena to the right or to the left. (See fig. 10.5, page 172 in Book One, if this still sounds confusing. And don't worry—you'll get used to it!)

This second group of lateral movements is performed in the collected gaits, and when done correctly they actually improve self-carriage. Here's why: the fact that your horse is bent while he's going sideways necessitates that he engage his hind legs and shift his center of gravity toward his rear. Think of it as a formula: Bend + Sideways = Engagement.

5.1

In this shoulder-in there is a gentle bend through the entire length of Special Effects' body. His hindquarters are parallel to the rail and his hind feet travel straight down the track while his forehand is brought toward the middle of the ring at a 30-degree angle from the rail. For the picture to be perfect, his ears should be level.

5.2

Here Special Effects' body is no longer bent and a movement that began as a shoulder-in has degenerated into a leg-yield. It's easy to see that there's no bend because his hindquarters have swung out and they are no longer parallel to the rail.

Since bend is the essential ingredient in changing a lateral movement into an exercise that increases self-carriage, you can see why it's so important to work on correctly executed school figures. The more flexible and bendable your horse is, the better he can negotiate small circles and the more the lateral work can improve his balance in the collected gaits.

Remember that if your horse isn't bending well while you're doing lateral work, you'll need to momentarily abandon doing these more advanced lateral movements. After all, without bend, your lateral movement just becomes a leg-yield (figs. 5.1 and 5.2). So if you need to, go back to practicing bending exercises like circles and serpentines for a

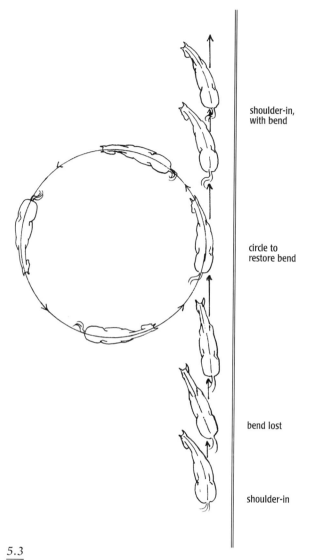

shoulder-in,
with bend

circle to
restore bend

bend lost

shoulder-in

5.3

If you are doing a shoulder-in and your horse starts to lose his bend, turn him on to a small circle and stay on it for as long as needed to recreate the bend before continuing the shoulder-in.

while. Then, as your horse becomes more flexible, you can resume going sideways. You'll find that as his bend improves, you'll be doing more productive lateral exercises.

For example, if your horse normally bends well but after a few steps of a lateral movement, he loses the bend, interrupt the lateral exercise and arc onto a circle instead. Once you've re-established the bend, continue with the lateral exercise. If you're doing a shoulder-in or a half-pass and your horse starts to lose his bend after a few strides, turn him onto a small circle immediately. Stay on that circle for as long as necessary to recreate the bend and then continue the movement (fig. 5.3).

When we get started shortly, you'll need to decide which pace you'll work in for your more advanced lateral movements. If you have a horse with a "safe" walk—meaning he has no tendency to lose the regular rhythm of his walk and he'll stay in front of your leg—it's easiest to start in the walk because it is slower and you'll have more time to get organized and coordinate your aids. If you're concerned about the quality of the walk degenerating or your horse getting behind your leg, you'll need to start in the trot. This might be a little more difficult for you because it's faster, but preserving the quality of the walk is always the priority. Plus, the greater impulsion in the trot will help you maintain the "forward" aspect of these "forward and sideways" movements.

I'm also going to strongly recommend that if you haven't already marked off an arena with letters, you do so before starting these lateral exercises. This will make it easier for you to have reference points so that you can ride accurately. Precision is essential so that your horse doesn't "cheat" and use his stronger hind leg more than his weaker one; sometimes his evasions can be so subtle that you won't realize it. Riding toward designated markers will give you confidence that your horse is making an equal effort with both hind legs. (See Chapter Ten for arena diagrams).

Shortly, I'll get into the first new lateral movement that you do with your horse—the shoulder-in. However, before I get started, I need to digress for a moment and review the use of the word "tracks" as it relates to lateral work (material I covered in Book One, Chapter Ten, but bears repeating).

TRACKS

We use the word "tracks" in so many different contexts. In the interests of clarifying the word, I'll describe all the different ways we use it in training.

First of all, the path that you make in the dirt as you go around your ring is a track.

Next, think of a working trot. In the working trot, your horse should "track up". In other words, if you looked on the ground, you'd see that the hoofprint made by each hind foot steps directly into the track of the hoofprint made by the front foot.

Then again, you ride around your ring with either your left or your right leg closest to the center of the arena. This determines whether you are "tracking to the left" or "tracking to the right." It might seem odd, but in order to "track to the right", for example, you'd have to enter the ring and turn to your left!

So far these usages of the word "tracks" are pretty clear-cut. But now we get to the fun stuff—lateral work.

To begin, let's consider the concept of *direction*. When you're just riding on a straight line, you're working on a "**single track**." In this case, the "single track" refers to the fact that you're only going in one direction—*forward*.

When you do any type of lateral work, you are working on "**two tracks**." The words "two tracks" refers to the fact that you're going in *two directions* at once—forward *and* sideways.

We also use the word "tracks" to describe how many *legs* we see coming toward us when standing directly in front of a horse. In each of the following examples, the horse will be going to the left and I'll start with the leg that is closest to the rail.

Leg-yields are done on "four tracks" because you can see all four legs coming towards you. If you are doing a leg-yield with your horse's head to the rail you see the right foreleg, the left foreleg, the right hind leg, and the left hind leg, in that order (fig. 5.5).

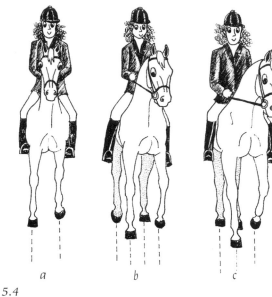

a   b   c

5.4

a) *Straight: horse moving on a single track, showing two tracks on the ground*
b) *Shoulder-fore: a two-track exercise on four tracks*
c) *Shoulder-in: a two-track exercise on three tracks*

Shoulder-fore is also on four tracks, but the legs are lined up differently. Starting from the rail, you see the right hind, the right fore, the left hind, and the left fore (fig. 5.4b).

During shoulder-in, shoulder-out, haunches-in, and haunches-out, the horse is on three tracks because you can only see three of his legs coming toward you. For example, in left shoulder-in, you see the right hind, the right fore, and the left fore. You won't see the left hind because it's hidden behind the right fore (fig. 5.4c).

To sum up: with single track movements you see two legs coming toward you; with two track movements you see either three or four legs coming toward you (figs. 5.4 to 5.7).

5.5

A good example of a leg-yield in the head-to-the-wall position. Special Effects' spine is straight, he's clearly on four tracks, and the angle of his hindquarters from the track is about 35 degrees.

5.6
During shoulder-fore Moxie is also on four tracks. Each of her four legs is visible and makes a separate track on the ground. But the angle is very slight compared to the angle created by the four tracks that you see in a leg-yield.

5.7
The haunches-in is one example of a two-track movement with bend being done on three tracks. Special Effects' outside hind leg isn't visible because it's lined up directly behind his inside foreleg.

Shoulder-In

USES

The first of the more advanced lateral movements that you need to learn is the shoulder-in. Shoulder-in is a suppling, straightening, strengthening as well as an "increasing self-carriage" exercise (figs. 5.8 and 5.9).

It supples the horse because it stretches and loosens the muscles and ligaments of the inside shoulder and forearm where the horse passes his inside foreleg across and in front of his outside foreleg. This suppling effect increases the horse's ability to move his forearm gymnastically in other lateral movements.

It is a straightening exercise because it enables the rider to place her horse's forehand in front of his hindquarters.

It strengthens and improves self-carriage because with each step the horse moves his inside hind leg underneath his body and places it in front of his outside hind leg under his center of gravity. By doing so, his inside hind leg gets stronger because it has to carry additional weight. Also, in order to move his inside hind leg in this way, the horse must lower his inside hip. When this is done, it contributes to the development of self-carriage.

Learning shoulder-in should be a simple concept for you to absorb because you're already familiar with shoulder-fore, which can be thought of as an "introductory" shoulder-in. To remind you, in shoulder-fore the horse is very slightly bent to the inside along his whole body. He should be positioned so that the rider can just see his eye and nostril.

The angle that the horse's forehand is brought in off the rail in shoulder-fore is about 15 degrees. His forelegs are brought slightly to the inside of the ring so that when viewed from the front, you would see the inside hind leg stepping in between the front legs. Since you can see all of the horse's legs from this position, you could say that during shoulder-fore, the horse is doing a two-track exercise on four tracks!

Shoulder-in is similar to shoulder-fore, but differs in that the horse's bend and his angle to the rail are increased and the horse travels on three distinct tracks rather than four—one for the outside hind leg, a second track for the inside hind leg which is lined up directly behind the outside foreleg, and a third track for the inside foreleg.

The exciting thing about learning shoulder-in is that once you master it, you'll have the main tool you need to do all of the other lateral movements. As you'll discover shortly, all these other lateral exercises are either near, or distant cousins of shoulder-in.

5.8

In shoulder-in, the horse's front legs are brought in off the track at about a 30-degree angle to the rail. Your horse's inside hind leg should be lined up directly behind his outside foreleg. He is on three tracks.

DESCRIPTION

Shoulder-in is a lateral movement in which the horse is flexed to the inside and slightly bent around your inside leg (in this case the one closest to the inside of the ring) and both his front legs and forehand are brought in off the track at approximately a 30-degree angle. At this angle, your horse's inside hind leg will be lined up directly behind his outside foreleg and he's on three tracks.

During shoulder-in, your horse's inside foreleg passes and crosses in front of his outside foreleg and his inside hind leg is placed in front of his outside hind leg.

It differs from the rest of the lateral exercises with bend because the horse is flexed at the poll to the inside, and bent around the rider's inside leg, but moving in the opposite direction from the way he's bent. For example, if your horse is bent to the right and traveling around the ring to the right, the direction that his legs and body move in a shoulder-in is to the left.

Some people bring their horse's forehand in to a greater degree than the angle that produces the three tracks I just described. When this is done, all four legs are visible (fig. 5.10). The three-track versus the four-track debate isn't an issue as long as the horse's bend is maintained so the exercise doesn't become just a leg yield. (Remember, a leg-yield is ridden without bend–the horse is only flexed slightly at the poll, away from the direction he is going. It is not as beneficial an exercise as the shoulder-in). What's more important is to be sure to do the shoulder-in with the same amount of angle in both directions rather than on three tracks one way and four tracks the other way. You want to be sure to develop your horse evenly in both directions.

To get the idea of shoulder-in, plan to ride a ten-meter circle in the second corner of the short side of your arena. Then, imagine that you discontinue riding that circle one stride after you start it. Maintain the bend that you established at the beginning of the circle, and send your horse straight down the long side of your ring instead. Your horse's hind

5.9

Shoulder-in: Galen is evenly bent from poll to tail around Deb's inside leg. Her forehand is brought in off the track at approximately a 30 degree angle. Because her inside hind leg is lined up directly behind her outside foreleg, three separate tracks on the ground are visible. Galen is bent and traveling to the right, but her legs and body are moving to the left.

5.10

Deb has brought Galen's forehand to the inside slightly more than before so that now she is on four tracks. However, she is still doing a good shoulder-in because she has maintained the bend around her inside leg. The wider angle to the rail is fine as long as she does it the same way when she goes in the other direction, so that both sides develop evenly.

5.11

Your horse's hind legs stay on the line of the circle and his forehand is brought to the inside to describe a slightly smaller circle than his hind legs.

legs stay on the track as if they were traveling straight forward parallel to the track, while his forehand is moved onto an inside track. Essentially, a shoulder-in is a first step of a small circle but repeated on a straight line.

You can also practice on a circle. Here, your horse's hind legs stay on the line of the circle and his forehand is brought to the inside, to describe a slightly smaller circle than his hind legs (fig. 5.11).

The Aids for Shoulder-In

The aids for left shoulder-in are as follows:

1. *Seat:* weight on left seatbone.
2. *Left leg:* on the girth for the horse to bend around as well as to ask for engagement of the inside hind leg.
3. *Right leg:* behind the girth to help bend the horse around the inside leg.
4. *Left rein:* vibrate for inside flexion.
5. *Right rein:* steady and supporting to prevent too much bend in the neck.
6. *Both hands:* stay low and move to the left. They should stay equidistant from your body and move sideways on the same plane. Be sure that your inside hand (left) does not get drawn closer to the saddle and that your outside hand (right) does not cross over the withers. Move both hands enough to the left to lead your horse's shoulders in that direction so that you place his outside front leg in front of his inside hind leg.

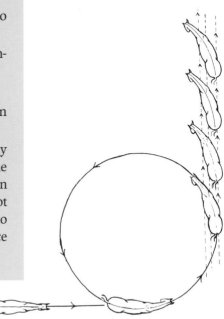

SEQUENCE OF AIDS

As with any of the lateral movements that have a bend, always ask for the bend before you ask for the angle. First, ride well into the corner to bend your horse. If he doesn't want to bend in the corner, ride a small circle until he bends easily. Think about your bending aids while on the circle. When circling to the left, your weight is on your left seat bone, your left leg is on the girth, your right leg is behind the girth, you vibrate the left rein for flexion while supporting with the right rein to prevent your horse from bending his neck too much to the inside. The supporting outside rein is essential because horses are more flexible in their necks than through the rest of their bodies and would happily overbend their necks to the inside if you let them. For the shoulder in to be correct, the bend must be uniform from poll to tail.

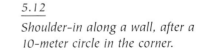

5.12

Shoulder-in along a wall, after a 10-meter circle in the corner.

You'll know your horse is bending easily when you can soften the contact on the inside rein, and he feels like he'll stay bent pretty much by himself. Then, once your horse is bending well on the small circle, start another one and interrupt it after the first step to continue down the long side while bent. Initiate this movement down the long side by looking straight down the track rather than between your horse's ears as you do on a circle, and increase your inside (left) leg to send your horse down the long side of the ring (fig. 5.12).

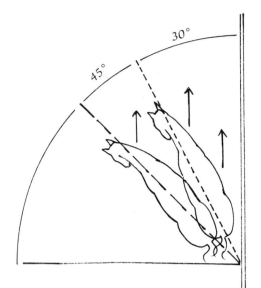

5.13

In shoulder-in the 30-degree angle your horse's body makes to the track is like a small wedge of pie.

Once he is headed in the right direction, ask for the angle of about 30 degrees by bringing your two hands to the left. This will bring your horse's forehand in. Think of the angle that your horse's body makes to the track or the rail as a small wedge of pie. Keep your hands side by side and place them low. It's important that your hands are low because if they aren't, your horse's shoulders can escape underneath the reins rather than being influenced and displaced by them. Think of using an opening left rein to help keep your inside hand in front of your inside hip and bring your right fist toward your horse's shoulders to create the angle (figs. 5.13 and 5.14).

Shoulder-in can only be done in the walk and trot. When in the canter, you should only ride shoulder-fore (See Book One, Chapter Ten). If you ask for the greater degree of angle required for a shoulder-in while in the canter, you might destroy the purity of the pace by making it four-beat.

• *Helpful Hints for Shoulder-In* •
MAINTAINING THE TEMPO

One of your major goals in all of riding is to keep your horse's tempo constant, and this rule applies to shoulder-in as well. He should neither slow down nor speed up. Because the movement makes a lot of new demands on your horse, when he is first learning it, he might lose impulsion and slow down or get so worried that he rushes off.

These reactions usually happen because he's not yet supple or strong enough to cope with the increased engagement of his inside hind leg. So, for the time being, make one of the following adjustments to decrease the difficulty of the movement until your horse becomes more able and athletic. You'll find that depending on the individual animal, some horses benefit from one exercise rather than the other.

1. Ask for less angle and bend by doing shoulder-fore instead (See Book One, Chapter Ten).

2. Ride shoulder-in for only a few steps. Straighten your horse and renew his desire to go forward by lengthening for several strides. Ask for only a few steps of shoulder-in again.

3. Ride shoulder-in at the walk. This exercise won't be helpful for the nervous horse who gets more tense when you ride on contact in the walk. Those "raring-to-go" types will do better in the trot because they'll have a forward outlet for their pent-up energy. For

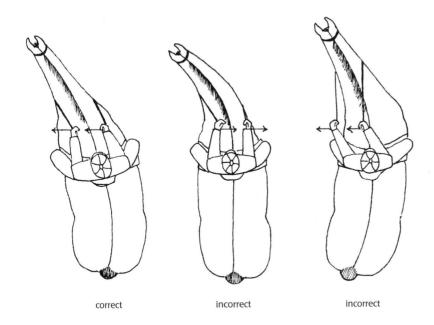

correct   incorrect   incorrect

5.14

Rein aids for left shoulder-in. Both hands stay low, are equidistant from your body, and move sideways to the left on the same plane.

most horses though, doing shoulder-in in the walk is a good idea because it gives you more time to get organized and apply your aids quietly.

MAINTAINING THE BEND

If your horse's hindquarters swing out toward the rail rather than staying parallel to it, he'll lose his bend and you'll be doing a leg-yield, not a shoulder-in. That's fine if your goal is to do a leg-yield with a straight body. But since one of your goals when doing shoulder-in is to engage your horse's inside hind leg, he needs to be bent through his body with his hindquarters parallel to the fence while he's going sideways.

You'll probably find that your horse will be perfectly happy to swing his hindquarters out towards the fence because by doing so he can evade the increased bending of the joints of his inside hind leg. You may actually be the cause of this evasion if you don't use your legs correctly. If you neglect to keep your outside leg back, it won't be in a position where it can control the haunches. To cut off this escape route, imagine that you "trap" your horse's outside hind leg and keep it from escaping by ap-

5.15

To keep your outside leg back where it can control the haunches, think of trapping your horse's outside hindleg to keep it from escaping.

5.16

If you tend to draw your inside leg back by mistake, exaggerate the correction. "Picture" tucking it up into the curve behind your horse's elbow and letting it nestle there.

plying your outside leg behind the girth (fig. 5.15).

To absorb this concept of preventing the hindquarters from swinging out with your outside leg, think about just riding the hind legs *straight down the track* while moving the shoulders in. Do many transitions from a few straight strides along the track to a few steps of shoulder-in and back to straight ahead again. Concentrate on maintaining the exact same position of your horse's hind legs—parallel to the fence—at all times.

You also need to be careful with the position of your *inside* leg. If you draw it back instead of keeping it on the girth, you'll push your horse's hindquarters out as if you were actually asking for a leg-yield (fig. 5.17).

Use a mental image to help you keep your inside leg on the girth rather than letting it slide back behind the girth. I call this position of your inside leg at the girth an "engaging" spot because your leg needs to be placed there in order to engage or activate the horse's corresponding hind leg. If you tend to draw your leg back, exaggerate the image by picturing that you tuck this leg right up into the curve behind your horse's elbow and let it nestle into that spot (fig. 5.16). This should counteract the urge to pull it back, so that it will end up on the girth where it belongs.

In either case, once you realize that either of your legs hasn't done its job correctly, first ride your horse straight down the track. Do this by leading his forehand back to the track by bringing both of your hands toward the rail. Then make sure you've repositioned your legs so that they are side by side. Once your horse's body is realigned so that he's on a single track and parallel to the fence, you can have another go at riding the shoulder-in, and as you do it, "think" that you want to bring his shoulders *in* rather than push his hindquarters *out.*

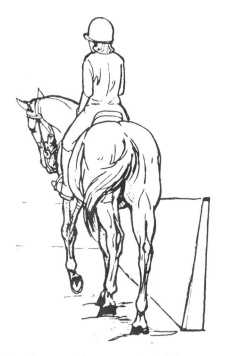

a) Shoulder-in ridden correctly with horse evenly bent and moving on three tracks.

b) If your horse's hindquarters swing out toward the rail rather than staying parallel to it, he'll lose his bend and you'll only be doing a leg-yield.

5.17 Position of hindquarters in relation to the rail during shoulder-in

Sometimes, rather than not having enough bend, a rider overbends her horse's neck to the inside. Remember that during shoulder-in (and all of the lateral exercises with bend, for that matter) the bend should be uniform from poll to tail. Often there's too much bend in the neck because a rider uses an unequal influence of the two reins. For instance, she uses too much inside rein without supporting with her outside rein. Or, she neglects to keep her hands side-by-side.

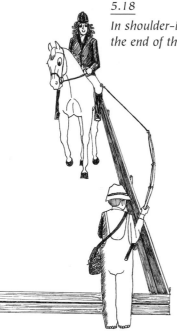

5.18

In shoulder-in, get a visual reference point for a steady angle. Line up your knee to a point at the end of the ring, and feel it being drawn to that point as if by an invisible line attached to it.

MAINTAINING THE ANGLE

Once you commit yourself to an angle with the rail, it shouldn't waver. Get a visual reference point for a steady angle by lining up your outside knee with a point at the end of your arena. Feel your knee being drawn to that point as if there were a line attached to it that was being reeled in by an imaginary fisherman (fig. 5.18).

Here's something else you can do to get a visual reference point for a steady angle. If your riding area or ring is mostly dirt and has pretty heavy traffic, you probably have a gulley along the well-used track. On either side of this depression, there's a lip of dirt. Take advantage of this. Place your horse's hind legs in the gulley and put his outside front leg on the inside edge of the track. Glance down at your horse's outside shoulder to check that his outside foreleg steps exactly on the inside lip of the track with every stride. This leg should not move back into the track or go any further beyond the edge toward the center of the ring.

One of my students had a real challenge riding the shoulder-in with an angle of 30 degrees in both directions. She consistently asked for too much angle when she went to the right and not enough angle when she went to the left. She knew that she did this habitually, but that information wasn't enough for her to make the necessary adjustments.

She needed to develop a sense of where her horse's shoulders were in relation to the rail. To develop this awareness, we divided the long side of the ring into three parts. I had her ride the first third of the long side in shoulder-fore at a 15-degree angle. Then she increased the angle and did a shoulder-in at 30 degrees for the next part. Finally, she increased the angle to about 35 degrees and did a leg-yield for the last third of the long side. I acted as her mirror and gave her feedback on the various angles.

Sometimes we'd change the order of the exercises. In time she developed her perception of what she needed to do with her aids to create a specific amount of angle, regardless of the direction she was going. Eventually she was able to place her horse's shoulders anywhere she wanted.

CONTROLLING THE SHOULDERS

One of the most common mistakes that I see is a shoulder-in ridden as a "head- and neck-in". What I mean by this is that if you were watching, you'd see the horse's head and neck brought to the inside, but his shoulders either stay directly in front of his hindquarters or, even worse, they fall out toward the rail (fig. 5.19).

5.19

This is not shoulder-in. I call it a "head- and neck-in." The horse's head and neck are brought to the inside and the horse falls out through the outside shoulder.

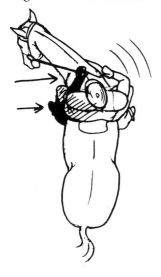

5.20 and 5.21

Kelly Weiss and Kousteau demonstrate different positions of the head and shoulders in these two photos. In both of these pictures Kousteau's head is brought to the left at approximately the same degree. However, in the first photo, Kelly does not have control of the horse's shoulders and they bulge out to the right so that Kousteau's right front leg is almost directly in front of his right hind leg. Also, because he is not stepping into the rein on his soft left side, he collapses away from it, bends only in the neck, and tips his head.

5.21

In this photo, Kelly has good control of his horse's shoulders. He has successfully moved them to the left so that we see a shoulder-in being performed on slightly more than three tracks. Also, he has created good engagement of the left hind leg and as Kousteau steps into the left rein, his ears become more level and his head is straighter.

A horse is inclined to adopt this position more frequently when his soft side is on the inside. This is because he often doesn't step solidly into the rein and accept it on his soft side. Since he's not really connected to this rein, when you go to use it, he collapses away from it and just bends his neck. As a result it's impossible to influence his whole body (figs. 5.20 and 5.21).

Although this might be an odd concept to absorb, you'll find that it's actually easier for you to do a shoulder-in when your horse's stiff side is on the inside. I realize that bend is a requirement of shoulder-in, and it's more difficult to bend your horse on his stiff side, but because he steps into the rein and accepts it on his stiff side, it'll be easier for you to influence his shoulders.

When you use your hand to correct a part of your horse's body that should be controlled by your leg, you'll get a "head- and neck-in." For instance, you start a shoulder-in but then feel your horse's whole body wanting to move off the track toward the inside of the ring. You attempt to hold his hind legs on the track by using your inside rein as an indirect rein rather than keeping it in front of your inside hip.

Here's how this cycle unfolds: you ask for shoulder-in and your horse realizes he's going to have to do more work by engaging his inside hind leg. This is very physically demanding for him because not only does he have to bend the joints of his inside hind leg to a greater degree, but he also has to take that leg and place it underneath his body in front of his outside hind leg. In an effort to avoid this extra work, he steps toward the inside of the ring.

To be more specific, during left shoulder-in, he steps sideways to the left with his left hind leg rather than stepping toward his center. He is attempting to avoid the increased closing of the joints of this leg. You feel him coming off the track and your instinct is to bring your hands back toward the rail (to the right) to hold his body on the track.

This is not going to help. When you feel this happening, you need to treat the cause and not the symptom. The symptom is that your horse comes off the track toward the inside of the ring. The cause is that your horse is drifting to the inside to avoid the increased bending of the joints of his hind leg. So you need to direct your correction to his hindquarters rather than to his forehand. Insist that he keep his hind legs on the track by using your inside leg actively. Since your legs control his hind legs, the correction must be made by using your inside leg actively on the girth.

In clinics I often try to give a rider the idea of moving the shoulders in by allowing her to counter-flex her horse at the poll. I realize that by doing this her horse won't be bending correctly for a shoulder-in. But this is only temporary. At this point my primary concern is to teach her the feeling of controlling her horse's shoulders. Once she feels how she can move his shoulders by moving her hands sideways as I described in the aids for this movement on page 102, I have her go back to correct flexion and bend.

Sometimes your horse refuses to move his shoulders, and they just seem glued to the rail. You feel that you're using your hands correctly, but your horse's shoulders don't budge and it's difficult to get any angle at all.

The problem here might be that your horse lacks suppleness and mobility in his shoulders. So do some "shoulder-mobilization" exercises to improve the horse's ability to slide his shoulders left and right.

I described these exercises in detail in my "Hard To Steer" section in Chapter Thirteen in Book One. All of them can be done in all three paces. In each case, you ask your horse to flex at the poll (by vibrating the rein) in the opposite direction from the way you want his shoulders to move. In other words, if you're going to slide his shoulders to the left, you'll want to first flex him to the right. You'll know you're gaining in the suppleness department when you can easily move your horse's shoulders around yet the weight of the reins in your hands doesn't get any heavier.

USING SHOULDER-IN
TO INCREASE SELF-CARRIAGE

During each step of shoulder-in, your horse's inside hind leg moves in the direction of his center of gravity and he lowers his inside hip. Doing so causes his hindquarters to lower and his hind legs to carry more of his weight than before. As a result, his shoulders are relieved and his forelegs can step more freely.

One way for you to determine that you've ridden a good shoulder-in is to do several strides and then ask yourself the following question. "When I'm finished, does my horse feel like he's carrying himself because he's more balanced back on his hindquarters and lighter in my hands than he was when I started?" In other words, has your shoulder-in increased his self-carriage? You've done a good shoulder-in if your horse's balance is more "uphill" and less on the forehand after the shoulder-in than it was before you started.

Here's an image to help you achieve that desired effect. Do you remember that earlier in this book (Chapter Three) I told you that one way of measuring the degree of self-carriage is to evaluate the relative height of the withers to the top of the croup? So, when you ride shoulder-in as an exercise to increase self-carriage, think of calling the movement "shoulders-up" instead. Picture your horse's withers becoming higher than his hindquarters. "Feel" a lighter rein contact as he comes into self-carriage because his entire forehand from the withers forward is raised.

Maybe your horse maintains his self-carriage pretty well while in a particular gait, but as soon as you do a downward transition, he falls on his forehand. If this happens, do the following exercise to teach him to stay in good balance throughout the transition.

Start by doing trot-walk-trot transitions. Ride down the long side of the ring while in a collected trot. Step into the walk and ask for shoulder-

5.22

To prepare to do shoulder-out, Amy first rides parallel to the long side on a line that is about three feet in from the track. She does this so that her horse has room to move his shoulders over.

in at the moment of the downward transition. Then straighten your horse and pick up the trot again.

You can also do canter-trot-canter transitions. Ask for a transition to the trot and at the moment that your horse steps into the the trot, immediately ride shoulder-in for a few strides. Then straighten him and ask for the canter depart again.

Shoulder-Out

When schooling, you can do an exercise that is the mirror-image of shoulder-in. (I say "when schooling" because it is not used in competition). I call this exercise **shoulder-out**, and I use it when I want to engage my horse's outside hind leg. For example, I might decide to do a shoulder-out prior to a canter depart if I have a horse that consistently

5.23

Next, she bends Special Effects around her leg that is closest to the rail. Finally, she brings his forehand toward the outside of the ring by moving both of her hands in that direction.

picks up the wrong lead because his outside hind leg—the strike off leg—is not engaged. I'll do shoulder-out to help activate that leg.

All of the same principals as well as the suppling and engaging benefits of shoulder-in apply to shoulder-out. It can be done only in the walk and the trot.

To do a shoulder-out, first ride your horse straight down a line that is slightly to the inside of the track around the ring. You need to do this so you'll have room to move your horse's forehand toward the rail (figs. 5.22 and 5.23). If you are riding to the left and you want to ride shoulder-out, flex your horse to the right and bend him around your right leg. Your weight is on your right seatbone. Your left rein supports; your left leg behind the girth helps bend your horse around your right leg. Both of your hands move to the right to lead your horse's shoulders in that direction.

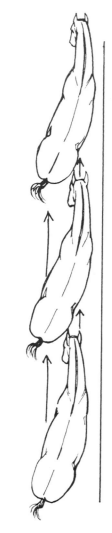

5.24 Haunches-in

Haunches-In

Haunches-in (also known as **travers**) is another exercise that you can do to help supple your horse and improve his balance and self-carriage. Doing haunches-in improves the mobility of the haunches by stretching and loosening the muscles and ligaments of the hindquarters. It also checks a horse's obedience to your outside leg. Haunches-in can be done in all three paces, and it can be performed on both straight and curved lines.

Once you know how to ride a shoulder-in, doing a haunches-in should be simple for you. Here's why. Remember when I told you to think of shoulder-in as the first step of a circle that is repeated on a straight line (page 93)? Well, you can think of haunches-in as the *last* step of a circle repeated on a straight line. If you imagine the arc of a circle where it touches the track, you can see that shoulder-in and haunches-in are close relatives (fig. 5.24). If you ride a small circle and don't finish it by one stride, but instead keep the bend you have on the circle while sending your horse forward on a straight line, you have a haunches-in.

DESCRIPTION

Haunches-in is a lateral movement in which the horse is slightly bent around your inside leg. Specifically, when tracking to the left, your horse is bent around your left leg. His front legs stay on the original track of the long side and his hindquarters are brought in off the track toward the center of the ring at about a 30-degree angle to the rail. His outside legs pass and cross in front of his inside legs and he looks in the direction he's moving.

With the horse's hind legs shifted toward the inside of the ring at a 30-degree angle from the rail, his outside hind leg is lined up directly behind his inside foreleg. So if you stand in front of a horse as he comes towards you in haunches-in, you see three tracks (fig. 5.25).

Some people are reluctant to introduce haunches-in because they have spent a lot of time straightening their horses who like to carry their hindquarters to the inside naturally. They are concerned that if they ask the hindquarters to come in, they'll be encouraging this form of crookedness.

I have two thoughts on this subject. The first has to do with obedience: there's a world of difference between asking your horse to move sideways from a specific aid and letting your horse take the initiative to move his hindquarters over. The other vital distinction is that during haunches-in, your horse is asked to bend through his entire body, thus making him engage his hindquarters. The crooked horse described above doesn't bend at all. His hindquarters are just drifting to the inside of the ring so he can avoid bending the joints of his inside hindleg (fig. 5.26).

5.25
Haunches-in showing a clear bend from poll to tail around Deb's inside leg. Galen's outside hind leg is lined up directly behind her inside foreleg so only three tracks are visible.

5.26 Haunches-in

a) *Traveling straight correctly; using both hind legs equally.*
b) *Traveling crooked on two tracks, to avoid carrying weight behind equally.*
c) *Traveling on two tracks doing a correct haunches-in with bend through horse's body.*

a   *b*   *c*

The Aids for Haunches-In

The following are the aids for haunches-in when tracking to the left:

1. *Seat:* weight on left seatbone. Because your outside leg is behind the girth asking your horse's hindquarters to move over, it's easy for you to end up leaning to the right with your whole upper body. Concentrate on keeping your weight over your inside leg by visualizing moving your right seatbone toward the middle of the saddle.

2. *Left leg:* on the girth for the horse to bend around as well as to ask for engagement of his inside hind leg. Feel your horse's rib cage softly yielding away from your inside leg rather than bulging or leaning against it.

3. *Right leg:* behind the girth to help bend the horse around your inside leg and to take his hindquarters away from the rail.

4. *Left rein:* vibrate for inside flexion.

5. *Right rein:* steady and supporting to prevent too much bend in the neck.

6. *Both reins:* hold your horse's forehand on the track but the outside one is dominant and is supported by the inside rein.

SEQUENCE OF AIDS

You'll base your decision about whether to start haunches-in at the walk or the trot by using the same criteria that you did for starting shoulder-in. Specifically, if your horse maintains the regularity of his rhythm, stays in front of your leg, and seems calm, start in the walk because you'll have more time to get organized and think about how to coordinate your aids. If the walk isn't "**safe**," start in the trot.

As with shoulder-in, be sure to ask for the bend before you ask for the angle. Otherwise, all you'll end up with is a leg-yield instead of a haunches-in. First, ask for bend in a corner. If your horse doesn't bend easily, stay on a small circle in the corner until he does. In your mind, run through the bending aids while on the circle as you did for the shoulder-in. Think about improving the bend by "embracing" or "enveloping" your horse's barrel with both of your legs. Feel the contact of your legs on your horse's sides all the way down to your ankles so you can "wrap him up" in between your legs.

Since I suggested that you picture doing a haunches-in from the last step of a small circle before it intersects with the track, apply the "angle" aids just before you finish a corner or a circle. Add the angle by increasing the pressure of your outside leg and leading your horse's shoulders to the rail with an opening outside rein. This way you'll prevent the hindquarters from completing the entire turn as you start down the long side, thus doing a haunches-in.

While you're doing this, be sure to maintain flexion and bend to the inside. Look straight down the track.

• *Helpful Hints for Haunches-In* •

MAINTAINING RHYTHM AND TEMPO

Sometimes when you introduce haunches-in, a horse loses his impulsion or his rhythm. He might also become worried and show his anxiety either by rushing off or "sucking" back. As in shoulder-in, any of these problems can occur because he's not yet supple or strong enough to cope with the increased engagement of his hind legs. If you feel him struggling either physically or mentally, decrease the difficulty of the movement by modifying it in the same way that you did for the shoulder-in:

1. Ask for less angle.
2. Ride only a few steps, then renew your horse's desire to go forward by turning onto a circle or by doing a few steps of a lengthening. Once he's "thinking" forward, ask for a few steps of haunches-in again.
3. Ride haunches-in in the walk as long as the quality of his walk doesn't suffer.

MAINTAINING BEND

It's absolutely vital that your horse stays bent during haunches-in. Otherwise, rather than riding an engagement exercise, you'll simply be riding a crooked horse whose hindquarters have drifted to the inside to avoid engagement.

If your horse resists being bent correctly when you start a haunches-in, circle first. Then, only do a few steps of haunches-in and quickly melt back onto a small circle before he loses his bend. It's better to do a couple of high quality steps than to overface your horse and end up with many strides of a leg-yield. As your horse becomes more supple, you can gradually increase the number of haunches-in steps.

Another way that your horse can lose his bend is if you allow his front legs to deviate from pointing straight ahead up the track. Proper coordination of the two reins (the steady outside rein, which functions as a slight opening rein and leads the forehand toward the rail, and the vibrating inside rein, which supports this position) as well as a firm inside leg will keep his front legs traveling in the right direction.

5.27

As you ask your horse's haunches to move toward the inside of the ring, make sure you maintain bend by keeping his front end pointed straight ahead, parallel to the rail. Imagine he has miners' lamps on his knees and they shine straight forward.

While on a straight line, your horse's front legs should travel straight forward parallel to the rail, while his hindquarters are displaced onto an inside track. If his forehand starts to point toward the fence, it means he's losing the bend. Once the bend is lost, the exercise becomes a leg-yield.

So one way for you to determine that you're maintaining bend is to make sure that the position of your horse's front legs during a haunches-in is exactly the same as it is when you ride straight down the track—parallel to the fence.

In your mind's eye, hold the image of his front feet pointing straight down the track like a car's headlights that are lighting your way. If the headlights are misaligned, they'll point out toward the rail and they won't help you see your way straight ahead (fig. 5.27).

You do a haunches-in on a circle in the same way as on a straight line. Your horse's front legs stay on the track of the circle, and his hindquarters are moved to the inside to make a slightly smaller circle. If his forehand starts pointing to the outside of the circle, the bend is lost, and, once again, you'll end up just doing a leg-yield (fig. 5.28).

I frequently see situations where a rider causes the loss of bend because she asks her horse to move his hindquarters over at too great an angle to the rail. She uses too much outside leg and she pushes her horse's hindquarters too far to the inside. At an angle greater than 30 degrees, it's difficult for a horse to bend and his only option is to straighten his body and do a leg-yield.

I'm not sure why this is such a common problem but I'm suspicious that the reason is that the rider can't see how far she's bringing her horse's hindquarters in from the rail when doing a haunches-in. She, therefore, tends to ask for more angle than she

5.28

Haunches-in on a circle follows the same rules as haunches-in on a straight line. Specifically, the forehand stays exactly on the line of travel. The hind legs move to the inside to make a slightly smaller circle.

needs. It's easier to do a shoulder-in because all you have to do is look down at your horse's forehand to see the angle at which the shoulders are brought in off the track.

MAINTAINING THE ANGLE

Some people find it difficult to move their horse's hindquarters in with enough angle. Be sure you're not part of the problem. Remember that your horse's front legs should be on the track parallel to the fence. He should be slightly bent and flexed toward the inside of the ring. I say "slightly" because many riders crank their horses' forehands too much to the inside of the ring in an effort to keep them bent and, as a result, only the horse's barrel is left on the track. But by bringing the front end in off the track so much, it becomes impossible for the back end to come in at the required 30-degree angle away from the rail. After all, your horse's body isn't a pretzel!

However, as I mentioned above, a more likely scenario is that you ask for too much angle because you can't see where the hindquarters are. Sometimes you are too strong with your outside leg. Other times your horse sees an escape route from engaging his hind legs, and he happily swings his hindquarters in too far. Remember that if there's too much angle, you'll probably lose the bend and the purpose of the haunches-in is lost. Make sure your horse stays on three tracks with his inside fore and outside hind on the same track so that his hindquarters are at an angle of approximately 30 degrees away from the rail.

Use a person on the ground or a mirror to help you to learn this feeling of the correct angle. Remember this isn't a huge shifting of his hindquarters. Lining up the outside hind leg behind the inside foreleg is merely the displacement of a few inches. If you tend to ask for too much angle, compensate by underriding it. It's better to bend your horse and perhaps not have enough angle than to lose the bend by asking for too much angle and end up with a leg-yield.

FURTHER USES OF HAUNCHES-IN

Controlling the Hindquarters in Shoulder-In

Since the rider's outside leg must be behind the girth during haunches-in, I use this movement as a way to teach her how to prevent the horse's hindquarters from swinging out when she's riding a shoulder-in. I ask the rider to alternate between a few steps of haunches-in and a few steps of shoulder-in without straightening her horse in between. Because her outside leg is clearly positioned behind the girth in haunches-in, she just keeps it in that exact same spot as she slides into shoulder-in. The bending aids are exactly the same in both movements. The difference is whether the front end, or the back end, of her horse is displaced off the track (fig. 5.29).

5.29

To learn the feeling of controlling your horse's hindquarters with your outside leg during shoulder-in, alternate between a few steps of haunches-in and a few steps of shoulder-in.

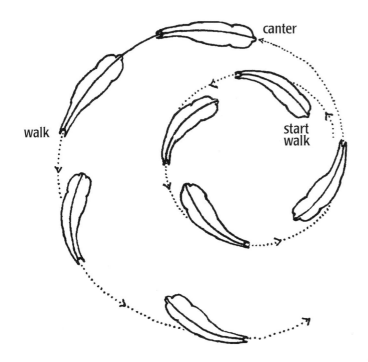

Developing Self-Carriage in the Canter

I often use haunches-in in the walk for horses that have a tendency to get strung out, fall on the forehand, and lose their self-carriage after a few strides of canter. Since the walk and canter are very closely related, I can often help the canter through good walk work. However, even though my objective is to improve the canter with this work, I make a special point of preserving the rhythm of the walk, which can be lost if you're not careful.

For horses with **"safe" walks** who always stay active and in a regular rhythm, you can proceed with the exercise in the following way. After warming up, walk around the ring in haunches-in. Stay in that position through the corners and the short sides until it feels "easy." (It's easy when you don't have to work hard to keep the bend.) You should almost feel as if your horse is bending all by himself. In fact, you should be able to soften by relaxing the tension on your inside rein and have your horse feel as if he'll stay bent without you having to hold him in position. When this happens, it'll feel as if your horse has gathered himself together and the contact will feel much lighter. Obviously, this should be done only with horses who are experienced and comfortable with haunches-in.

Once you have accomplished these "feelings" as you ride down the long side in haunches-in, try turning on to a small circle here and there while still riding haunches-in. Place your horse's front legs on the track of your circle and move his hind legs toward the inside so that they make a smaller circle than the front legs do. The addition of the circle makes the exercise more demanding than by just doing it the whole way around your ring.

Finally, when your horse feels very soft in haunches-in on this small circle at the walk, it's time to try the canter. While still in the walk, arc out onto a larger circle. Straighten him along the arc of that circle and do a normal walk-to-canter transition. Canter for just a few strides. Then, before he falls on his forehand and his balance degenerates again (sometimes it takes only five or six strides), walk and resume the haunches-in position. In this way, your horse learns to carry himself in the canter a few strides at a time (fig. 5.30).

5.30

To improve self-carriage in the canter, ride haunches-in at the walk on a small circle. Arc out onto a larger circle, straighten, and do a transition from walk to canter. Canter a few strides, and before your horse loses his balance again, walk and resume the haunches-in position.

5.31

Haunches-out: Galen is bent from poll to tail around Deb's right leg. This was her outside leg when she was traveling on a straight line, but now that she has bent her horse around it, it has become her inside leg. (Remember, "inside" and "outside" is determined by the bend of the horse—not by where the rail is.)

Once her horse is bent, she moves her forehand about 30 degrees away from the rail. Since the horse's left hind leg is hidden behind her right front leg and we can only see three legs, Galen is on three tracks.

Haunches-Out

Just as shoulder-out is the mirror image of shoulder-in, **haunches-out** (also known as **renvers**) is the mirror image of haunches-in. Consequently, it provides the same loosening, suppling and engaging benefits as the haunches-in.

To do haunches-out when tracking to the left, flex your horse to the right and bend him around your right leg. While his hind feet remain on the track, bring his forehand onto an inside track at about a 30-degree angle from the rail (fig. 5.31).

At this angle, your horse is on three tracks. Specifically, when tracking to the left, one track is made by the outside hind leg, the second track is made by the inside hind leg lined up directly behind the outside foreleg, and the third track is made by the inside foreleg. All of the same principles of haunches-in apply to haunches-out (fig. 5.32).

5.32

Haunches-out

KEY POINTS

🐎 The more advanced lateral movements are distinguished from the easier lateral movements (turn on the forehand and leg-yielding) because the horse is bent through his body as he moves sideways.

🐎 Think of this formula when you ride these lateral movements: Bend + Sideways = Engagement.

🐎 Shoulder-in supples, straightens, and improves self-carriage. Think of shoulder-in as the first step of a small circle that is repeated (maintaining the bend) along the straight line of the track.

🐎 Haunches-in supples and improves self-carriage. Think of haunches-in as the last step of a small circle just before it joins the track that is repeated (maintaining the bend) along the straight line of the track.

CHAPTER SIX

Advanced Lateral Movements

Half-Pass

DESCRIPTION

With haunches-in firmly in your repertoire, it should be fairly easy for you to do a **half-pass.** I find it puzzling when a rider tells me that her horse can do a good shoulder-in and a good haunches-in but he can't do a half-pass yet. If a horse can do haunches-in, he can certainly do a half-pass, because this lateral movement is simply haunches-in done on a diagonal line across the arena instead of along a straight line or on a circle.

Half-pass is a lateral movement along a diagonal line in which your horse is slightly bent around your inside leg and his body is parallel to the fence, with his forehand slightly in advance of his hindquarters. His outside legs pass and cross in front of his inside legs, and he looks in the direction of movement (figs. 6.1 to 6.5).

You're already familiar with this idea of going forward and sideways along a diagonal line from the work you've done with leg-yielding. But what makes a half-pass so much more difficult than a leg-yield is that you're now asking your horse to go sideways while he's bent around your inside leg. This bend makes the movement much more demanding.

You can do half-passes in all three paces to supple your horse, improve his self-carriage and lighten his forehand so that he can "dance" with greater fluency and grace.

PLACES AND PATTERNS FOR THE HALF-PASS

When you're in a large arena, you can do a half-pass from the long side to the center of your arena, from the centerline to the long side, or all the way across the diagonal. (See Chapter Ten for arena charts). Be sure that you do half-passes from, and to, specific points so that you work both hind legs equally.

6.1 *Half-pass*

6.2

6.3

6.2 to 6.5.

Half-Pass Sequence

A half-pass sequence from the beginning of the long side to the centerline: in this half-pass to the left, Chris Hickey bends Dwight around his left leg. His body is basically parallel to the long side, but his forehand is slightly in advance of his hindquarters. His outside (right) legs cross in front of his inside legs and he looks in the direction that he's going.

For our purposes we will limit the angle of the line you ride sideways to approximately 22 degrees from the rail. In a large arena (fig 6.6), for example, this angle would take you from the letter marked D, over to E; or E, over to G. It's also the angle that would be made if you did a half-pass along the entire diagonal from M to K or from H to F.

(More advanced horses in dressage competition are hardly ever asked to exceed a 30-degree angle, while at the highest level, the Grand Prix, the maximum angle required is 40 degrees.)

6.4

6.5

The Aids for the Half-Pass

The aids for a half-pass to the left are as follows:

1. *Seat:* weight on the left seat bone.
2. *Left leg:* on the girth for bend through the body, impulsion, and engagement of the inside hind leg.
3. *Right leg:* behind the girth to help bend the horse around the inside left leg and to initiate movement sideways.
4. *Left rein:* vibrate for flexion.
5. *Right rein:* steady and supporting to limit bend in the neck.

Note: the left rein and left leg are responsible for maintaining the bend. The right leg supported by the right rein is responsible for the degree of sideways movement.

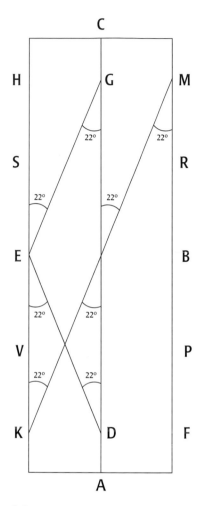

6.6

Some of the lines—with 22-degree angles to other lines—on which you can ride a half-pass.

SEQUENCE OF AIDS

First, ride a small circle in the corner as you did before beginning a shoulder-in or haunches-in (see fig. 5.12). Next, upon leaving the circle, do a step or two of **shoulder-fore** to insure that your horse's shoulders will be slightly in advance of his hindquarters when you start going sideways. Then, initiate sideways movement by "stepping down" into the inside (left) stirrup and using your outside aids. One way for you to learn this feeling of "stepping down" in the direction of the half-pass is to imagine that you want to shift the saddle over to the left side of your horse's back.

There is another school of thought that recommends starting the half-pass without doing the step or two of shoulder-fore. Instead, teach your horse how to do the half-pass by first turning straight onto the diagonal line for a few strides. Then, keeping the forehand on the diagonal line, ask for a haunches-in. This is the half-pass.

The reasoning behind this different approach is that in shoulder-fore, the horse's inside front leg has to cross over and in front of his outside front leg. However, in a half-pass he does the opposite. His outside front leg crosses over and in front of the inside front leg. This change in the way the legs move can cause a loss of rhythm and impulsion.

I suggest that you try both methods to see which approach is easiest for your horse. In either case, while you're applying the aids, do some imaging to help insure the correct bend and positioning of your horse's forehand. Pretend he has eyes in the front of his shoulders and make him "look" at the specific point that you're riding toward (fig. 6.7).

• *Helpful Hints* •

MAINTAINING IMPULSION

Some horses lose impulsion during a half-pass because their riders try to push them sideways too much. If this is what you tend to do, think of riding the movement "forward and sideways" rather than "sideways and forward." This idea, plus an active inside leg and a light, non-restrictive inside rein, will help you to maintain his activity. If your horse still struggles and feels like he's losing power, do only a few steps of half-pass and then ride him straight forward or onto a circle to renew the impulsion.

You can also help maintain impulsion by asking for less engagement. One way to do this is to decrease the bend. Another way is by going more forward and less sideways, so that rather than going from D on the centerline over to E, (or B), go from D over to S, (or R). Either of these options will reduce the required amount of engagement. Then, when your horse becomes stronger and is able to maintain his impulsion, gradually increase the bend or resume going more sideways.

It can also be difficult for your horse to go forward and sideways fluidly and with energy if you lose your own balance by getting left behind the movement. This is happening if you notice that you are leaning to the right as your horse moves to the left. You might feel like you are getting left behind, and you've probably experienced this sensation before. Remember when you were first learning how to post to the trot? You most likely fell behind your horse's movement a lot. But then you got used to the forward momentum, and as you became more balanced, you were able to "go with" your horse's motion. In the half-pass, you need to "go with" your horse's motion when he's going sideways and forward, too.

In order to help you with this problem in the half-pass, try to place your body weight in the direction of movement. Visualize moving your outside seat bone more toward the center of your saddle. Or, practice sitting in the direction of the half-pass by doing the following exercise. You'll need a friend or instructor to help you.

Since you're doing a half-pass to the left, your helper should stand on your left. While sitting on your horse, close your eyes and without warning have your helper grab your belt on the left side of your waist and pull your body toward her. Have her do this several times until you memorize this feeling of moving your body over to the left. Then start a half-pass and recreate the feeling of being pulled sideways so that you can counteract the effects of getting left behind.

You can also end up getting left behind the movement if you use too much outside leg to send your horse sideways. When you use this leg too strongly, your body will be pulled to the outside. Don't fall into this trap of using your outside leg too hard, too often, or too far back on your horse's side. If your horse doesn't move away from your outside leg readily, try a "wake-up call." Give one good kick, or tap him with the whip, in a way that sends him sideways rather than forward. Then, expect him to go eagerly sideways from a polite leg. If he doesn't, repeat your warning until he believes you and obediently moves away from your leg when it's applied lightly behind the girth.

MAINTAINING THE TEMPO

Many riders find that their horse's **tempo** changes when they introduce the half-pass. The first thing you should do is check that the tempo is good before you even start. Keep in mind that tempo is controlled by your seat. Your horse should adjust his tempo to match the one designated by your seat; you should not succumb to the tempo that he offers.

6.7
To help with the bend during the half-pass, pretend your horse has eyes in front of his shoulders, and make them "look" at the specific point you are riding toward.

So, if your horse goes faster, you can steady the tempo by tightening your stomach muscles. This action causes your seat to have a non-following, retarding effect.

If the horse gets slower during the half-pass, speed up the tempo by quickening the action of your seat. Do this by moving your seat faster than the tempo that your horse is going.

I haven't mentioned this "speeding up of tempo" with the seat before, because I don't want you to get into the habit of driving with your seat every stride. You'll end up on the same dead-end street as you will by using your legs constantly, where you do a lot of work and your horse soon gets dull to your aids. When you quicken the action of your seat in the half-pass, do it briefly to speed up your horse's tempo. Then go back to sitting quietly and in harmony with your horse at his new and improved tempo. If the tempo doesn't improve as a result of a brief increase or decrease in the action of your seat, try decreasing the angle of the half-pass, or do the half-pass in posting trot, until the tempo can be maintained easily.

MAINTAINING THE BEND

The most common fault that I see riders make when riding a half-pass is that their horses lose the bend. And without bend, the half-pass becomes a leg-yield. Usually a horse loses his bend in an effort to avoid the difficulty of the movement. When your horse has lost his bend, it's advisable to use the same exercise as you do when training shoulder-in and haunches-in. Do a couple of good steps of half-pass, arc onto a circle to renew your horse's bend, and then continue in half-pass for a couple more good steps. This is infinitely preferable to doing many more steps without bend.

It's also possible to lose the bend if your horse's front end isn't facing toward a specific spot. Place your horse's entire forehand so that it's positioned toward the place you're riding to and stick to it. You need to do this because if his front feet are not pointed exactly where you're headed, you've lost the bend. For example, if you're headed toward the letters just before the corners, such as H, M, K or F, and the position of your horse's front feet has shifted so that they're now aiming directly toward the corner itself, or even toward the short end of the ring, it's a sure sign that the bend has been lost.

To help a student absorb this concept, I explain that a half-pass should be thought of as a haunches-in ridden on a diagonal line instead of a straight line. To emphasize my point, I first have her ride haunches-in along the rail. Once she gets comfortable with the aids and familiar with her horse's positioning along this straight line during a haunches-in, I tell her to imagine that she's working in a triangle instead of a rectangle.

All she has to do is ride haunches-in along the longest side of the triangle (the diagonal line) as easily as she rode haunches-in along the track by the rail. This is the half-pass. It's important, as I said earlier, to remember that the horse's front feet and ears must remain pointed at the exact spot he's headed toward (fig. 6.8).

PREVENTING LOSS OF ENGAGEMENT

For a half-pass to be effective, your horse must engage his hind legs. Often, it's not that easy to tell if your horse has escaped this engagement. A good test of engagement is to check if you could leave the half-pass and ride straight ahead parallel to the long side in a shoulder-in.

For example, do a few steps of half-pass across the diagonal, ride a few steps of shoulder-in, and then go back to half-pass again. Initiate the transition to shoulder-in by increasing the influence of your inside leg and driving your horse's inside hind leg toward your outside rein. Concentrate on the transition into the shoulder-in, and ask yourself if it's easy for you to go from one movement to the other. The answer to that question tells you whether your horse has maintained the engagement of his inside hind leg during the half-pass or merely stepped sideways as he would in a leg-yield.

He can escape this engagement if you don't keep him correctly positioned in relation to the rail on the long side. This correct alignment of your horse's body in a half-pass dictates that his bent body is basically parallel to the rail but his forehand is ever so slightly in advance of his hindquarters. If you find your horse's hindquarters either leading or trailing rather than being positioned just slightly behind his forehand, that means there is insufficient engagement of his inside hind leg (figs. 6.9 to 6.13).

If your horse's hindquarters tend to lead, it's vital that you set him up with a step or two of shoulder-fore before you start the half-pass. Then take care not to push too much with your outside leg as you start moving sideways.

If your horse prefers to trail his haunches behind his forehand, or his forehand gets too much in advance of his hindquarters, realign both ends of his body. Use a slight opening outside rein to hold his shoulders back and close your outside leg behind the girth to send his hindquarters over. As you work on the correct alignment of your horse's body, you'll probably notice that if he tends to trail with his hindquarters when going to the left, he'll probably want to lead with them when he goes to the right.

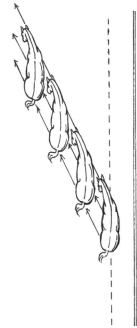

6.8

If you have trouble with your horse's positioning during a half-pass, think of the movement as a haunches-in on a diagonal line.

6.9

A half-pass showing correct alignment of Dwight's body. He is almost parallel to the long side of the arena and his forehand is ever so slightly in front of his hindquarters. This position encourages good engagement of the hindquarters—the purpose of the movement.

CORRECTION FOR A "TOO-MUCH-SIDEWAYS" HALF-PASS

If a horse doesn't go sideways to the proper degree, which is an angle of approximately 22 degrees (see diagram on page 118), he can't be using his inside hind leg correctly. If he goes more sideways than forward at an angle much greater than 22 degrees from the rail, it means he's not listening to your inside leg–the leg that is responsible for the bend as well as sending him forward. By stepping sideways too much, he can avoid closing the joints of, and engaging, his inside hind leg. To be engaged, your horse must step under *and forward* with his inside hind leg. Focus on this leg and picture it stepping forward toward your inside hand with each step.

6.10 and 6.11
In this half-pass sequence, Dwight has not been positioned correctly and his hindquarters are trailing too far behind his forehand.

CORRECTION FOR A "TOO-LITTLE-SIDEWAYS" HALF-PASS

On the other hand, if your horse goes forward too much and doesn't cover enough ground sideways, he's also escaping engagement. When you first train your horse to do half-passes, an angle of less than 22 degrees from the rail or the centerline is fine. You can do it as a preliminary exercise to give your horse the idea of going sideways with bend, but eventually you want to make the angle sideways more sharp so that he travels at about a 22-degree angle to the rail.

6.12 and 6.13

In this half-pass sequence, his haunches are leading because Chris has used too much outside leg. If the haunches are trailing or leading, there is insufficient engagement of the inside hind leg—the reason for the exercise.

Here's an image to hold in your mind's eye if you're having difficulty moving sideways at the proper angle. Pretend there's a magnet on the fence and your horse's body is made of iron. You are being drawn inexorably toward the fence by the force of the magnetic attraction (fig. 6.14).

You also need to be sure that your horse bends the same and goes sideways at the same angle to the fence in both directions. When his hollow side is on the inside, it's easier for him to bend and he'll probably want to go too much sideways. However, when his stiff side is on the in-

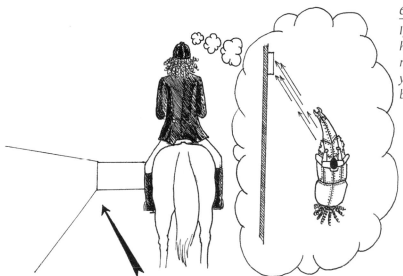

If you have trouble going sideways in half-pass at a 22-degree angle to the rail, visualize a magnet on the fence and your horse made of iron! Your horse will be drawn toward it by magnetic force.

side, it's more difficult to go sideways with enough bend. In order to be certain that you're always doing half-passes the same in both directions, check your bend and be sure to ride from and to specific points.

FURTHER USES OF THE HALF-PASS

I like to use the half-pass to point out to the rider just how much she can influence the various parts of her horse's body with her aids. I use it as an exercise to help her develop the ability to influence her horse's shoulders.

To do this, I'll have her start a half-pass and take both of her hands in the direction of the movement to guide her horse's forehand over. Next, while maintaining bend and sideways movement, I'll have her move both arms slightly away from the direction they are traveling. This will slow her horse's shoulders down. I'll once again have her put both hands in the direction of the half-pass to allow his front legs to go in advance. By doing this several times as she works her way across the arena in half-pass, she gets a chance to practice using the reins to control the position of her horse's shoulders—either allowing them to advance or slowing them down.

I have one caveat for you here, though. The exercise I just gave you is a wonderful rider exercise, but it's not necessarily a great exercise for the horse. This is because the ultimate purpose of a half-pass is to increase self-carriage. If you carry your hands away from the direction of movement for many strides, (that is, you move your hands to the right in a left half-pass), you'll succeed in bending your horse okay, but you'll lose self-carriage and put him on his forehand. Other than a stride here and there, your inside hand should remain in front of your inside hip and your outside rein should come toward your horse's neck so that both hands guide him over by moving in the direction of the half-pass.

I also like to use half-passes to help horses learn how to do clean flying changes. I'll explain how to do this in Chapter Eight.

Turn on the Haunches

Another distant cousin to shoulder-in is the **turn on the haunches**. It's actually a closer relative to haunches-in. In fact, a haunches-in on a small circle is one of the exercises that I do to introduce the concept of the turn on the haunches to both horse and rider.

DESCRIPTION

The turn on the haunches is a 180-degree turn executed at a walk (fig. 6.15). The horse is bent in the direction of the turn and his forehand moves around his hindquarters until he is facing in the opposite direction. His forefeet and his outside hind foot move around his inside hind foot, which forms a pivot. As with all of the movements in the walk, care must be taken that the regularity of the rhythm is maintained. Even though it forms the pivotal point of the turn, the inside hind leg must be picked up and returned to a spot slightly in front of where it left the ground (figs. 6.16 to 6.22).

The turn on the haunches engages a horse's hindquarters and encourages good flexion of these joints. Earlier, I told you that when you execute a shoulder-in correctly, the end result is that your horse's body feels more packaged at the finish than when you started. The same holds true for a turn on the haunches.

In order to enhance your aids with an image, as you turn, picture your horse's hind legs stepping more underneath your seat and his body becoming a more compact package from poll to tail. As you ride each step of the turn, visualize the joints of your horse's hind legs bending as if he were doing some deep knee bends (fig. 6.23).

The turn on the haunches is also used as a safe way to introduce a walk pirouette to a horse who will later on be asked to do this more advanced movement. This is because the turn on the haunches has all the good qualities of a walk pirouette (desire to go forward, bend, and rhythm) but is less demanding for a horse both physically and mentally. However, the turn on the haunches differs from a pirouette because it is done from a medium walk, which is just slightly shortened prior to the

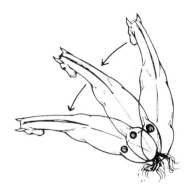

6.15

The first steps of a turn on the haunches to the left.

6.23

The turn on the haunches encourages good flexion of the joints of the horse's hindquarters. In order to help him engage, visualize these joints bending as if he were doing some deep knee bends!

6.16 to 6.22
Turn on the Haunches Sequence

6.16
Deb prepares for a turn on the haunches to the left by shortening Galen's walk stride while maintaining a clear four-beat walk. She also flexes her slightly to the left in preparation for the turn. Her poll should be a bit higher so that it is the highest point of her neck.

6.17
She starts the turn by putting her weight on her left seat bone, keeping her left leg on the girth, her right leg slightly behind the girth, and moving both hands to the left to lead her forehand around her hindquarters.

turn, rather than from a collected walk as in the pirouette. Plus, in a turn on the haunches, the horse's hind legs are allowed to describe a small circle (about the size of a dinner plate), while in a walk pirouette, the inside hind leg should be picked up and put down on the same spot—obviously a more difficult movement.

6.18

6.19

6.18 to 6.21

Deb keeps her horse nicely bent around her inside leg throughout the turn. Note the activity of the inside hind leg as it is clearly picked up and placed down with each step.

6.16 to 6.22 Turn on the Haunches Sequence con't.

The Aids for the Turn on the Haunches

The aids for a turn on the haunches to the left are as follows:

1. *Seat:* weight on the left seat bone.
2. *Left leg:* on the girth to promote bend through the body and engagement of the inside hind leg.

6.20

6.21

3. *Right leg:* place behind the girth to help bend the horse around the inside leg and to prevent his hindquarters from swinging out.

4. *Left rein:* vibrate for flexion.

5. *Right rein:* steady and supporting to limit the amount of bend in the neck.

6. *Both hands:* move in the direction of the turn (to the left) to lead your horse's forehand around his hindquarters. Your hands should stay side by side and equidistant from your body. Your left rein is used as an opening or leading rein while your right rein is brought closer to the neck to guide your horse's forehand around.

6.22
This well-executed turn on the haunches has improved Galen's balance. Her forehand is lighter, higher, and freer than before the turn. Her poll is now the highest point and her nose is just slightly in front of the vertical.

6.16 to 6.22 Turn on the Haunches Sequence con't.

SEQUENCE OF AIDS

When you're ready to ride a turn on the haunches, give the aids in this order. First, prepare for the turn by shortening the length of your horse's stride in the walk with a retarding action of your seat—the **"stilled"** seat I have mentioned previously. Do this by stretching up tall and tightening your stomach muscles so your seat doesn't follow along with the longer steps. Make sure that you keep your legs on in order to maintain the activity of your horse's legs as you still your seat. Next, bend him to the inside. Then, set him up for the turn on the haunches by riding in a slight shoulder-fore position. Finally, bring both of your hands in the direction you want to turn in order to guide your horse's forehand around his hindquarters.

• *Helpful Hints* •

USING HAUNCHES-IN AS PREPARATION FOR TURNS ON THE HAUNCHES

Haunches-in on a small circle is a very useful preliminary exercise before doing turns on the haunches. Asking for a "competition-size" turn on the haunches right off the bat is difficult for your horse. As a result, you risk losing one or more of **the Basics** such as his desire to go forward, his bend, or his regular rhythm in the walk. However, if you introduce the idea of a turn on the haunches by doing haunches-in on a circle, you have a greater chance of preserving these basic qualities.

MAINTAINING RHYTHM

During a turn on the haunches your horse must maintain the rhythm of his walk at all costs. His inside hind leg should step in that rhythm and never stay on the ground as a pivot. So use some good imaging to help you with this. "See" your horse's hind legs working like pistons as they go up and down in a regular rhythm. Or, visualize that your horse is in a marching band and those hind legs stay in a well-marked rhythm as you gently guide his forehand around (fig. 6.24).

REDUCING TENSION

I've worked with some horses that get extremely tense as soon as you begin to shorten their walks. They'll begin to jig, or even think about rearing. For these horses, I stay in the medium walk rather than trying to shorten it, and ride several small circles in haunches-in with many relaxing breaks in between each series of circles. Doing several circles gives these tense horses time to settle into their rhythm and to realize nothing terrible is going to happen to them. Over time, I'll decrease the size of the circle in direct proportion to the degree of my horse's relaxation. In my mind I prevent these horses from jigging by pretending their legs are in molasses, and that they have to slowly and deliberately pick those legs up out of the "goo" and put them back down again (fig. 6.25).

6.24

In a turn on the haunches, visualize your horse in a marching band, his hind legs working like pistons in the regular rhythm of the walk.

6.25

To prevent my horse from jigging when I shorten his walk to prepare for a turn on the haunches, I imagine that his legs are in molasses and that he has to slowly and deliberately pick them up out of the "goo."

ADJUSTING THE SIZE OF THE TURN

As with all work you do with your horse, maintaining his desire to go forward is one of the priorities (regular rhythm being the most important). If he loses this desire during the turn on the haunches and feels like he might even step backward, try riding one or two steps around the turn, then close your legs and ride him straight forward for a couple of steps. Continue alternating even if you go 360 degrees or more around, until you feel that your horse is happy to react by immediately going forward at any point during the turn.

Although it's much less of a fault than losing energy or stepping backward, sometimes the turn will be too large because you haven't placed enough emphasis on your outside rein. The outside rein is the rein that defines the size of the turn. To make the turn tighter, close your outside hand in a fist and firmly support with it. Pick a definite spot in the arena and mark it with an imaginary "X." Visualize keeping your horse's hind legs marching up and down on that spot.

Sometimes the turn is too large and it seems to take forever to bring your horse's forehand completely around. Often this is caused because you're restricting his shoulders by using an indirect inside rein away from the direction of movement. Some people use this in an effort to maintain the bend, but this is wrong. If you're doing a turn on the haunches to the left, both hands should move to the left to lead your horse's forehand around the turn.

You might also find that it takes too long to finish the turn if you lose your balance and get left behind the motion. This is the same sensation of falling to the outside that I discussed in the previous section on half-passes (page 119). Your horse is moving to the left but your upper body gets shifted to the right. Or, you squeeze too hard with your outside leg, and your upper body leans to the outside as well.

Use the same corrections that we did for the half-pass. First, be sure your horse is responsive to your outside leg so you don't have to push too hard with it. Then, step down into your inside stirrup to encourage your horse to move under your weight while you think about moving your outside seat bone toward the middle of your saddle.

MAINTAINING THE BEND

Remember, if your horse loses his bend, there will be little engagement of his inside hind leg, so you need to make your bending aids more active. To do this, ask for flexion by vibrating your inside rein. Then lighten or ease the tension on the rein. Your horse should stay flexed to the inside by himself when you soften the contact.

While you're asking for flexion, use your active inside leg on the girth with the idea of pushing your horse's ribcage away from it and to the outside of the turn. At the same time, make sure that you remember to "trap" the outside hind leg so that it doesn't swing to the outside. Use your outside leg, which is placed behind the girth.

CONTROLLING THE HIND LEGS

Most of the mistakes I see in turns on the haunches revolve around how the hind legs step. Your horse's hind legs must maintain the regular rhythm of the walk and be picked up and put down slightly in front of the same place where they left the ground.

If your horse pivots on his inside hind leg as though he is screwing it into the ground, you've lost the rhythm of his walk. As you know by now, maintaining the regular rhythm is the priority, so this is a serious fault. If this is your horse's tendency, ride larger turns as a schooling exercise. Then when you do make the turn somewhat smaller, be sure to maintain the activity of your horse's inside hind leg by squeezing and releasing with your active inside leg. Also, soften your inside hand forward so you don't block or interfere with the stepping of his inside hind leg.

Then again, I often see a horse step toward the inside of the turn with his inside hind leg. Specifically, in a turn on the haunches to the left, his left hind leg steps sideways to the left as if he's leg-yielding away from your outside leg. A horse will do this to avoid the bending of the joints of his hind legs. Engage his inside hind leg in preparation for the turn by riding shoulder-fore before you start. Then use an active inside leg during the turn to remind him to keep using it.

You can also do the following exercise as a check that you're maintaining control of your horse's inside hind leg. During the exercise, stay away from the rail so you don't run into any obstacles. First, walk your horse forward in shoulder-fore. When you're ready, do one step of a turn on the haunches, and immediately walk forward in shoulder-fore again. Make sure your horse's hind legs stay on whatever line you choose rather than drifting to either side of that line. Think about using your inside leg and driving it toward your outside rein as you move your horse's shoulders slightly to the inside. Then when you're ready, do another step of your turn and then proceed forward in shoulder-fore again.

Sometimes you'll manage to capture your horse's inside hind leg and prevent it from stepping to the inside of the turn, but you'll find that he'll look for an escape route by stepping to the outside of the turn with his outside hind leg. That is, on a left turn on the haunches, his right hind leg will swing out to the right.

Generally, this can be prevented by passively guarding and supporting with your firm outside leg. If your horse persists in swinging out with his outside hind leg, prepare for the turn by riding haunches-in before you begin. Try to keep the feeling of pushing his haunches to the inside of the turn as you make your way around the turn on the haunches. Keep in mind that this is only a schooling exercise to give your horse the idea of where to place his outside hind leg. In competition, or done correctly for maximum benefit, the turn on the haunches should always be started from the shoulder-fore position.

USING TURNS ON THE HAUNCHES FOR DEVELOPING SELF-CARRIAGE

With horses that have a bit of education, I've used turns on the haunches to develop self-carriage in all three paces. First, I'll have a student cruise around in the walk, trot, or the canter, and simply evaluate her horse's balance. How much weight is on his hind legs and how much is on his forelegs? What's the weight in the reins? How long is her horse's body from poll to tail? Then, I'll have her ride several turns on the haunches. Sometimes I'll even have her do turns of 360 degrees or more as long as she is keeping the rhythm and the bend correctly.

Next, she'll resume whatever pace she was in before and take a moment to reevaluate the horse's balance. If the turns on the haunches have been ridden correctly, the balance will be shifted somewhat toward the hind legs, the contact will be lighter, and her horse will be shorter and more "packaged" from poll to tail.

KEY POINTS

🐎 The half-pass supples and improves self-carriage. Think of a half-pass as a haunches-in position ridden on a diagonal line across the arena.

🐎 Turn on the haunches is an engagement exercise and a preparatory exercise for walk pirouettes. Think of it as a haunches-in position done on a tiny circle.

CHAPTER SEVEN

Shifting into Second Gear: Medium and Extended Gaits

I n Book One (Chapter Nine) you learned about lengthening your horse's strides and frame in the working trot and canter. The horse in training at the basic levels in dressage is able to show two "gears" in each of those paces. He can trot and canter and he can show a lengthening—a longer stride and frame—of those paces. Remember that during a lengthening, your horse covers the maximum amount of ground with each stride that he's capable of doing at his current stage of development.

In this chapter, I'm going to introduce two additional types of lengthenings that are more advanced: the **medium** and the **extended** gaits. Just as the lengthenings are the "covering-more-ground" expression of the basic **working** gaits, the mediums and extensions are the "covering-more-ground" expressions of the **collected** gaits which I described in Chapter Four of this book.

So this means that rather than only having two "gears" in the trot and canter, the educated horse is also able to show three more "gears"—collected, medium, and extended—in all his paces. As an analogy, you can think that a lengthening is to a working gait what an extension is to a collected gait—the maximum lengthening of stride and frame that the horse can show at his stage of development.

DESCRIPTION

The medium gaits share certain qualities with extended gaits in that they are produced from a collected gait, but rather than being extended to their utmost, the horse's strides and frame are only moderately extended (figs. 7.1).

The medium and extended gaits are similar to lengthenings in two respects. The horse elongates his frame as well as covers more ground with each stride, as he does in a lengthening. He also maintains the same tempo that he had established in the collected gait.

Lengthening from a working gait

Extending from a collected gait

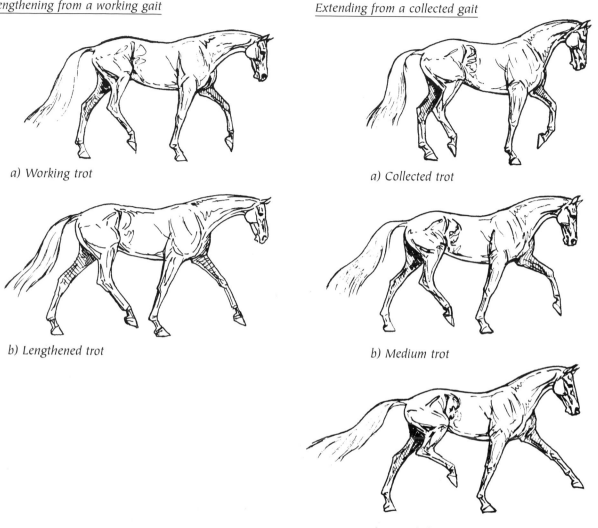

a) Working trot

a) Collected trot

b) Lengthened trot

b) Medium trot

c) Extended trot

7.1 The different "gears" in the trot

Because of these similarities I often hear people use the words **"lengthenings"** and **"extensions"** interchangeably. This is incorrect because there is a very real difference between a lengthening of the basic working gaits where the horse's balance is more or less on his forehand and the medium and extended gaits, which can only be developed from a collected gait with a horse who is in self-carriage.

To help you understand the difference between a length-ening and a medium or extended gait, imagine that your legs are the horse's hind legs. Now, bend your knees just a little bit and then jump in the air. You'll probably get a few inches off the ground. The slight bend in your knees is equivalent to the amount the horse engages his hind legs in the working gaits. This minimal **engagement** of the horse's hind legs is the reason you're only able to generate a lengthening from a working gait.

Now, bend your knees a lot more, and jump again. You'll find that you can now spring a lot higher off the ground. The more the joints bend, (or engage), the higher you can jump. This is how your horse is able to produce an exten-sion from collection. Think of coiling the spring of the hind legs when riding a collected gait so your horse can propel himself, or "boing," into an extension (fig. 7.2).

7.2

Think of coiling the spring of your horse's hind legs when riding a collected gait, so he can "boing" into an extension.

During the collected gaits there is an increase in the engagement of the hind legs, which causes the horse's center of gravity to shift more toward his hindquarters. As a result, the horse's balance is more "uphill." So it follows that the balance in mediums and extensions should remain uphill as well.

To sum up, the common denominator for the collected, medium, and extended gaits is the engagement of the hind legs, which causes a low-ering of the hindquarters and results in a lightening and elevation of the forehand. I call this phenomenon **uphill balance**. Also, the length of the horse's strides and frame will vary, of course, becoming either shorter or longer depending on which "gear" you're in, but the tempo always re-mains the same.

In the collected gaits, the horse's balance is uphill: his strides are short and active, and they make an up and down arc; his frame is more com-pact than it is in the working gaits. In the medium and extended gaits, the horse's uphill balance is the same as it is in the collected gaits, but his strides are longer and his frame elongates.

Now, let's discuss the extended walk and look at how the medium and extended gaits differ in the trot and canter.

THE EXTENDED WALK

I am not going to cover the medium walk here (you have already learned this term in Book One, Chapter Seven, as the name for the basic walk). Years ago, the **AHSA** had a walk called "medium," for more advanced horses, which was described as the "gait between the collected and ex-tended walk." This medium walk followed the same rules, as far as length of stride, length of frame, and self-carriage are concerned, as *medium* trot

7.3 Collected Walk

In collected walk Woody remains on the bit as he marches forward with his head and neck raised and arched, showing clear self-carriage. Each step covers less ground but comes higher off the ground than at the medium walk.

and canter still do. Specifically, in these gaits the horse must show a *moderate* lengthening of his stride and frame while his balance remains up-hill.

Now, the AHSA has "borrowed" the medium walk for use with younger, or uneducated horses, and it replaces the previously named "working" walk. Medium walk no longer falls under the same rules regarding uphill balance as medium trot and medium canter. The name was changed because the term "working walk" seemed to encourage riders to restrict their horses and "cram" them together, rather than letting them march on actively.

Keep it straight in your mind by thinking of it this way. We work young horses in the medium walk. We work more advanced horses in the collected and extended walk.

In the *extended* walk, the horse covers as much ground as possible without hurrying, and the hind feet touch the ground clearly in front of the footprints of the forefeet (figs. 7.3 and 7.4).

7.4 Extended Walk
Woody covers as much ground as possible without hurrying. His hind feet touch the ground clearly in front of the hoof prints of the forefeet. He is allowed to stretch out his head and neck but the reins do not become slack.

THE MEDIUM AND EXTENDED TROT

In the medium trot the horse goes forward with free, moderately extended steps. He lowers his head and neck slightly and carries his nose a little more in front of the vertical than at the collected trot (figs. 7.5 to 7.7).

7.5 Collected Trot

Dwight remains on the bit with his neck raised and arched. His steps are shorter than in the other trots, but his hocks are well engaged.

In the extended trot the horse lengthens his steps to the utmost as well as lengthening his frame. His forefeet should touch the ground on the spot toward which they are pointing. They should not retract before being placed on the ground. (If this happens, it's usually because the rider restricts her horse with her hands and has not allowed him to lengthen his frame.)

7.6 Medium Trot
Dwight goes forward with moderately extended steps. His frame is slightly longer and his neck is somewhat lower than in collected trot, but his balance remains uphill rather than shifting onto the forehand.

7.7 Extended Trot
Dwight lengthens his steps and frame to the utmost. Ideally, his poll should be the highest point and his nose a bit more forward. That position would give the extension a slightly more uphill feeling.

7.8 Collected Canter
Woody remains on the bit and moves forward with his neck raised and arched. His strides are shorter than in the other canters, but they are active and energetic.

THE MEDIUM AND EXTENDED CANTER

In the medium canter the horse goes forward with free, moderately extended strides. He carries his head a little more in front of the vertical than at the collected canter and lowers his head and neck slightly.

In the extended canter, the horse covers as much ground as possible with each stride, while remaining calm and in good balance. He should lower and extend his head and neck, and the tip of his nose should point more or less forward (figs. 7.8 to 7.10).

When training, I usually work on the medium gaits first. Once I know my horse has the strength and understanding to maintain an even rhythm, constant tempo, and an uphill balance in the medium gaits, I begin to ask for the greater effort needed to do extensions.

Practicing the medium and extended gaits is valuable, not only as a way to supple your horse, but as a way to freshen him mentally and physically. For example, I intersperse them into my lateral work and collection exercises to relax his muscles and renew his desire to go forward.

7.9 Medium Canter

Woody goes forward with free, moderately extended strides. His frame is slightly longer and his neck is lower than in collected canter, but it's apparent that he stays in self-carriage as his body has the uphill look of an airplane taking off.

7.10 Extended Canter

Woody covers as much ground as possible while remaining in self-carriage. Note the spread between his hind legs as he reaches well under his body to cover ground with long strides. He has lengthened his frame, lowered his neck, and the tip of his nose is slightly more forward than in collected canter.

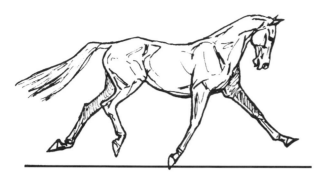

a) Although the action of this horse's front leg might look extravagant in this extended trot, the extension is incorrect. Rather than showing good engagement, the action of the hind legs is backward. Because his back is stiff and his neck is short, he flips up the toe of his front foot.

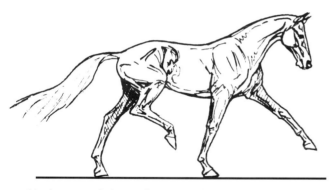

b) This extended trot shows good engagement of the hind legs. The energy flows over the horse's back, through a long neck, and his nose is pointed toward the spot where his front foot will come to the ground.

7.11 Extended trot

The Aids for Medium and Extended Gaits

Before asking for a medium or extended gait, first make sure that your horse's hind legs are sufficiently engaged in the collected gait to give him enough energy to be able to extend. If they aren't, you need to "coil the spring" of his hind legs by riding some good collecting half-halts (see Chapter Four).

When the hind legs are engaged as the result of these half-halts, you will be ready to ask for an extension. The aids for medium and extended gaits are as follows:

1. *Seat:* use a driving seat that feels like you're sweeping the back of the saddle toward the front of the saddle.
2. *Legs:* press lightly with both legs to signal your horse to go forward over the ground in longer strides.
3. *Reins:* soften your hands a bit forward to allow the frame to become longer, but keep a contact with your horse's mouth and a bend in your elbows.

• *Helpful Hints* •
INCREASING ENGAGEMENT WHEN DOING EXTENSIONS

It's not unusual to see a lack of engagement in extensions—even with a naturally big-moving horse whose strides are ground-covering and powerful. Sometimes, although the horse's strides get long, the action of the hind legs is backward: the hind legs push rather than come under the body to carry. Another common sight is the horse who widens or spreads his hind legs apart during extensions. In both cases the hind legs are pushing backward, rather than carrying, because of a lack of engagement (fig. 7.11).

To increase the engagement, start a half-halt (combine your driving aids, bending aids, and your **rein of opposition**) and "blend" that half-halt into the upward transition from the collected gait to the extension. This will remind the horse to keep his hind legs coming under his body. By "blend," I mean that you'll start the half-halt and continue to apply it while changing the emphasis of the driving aids or one of the other elements of the half-halt.

For instance, to blend the half-halt into the extension, you can gradually increase your driving aids over the course of three seconds. You can also keep the driving aids the same, but soften your hands a bit, or you might do a combination of both of these things.

You can also increase the engagement of the hind legs in preparation for extensions by riding some of the movements that you learned for improving **self-carriage** (Chapter Four). For instance, ride a small circle to increase self-carriage, and then immediately after leaving the circle, ask for a few extended steps. Or, do some frequent upward and downward transitions from pace to pace. For each downward transition, remember to close both legs to drive your horse's hind legs more underneath his body. Once you feel him carrying himself better (and you'll be able to tell that he's doing so because his balance feels more uphill and he's lighter in your hands), ask for your extension.

Another way to increase engagement is to use the shoulder-in as an exercise to set your horse up for the extension. Ride a few steps of shoulder-in, do three or four steps of an extension, then go right back into shoulder-in. Repeat this pattern as often as you like. The first shoulder-in insures that you start with engaged hind legs, and the transition back into the shoulder-in assists in the maintenance of that engagement. Don't feel like you have to extend for a long time; keep the extensions brief so you can do a few strides that are of a high quality rather than many strides that are not (figs. 7.12 to 7.14).

If your trainer has told you that this lack of engagement in extensions is a chronic problem for you (or perhaps you've seen it for yourself on a video), do some imaging to support all the actual exercises that I've just discussed. As you ask for the extension, focus solely on your horse's hind legs. Visualize them staying close together and stepping well under his body as he extends.

This is what I did with my horse Zapatero, the reserve horse for the 1992 United States Olympic Dressage Team, who used to find it difficult to stay engaged during the extended trot. I practiced by riding the "perfect" test in my mind's eye and I'd zoom my focus in on his hind legs only. I'd exaggerate the engagement by "seeing" him bending his hocks and bringing his hind legs so far under his body that he'd practically hit his belly with every step! (See fig. 7.15).

DEVELOPING BIGGER EXTENSIONS

If your horse does a good extension while correctly maintaining the tempo of the collected gait, but you'd like him to be more expressive—to float over the ground more with each stride—work on developing the energy in the collected gait. It's impossible for a horse to magically produce powerful strides out of "thin air." The magnitude of the extended stride is a direct result of the degree of engagement of the joints of the hind legs in the collected gait ridden right before the extension. Remember, the term "engagement" refers to the increased bending of the joints of the hind legs and of the lumbosacral area. When a horse engages his hind legs, his hindquarters lower and they support a greater proportion of the load. This engagement of the hind legs is a prerequisite for **thrust**—also known as **impulsion**.

7.12

This extended trot across the center of the ring lacks engagement. The loss of engagement can be seen as Kousteau takes the load off his left hind leg by pushing backward and sideways to the left with it. (Compare this leg to its position in photo 7.14).

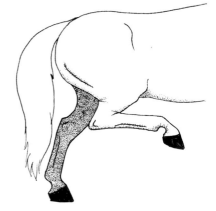

7.15

To increase engagement in extensions, in your mind's eye zoom your focus in on your horse's hind legs. "See" him bringing them so far under his body that he practically hits his belly with every step!

7.13

Riding the same line, Kelly increases the engagement of Kousteau's left hind leg by riding him in left shoulder-in. His left hind leg is lined up behind his right front leg; this position encourages him to carry weight on his left hind leg.

7.14

After a few steps of shoulder-in, Kelly straightens his horse and immediately asks him to extend again. Here Kousteau is able to carry himself in the extension because he brings his left hind leg directly under his body rather than pushing backward and sideways with it.

7.16

In any correct trot the front and hind legs that make up the diagonal pair that is in the air should be parallel. You should be able to see the upper part of the front leg (the forearm) match the lower part of the hindleg (the cannon bone).

Once again, you can use some of the movements and exercises that we did in the section on developing self-carriage (Chapters Four and Five) to engage the hind legs prior to asking for a bigger extension. The more you engage your horse's hind legs, the easier it'll be to ask for more.

1. While in trot, ride some steps of shoulder-in; in the canter, do some steps of shoulder-fore to engage the inside hind leg. Then straighten your horse and extend.

2. Do several trot-halt-trot or canter-walk-canter transitions to engage your horse's hind legs, and then ask for an extension.

3. Ride a 10-meter circle in either trot or canter and then ask for the extension as you leave the circle and go on to a straight line.

4. Go on a 20-meter circle and ride a shoulder-in (if you're in the trot) or a shoulder-fore (if you're in the canter). Be sure to keep your horse's hind legs on the original track of the circle. (If he even slightly decreases the size of the circle by drifting in toward the center during the lateral movement, he's avoiding the engagement of his inside hind leg.)

Staying on the circle, straighten your horse from the shoulder-fore or shoulder-in position (which in this case does not mean literally straighten, rather that you bend him along the arc of the circle), ask for a few steps of an extension, and then collect the gait again in shoulder-fore or shoulder-in (depending on whether you're in canter or trot). Make sure you maintain the bend around your inside leg during the extension. Losing the bend is another way that your horse avoids the engagement of his inside hind leg.

KEEPING THE DIAGONAL PAIRS OF LEGS PARALLEL IN THE TROT

In any trot, the front and hind legs that make up the diagonal pairs should be parallel. In an extended trot, the legs should remain parallel. One way for you to learn how to see "parallelness" is to look at a photograph of a horse in trot and examine the diagonal pair of legs that is in the air. In a correct trot, you'd see that the upper part of the front leg (the forearm) and the lower part of the hind leg (the cannon bone) are parallel (fig. 7.16).

I often see a horse flinging out his front legs while his hind legs do very little. This is described in "dressage speak" as "promising more in front than delivering behind." This usually happens because the horse lacks engagement and connection; the freedom in his shoulders and the reach of the front leg is not coming from the power of the hindquarters. Instead, the horse "cracks" his back by breaking at a point just behind the withers and raises his front end without the corresponding lowering of the hindquarters.

Some people aren't sure if their horses extend more with their front legs than with their hind legs. If you have no ground person to instruct you, you can check that the diagonal pairs are parallel by having someone take a photograph or video of you while doing a medium or extended trot. If you see that the front legs are really reaching forward but the hind legs are dragging indicating a lack of engagement and connection, direct your attention toward the hind legs to improve the trot.

Give a half-halt to insure the **connection** from back to front, and then do some engaging exercises such as shoulder-in, frequent transitions, and small circles in order to increase the impulsion from the hindquarters. Then, ask for an extension, being sure to soften your hands slightly forward so your horse can lengthen his neck.

Help the horse's hind legs become closer to parallel with the front legs by visualizing "taking the hind legs with you." "See" your horse coming forward and under more with his hind legs. Visualize the engagement of the hind legs and the bending of the hocks by pretending the horse is sitting and snapping the hind legs forward like a Cossack dancer (fig. 7.17).

MAINTAINING ENGAGEMENT DURING EXTENSIONS

When your horse is engaged and in **self-carriage** which he should be in medium and extended gaits, the contact will be light. Even though you're doing an extension, you should still feel the lightness and **uphill balance** of the collected gaits in the medium and extended gaits. If you feel a great deal of weight in your hands

7.17

During extensions, visualize your horse's hind legs engaging by pretending that he is sitting and snapping them forward like a Cossack dancer.

when riding an extension, this is probably because there's a lack of engagement as described in the previous example. The feeling in your hands is the direct result of what's happening, or not happening, with the hind legs.

In other words, if the hind legs are not engaged, you're going to feel like you have to hold your horse up. Before you ask for the extension, you need to activate the hind legs so your horse is in self-carriage and, therefore, the contact is only the weight of the reins—pleasantly light.

Quite often, a horse will start off in self-carriage but after six or eight strides, he loses engagement and ends up lying in your hands because he's no longer carrying himself. Perhaps the extra speed over the ground contributes to the loss of balance—the center of gravity gradually moves somewhat to the forehand. Maybe it's because he's not yet strong enough to maintain his engagement for so many strides. Whatever the cause, once you lose the feeling of self-carriage while extending, the horse's balance will shift to the forehand and he'll lean on your hands.

To sum up, remember this: always feel collection in extension and extension in collection! By this I mean you need to do an extension in an uphill, collected balance and you need to have the feeling of the barely controlled power of an extension when riding a collected gait.

The canter presents an added challenge to the maintenance of engagement. After all, even in a working canter when asking for minimal engagement, a horse generally chooses to be crooked and carry his hindquarters to the inside in order to avoid bending the joints of his inside hind leg. He might do this as an escape route to carrying weight behind because he's lazy or weak. Or perhaps he simply hasn't been taught the mechanics of bending his joints and placing that inside hind leg toward his center through canter work done in shoulder-fore position.

Remember when you ride a shoulder-fore in left lead canter, you ask the horse's left hind leg to step in between the front legs by using your left leg on the girth while you displace his forehand to the left by bringing both of your hands slightly to the left.

If lack of engagement and crookedness is not dealt with at an earlier stage, it becomes even more obvious when a horse is asked to collect his gaits. After all, if he hasn't learned to carry weight with his inside hind leg when his center of gravity is more toward the forehand, he certainly isn't going to start when the work becomes harder in collected gaits when the center of gravity is shifted more towards the hindquarters.

If he's crooked and avoiding carrying weight behind in the collected canter, it's inevitable that he will "unload" and carry his hindquarters to the inside during an extended canter (fig. 7.18). To correct this fault, stay in a slight shoulder-fore position before, during, and after extensions.

7.18
This horse is crooked in the canter. His hindquarters drift slightly toward the inside of the ring so that he can take the load off his inside hind leg. If the rider doesn't straighten him at this stage so that he learns to carry weight behind, he'll undoubtedly be crooked when asked to do extended canter.

KEEPING YOUR HORSE ON THE BIT

Not only can you lose engagement (and therefore, self-carriage) as just discussed, but you can lose the connection over your horse's back as well. For example, you're doing a collected trot around the ring and you feel like there's lots of impulsion in the trot. Because you feel so much power, you don't bother to prepare for the extension by blending a half-halt into the upward transition. Instead, you just close your legs to ask for the extension. As a result, your horse runs off his hind legs by pushing backward with them and his back becomes hollow (see fig. 7.11a).

If this happens to you frequently, it's essential that you once again blend or "superimpose" a half-halt into the upward transition to the extension—not so much to coil the spring of the hind legs as you did before to increase engagement, but to insure the connection from your horse's hind legs over his back to his front end. Prepare for the extension by starting the half-halt while still in the collected gait and continue the half-halt right through the transition into the extension as I described earlier. Maintaining the half-halt through the transition helps the horse stay connected because you're asking the hind legs to come under the body rather than letting them push "out the back door."

I realize that blending a half-halt into the transition for an extension might necessitate sustaining that half-halt for a little longer than the three seconds that you're accustomed to. In fact, your half-halt might last as long as four to six seconds. But after that amount of time, be sure to soften the aids so the horse gets his reward. If you forget to relax, you'll be constantly driving and holding without giving your horse any relief, and he'll probably end up stiffening against your aids.

IMPROVING THE DOWNWARD TRANSITION FROM EXTENSION TO COLLECTION

My tips for improving the downward transitions refer only to negotiating the transition from the extended trot to the collected trot and from extended canter to collected canter. You probably won't have to do this in the walk because it's a slow pace, but since you can get barreling along at a pretty good clip in a fabulous trot or canter extension, you might need a little help bringing your horse back to the collected gait again. Your extension shouldn't gradually fade over the course of several strides. An observer should be able to pick a particular point where a distinct transition to the collected gait occurred.

Ideally you do this with a half-halt, but if your horse ignores you or takes too long to come back to the collected gait, sharpen up his response to your half-halt by doing the following:

Ride an extension and come to a full halt, using the same combination of aids that you use for the half-halt (seat, legs, and outside rein). You'll probably need to be a bit stronger with the aids initially in order to do this dramatic transition from the extension to the halt. But be sure not to be too harsh. When the horse responds by going from the extension to the halt within four or five strides, try a transition from an extended gait to the collected gait with a regular half-halt. If he doesn't shorten his stride to the collected gait within a couple of strides, don't just give him a stronger half-halt. Instead come to a complete halt again.

In other words, if he ignores the regular half-halt, don't make your half-halt stronger to accommodate his lack of reaction. Sharpen his response to the half-halt by doing a quick full halt. Remember that, as I told you way back at the beginning of Book One, you want to "whisper" with your aids and have your horse "shout" his response (Book One,

Chapter Six). You don't want to shout with your aids and get a half-hearted response.

Another situation that often occurs during the downward transition is that your horse leans on your hands because he's lost his balance and his center of gravity shifts to the forehand. This can happen if you're too strong with the reins.

One solution to restoring engagement, which insures that he stays in self-carriage and, therefore, light in your hand during the downward transition, is to step into shoulder-fore as you ask for the transition. Let the shoulder-fore slow him down and collect the gait rather than giving a half-halt. During the transition, use your inside leg to drive his inside hind leg diagonally toward his center and lead his shoulders slightly to the inside. The shoulder-fore engages your horse's inside hind leg and he'll have to carry himself. As a result, he won't need to lean on your hands for support.

KEY POINTS

- Medium and extended gaits are a more advanced type of lengthening. The horse remains in self-carriage and has the uphill look of an airplane taking off.

- In medium and extended gaits, both the frame and the strides get longer while the rhythm and the tempo stays the same as it was in the collected gaits from which it was developed.

- In medium gaits, the strides and frame are moderately extended.

- In extended gaits, the strides and frame are lengthened to the utmost.

- Since medium and extended gaits are developed from the collected gaits, the best way to improve them is by increasing the engagement of the hind legs while in the collected gaits.

CHAPTER EIGHT

Flying Changes

L et's do a little "historic" review of how you've changed from one canter lead to the other with your horse so far. When I first discussed the working canter with your green (uneducated) horse in Book One (Chapter Nine), you did a **change of lead through the trot** when you wanted to switch from one inside foreleg leading in the canter to the other one. This meant that you'd do a few steps of trot between changing leads.

As your horse became more trained, I asked you to do **simple changes of lead** (Book Two, Chapter Four). This is a downward transition from one canter lead directly into a few steps of walk and then an upward transition to the other canter lead. Remember that if you don't hear or read the words "through the trot," you can automatically assume that the change of lead is a simple change through the walk rather than through the trot.

Now it's time to address a more advanced way to change your canter leads—the **flying change**. In a flying change, your horse stays in the canter the entire time, without walking or trotting. He switches his canter lead while he's in mid-air. He does this by changing which hind leg he places on the ground first after the period of suspension when all four of his legs are off the ground.

For example, when your horse is on the *left* lead, his *right* hind leg is the first beat of his canter stride. To negotiate the flying change of lead to the right lead, your horse must change the sequence of legs of a canter stride so that the first beat is made by the *left* hind leg as it comes to the ground (figs. 8.1 to 8.5).

In dressage, flying changes aren't required until the horse has acquired some degree of self-carriage, so a dressage horse is first asked to show flying changes in the tests that are of a medium degree of difficulty (Third Level tests). Western horses are asked to do flying changes at

8.1 to 8.5
Flying Change Sequence

8.1

Dwight is coming across the diagonal in right lead canter. This is the first beat of the canter, which shows Dwight's left hind leg on the ground.

8.2

The second beat of the canter, when the diagonal pair of inside (right) hind leg and outside (left) foreleg are on the ground at the same time.

8.3
The third beat of right lead canter, when the right front leg is on the ground. This is the moment when Chris gives the aid for the flying change. This gives Dwight a second to recognize that the aid has been given, so that he can switch the sequence of his legs during the period of suspension, which comes as soon as his right front leg leaves the ground.

8.4
This photo has been taken just after the period of suspension. Dwight has switched his canter lead by placing his new outside hind leg—the right hind leg—on the ground first. This is the first beat of the new canter the left lead canter.

8.1 to 8.5
Flying Change Sequence con't.

8.5

The second beat of left lead canter, showing the diagonal pair of inside (left) hind leg and outside (right) foreleg on the ground at the same time.

about the same stage of their training as are dressage horses—all should be able to walk, trot, and canter in balance, as well as lengthen and shorten their strides.

Most hunters, combined training horses, and show jumpers, however, learn flying changes earlier in their training. It's a distinct advantage to have a horse who can switch his leads quickly when changing direction around a course of jumps.

DESCRIPTION

In a flying change, a horse switches his canter lead during the period of suspension when all four of his legs are off the ground. In the higher levels of dressage, flying changes can also be done in a series. For instance, they can be done at every fourth, third, second, or at every stride. It is one of the most exciting movements to watch in dressage competition. When done in a sequence like this, they are commonly called "tempi changes." A horse can be trained to do four-tempi (every fourth stride), three-tempi, two-tempi, and one-tempi changes. But that is beyond the scope of this book, which focuses on cross-training your horse for improved performance with more fundamental dressage.

PREPARATORY WORK

Before schooling the flying changes themselves, you should spend many months laying a solid foundation by working on the following: simple changes of lead, self-carriage in the canter, and counter-canter.

1. Simple changes of lead. Before you try to do flying changes, you need to know that your horse is schooled enough and has sufficient engagement to be able to do clearly the downward transition from canter to walk. "Clearly" means that your horse doesn't do any "dribbly" trot steps in between the canter and the walk. If he's not balanced enough to do this yet, he's going to fall on his face when you ask for the flying change. In addition, for the upward transition he needs to be **"hot off your leg"** (see Book One, Chapter Six) so that he reacts immediately when you ask him to go from the walk to the canter.

If you need to review how to ride transitions from the canter to the walk, and simple changes of lead, see page 81.

2. Self-carriage in the canter. You must develop and maintain the quality of your horse's canter. If your horse's canter is four-beat or it's too "flat," you need to improve it before you work on flying changes. This is important because a flying change is simply a canter bound, and the flying change itself should look like every other canter stride. Therefore, your horse should canter in some degree of self-carriage with big, "round," expressive bounds.

When a canter is flat, the horse doesn't get off the ground very much during the period of suspension. As a result, he'll find flying changes difficult to do because there won't be enough time for him to switch his legs. Sometimes, horses with flat canters end up doing a step of trot with their hind legs when they go to change leads because they can't figure out how to negotiate rearranging their legs if there's not enough "air" time. In this case, rather than switching canter leads with both hind and front legs at the same time, they change leads with their front legs while doing a step of trot with their hind legs. Then one stride later, the hind legs catch up to the front legs and also begin to canter on the new lead (fig. 8.6).

Once you have a pure three-beat canter, work on exercises that increase the self-carriage, such as shoulder-fore (remember that we don't ask for a shoulder-in with a 30-degree angle from the rail while in the canter), both on straight lines and on large and small circles; haunches-in on a small circle; and frequent canter-walk-canter transitions. When

8.6
Your horse needs to bound over the ground with each canter stride, so that he has enough "air time" to switch his legs for a flying change.

I say "frequent," I mean you can do as few as five strides of canter, five strides of walk, five strides of canter, then five strides of walk.

You can also improve self-carriage in the canter by giving **collecting half-halts**. You learned these half-halts in Chapter Four. As you give one of these half-halts, drive your horse's hind legs further under his body as you always do during a half-halt. But, in this case, shorten the reins and increase the influence of your outside rein by using it more firmly so that your horse ends up covering less ground with each stride. As you close your outside hand in a fist, think about holding your horse almost on the spot in the canter during the three seconds of the half-halt. Then, go more forward over the ground for six or seven strides.

After the half-halt, your horse's balance should also be more **uphill**, It's important that you don't let him go back down on his forehand when you send him forward again. So make sure the reins stay short and that your horse doesn't pull them through your fingers in order to lengthen his frame and go back down on his forehand. Also, sit up tall and hold him in self-carriage by keeping your back erect and strong. Repeat this sequence of collected strides and shorter strides that are almost on the spot several times.

While asking for those short but very active and engaged strides, imagine you're convincing your horse to canter in a teacup (fig. 8.7). Do these transitions forward and back from the shortened canter to normal collected canter until your horse is easily adjustable and willingly responds to the "collecting half-halt" that asks him to canter almost on the spot.

Another way to determine that you've done good "collecting half-halts" is when you can feel that the canter has the same activity, rhythm, and tempo as it did before, but your horse does more strides per meter than he did prior to the half-halts. For example, if it normally takes a horse three to four canter strides to go through a corner, in a more collected canter he will cover less ground per stride and do it in five or six strides.

8.7

When you want short, but very active engaged strides in the canter, imagine you are asking your horse to canter in a teacup!

3. Counter-canter. As part of your "preparation-for-flying-change" homework, you'll need to develop a balanced counter-canter. (Should you need to review counter-canter, refer to Book One, page 158.) Work on it until you feel confident that you can ride counter-canter without tension on both circles and straight lines. Your horse should be able to do extensions in counter-canter as well as the transition back to collected canter without breaking to the trot or switching leads on his own. Ride the same exercise that I described in number two above, where you do transitions from collected canter to several shorter strides (canter in a teacup) to adjust your horse's center of gravity and create more self-carriage in his counter-canter.

The Aids for the Flying Change

Since a flying change is merely another canter "bound," the most important prerequisite for a successful flying change is the quality of your horse's canter. Another factor that contributes to completing a successful flying change is the timing of your aids. Normally you give the aids when your horse's leading front leg touches the ground, immediately before the period of suspension. This is because it takes your horse a moment to understand and carry out your request for the change, which will be done during the period of suspension. When doing a flying change from left lead to right lead, the aids are applied as follows:

1. *Seat:* a forward push with your right seat bone.
2. *Right leg:* squeeze on the girth to remind the horse to go forward.
3. *Left leg:* swing behind the girth to signal the new outside hind leg to strike off.
4. *Left rein:* close your hand in a fist to stick your horse's new outside hind leg on the ground and to maintain his uphill balance. Imagine closing and opening that hand so quickly that you could snatch a fly out of the air and then let it go.
5. *Right rein:* soften forward to allow the new leading leg to change.

GETTING STARTED

I find the easiest place to introduce flying changes for most horses is on a small figure eight where each of the two circles has a diameter of about 10 meters. Ride the first small circle of the figure eight in canter, and when you come to the point where you're ready to start the second circle, do a simple change of lead. Then ride the other half of the figure eight in the direction of the new lead. Go back and forth between the two circles with simple changes of lead until you feel that your horse understands and almost anticipates the transition from one lead to the other. At this point, give the aids for a flying change instead of asking for a simple change of lead.

More often than not, your horse will do a clean flying change. When he does, stop immediately and praise him lavishly.

However, don't be surprised if your horse offers any number of alternative reactions to your request for a flying change. For example, he could do a clean change, but then rush off with excitement. When this occurs, you can either stay on the new circle and canter until he relaxes and slows down or do a downward transition to the walk. In either case, praise him generously for doing the flying change. Eventually, his exuberance will go away.

He might also do a flying change with his front legs without switching his hind legs or change his hind legs without switching his front legs. In both cases, he ends up doing a disunited canter. Don't make a big fuss about it. Just come back to either the trot or the walk. Then re-establish a true canter. Do a few more simple changes of lead between the two circles to remind him about the task at hand, and then ask for the flying change again.

Then again, some horses don't do the flying change at all. They just canter merrily along on the 10-meter circle in counter-canter. In this situation, you can make your horse more alert by giving a slightly sharper outside leg aid or by tapping him with the whip a couple of times just before you give the actual aid for the flying change. But if you aren't making any progress after several attempts, you might want to abandon this exercise in favor of an alternative plan.

For example, forget about changing from one direction to the other because your horse might feel that this just complicates the issue. Instead, just ask for the flying change from the counter-canter. The first pattern to try is to simply ride a large circle in counter-canter. Engage your horse's "new" outside hind leg by tapping him with the whip, and then ask for the flying change anywhere on the circle. (If you're circling to the left, and you're in right lead canter, carry the whip in your right hand so you can engage his right hind leg.)

You can also just go all the way around the ring in counter-canter. Stay in counter-canter for as long as you need to feel organized before you ask for the flying change, but do wait until you're on the straight line of a long or short side of the ring. It's more difficult for your horse to be correctly balanced for the flying change when he's in a corner.

• *Helpful Hints* •

DEALING WITH TENSION
Sometimes when you start schooling flying changes, you'll find that your horse gets tense because he's worried or confused about changing his leads. Because he's anxious, he might begin to anticipate the flying change and nervously offer it before you ask.

8.8

If your horse gets tense because he's anticipating and worrying about doing a flying change, help him to relax by riding him in a deep frame in counter-canter as Ruth is doing here with Mastermind. While lowering his neck, she has done an excellent job of keeping his hind legs coming well under his body.

Never punish him if he does a flying change on his own. If you do, you'll only add to his anxiety. Just quietly trot or walk, and resume cantering on whatever lead you were on originally. Then, help him to stop "obsessing" about the flying changes by doing a lot of counter-canter without asking for any changes at all. While in counter-canter, you might alternate between riding him in a normal balance and putting him in a **deep frame** as described on page 46. The deep frame helps to loosen and relax his muscles, and in turn, his mind unwinds.

Once your horse is calm, simply finish the session with this relaxed counter-canter. In this way you won't have more tension to deal with the next time you school flying changes (fig. 8.8).

Many young horses get a bit excited when they start flying changes and can rush off. If I can, I always try to start these horses either in an indoor arena or within the confines of a well-fenced in area outside. The rail or wall acts as a sort of psychological barrier that backs the horse off and slows him down. To use this "barrier" to my advantage, I position my horse so I ask for the flying change when I'm cantering toward the solid wall or the railing rather than when heading toward a wide open space.

Sometimes an exuberant horse will speed up considerably after doing a flying change (often happily bucking!). In order to counteract this horse's excitement, I ask for the flying change and then immediately halt. Then I'll reward him with lots of pats or a treat. In this way my horse anticipates stopping for his reward rather than frolicking off enthusiastically.

HORSE IGNORES THE AID

When I introduced flying changes to Eastwood, I found that he was an interesting combination of nervous tension and dullness to my leg. He was worried about the flying changes, but he was slow to react to my leg aid. I made him hotter off my leg by doing a lot of simple changes of lead from the walk to the canter back to the walk and then to the counter-canter. If he wasn't quick to answer, I'd kick him once and then ask for the canter depart again.

As soon as he gave an electric response to my leg, I worked on relaxing him in the canter. I put him in a very deep frame and made sure his tempo didn't get too quick. We did lots of transitions to medium canter and back to collected canter in this frame to make sure he stayed relaxed yet still immediately responsive to my leg aids. When he was quick to my leg and relaxed, rather than dull to my leg and tense, I asked for a flying change.

I remember Gary Rockwell, World Equestrian Games bronze medalist, telling a story of a young horse he had in for training that just didn't understand the concept of doing a flying change with a rider on his back. He said this horse was perfectly happy doing counter-canter on the tiniest circle imaginable! Gary did all sorts of acrobatics to knock him off balance, thinking it had to be easier for the horse to change his leads than to stay in counter-canter. But this horse just kept cantering calmly around the small circle on the original lead. Interestingly enough, when Gary finally managed to get him to do his first flying change, a light bulb must have gone off in the horse's head. As soon as he realized that he was supposed to "swap" leads, the rest of his flying change education, including learning how to do tempi changes, came easily.

Now, Gary Rockwell is a lot more athletic than I am, and he was able to cleverly maneuver that horse into a position where he either had to change canter leads or he'd feel like he was going to tip over. But rather than doing all sorts of acrobatic contortions as Gary did, I usually use a pole on the ground or a low cavaletti to help give my horse extra "air" time, so it's easier for him to change the sequence of his legs during the period of suspension. If my horse approaches the pole on the left lead, I'll turn him with an opening right rein while he's in the air over the pole and ask for the flying change at the same time with my left leg behind the girth.

IMPROVING FAULTY CHANGES

Changing Late Behind

When a horse changes "late behind," he changes with his front legs first and then a stride or more later he finally changes with his hind legs. This is the most frequent mistake I see when riders begin to school flying changes, and it's a serious fault. In the beginning stages of training I might make a lot of compromises, but doing a clean change is the priority for me. For instance, I won't make an issue about whether my horse stays on the bit, is a little late to react to the aids, or gets somewhat tense. All of these things will go away in time. But I do insist that my horse change "cleanly," and I have several exercises for the horse that doesn't do so. Here are some of them:

1. I find that some horses don't change "clean" because they are not **"through"** the outside of their bodies (the side that will become the "inside" after the flying change). By "not through" I mean it feels as though they aren't connected because they've stiffened against the outside rein and their hind legs seem "paralyzed" and unable to jump under their bodies.

I had a horse like this in training several years ago who had been doing his flying changes late behind for over a year. This had become a very bad habit, and it was difficult to get him to change his established way of doing things. For the first six weeks of riding him, I didn't do any flying changes at all and just worked on his connection and "throughness" because he was so confirmed in this bad habit. I did a couple of unusual things (chronic problems sometimes need drastic measures).

The first was to school him a lot in counter-canter but with one slight modification. Normally, when you do counter-canter, your horse is flexed at the poll toward the lead that he's on. Specifically, if he's in counter-canter while going to the right, he should be on the left lead and flexed at the poll so that he looks slightly to the left. Instead, I flexed this horse to the right when we were doing counter-canter on the left lead while going to the right. And, I flexed him to the left when we were doing counter-canter on the right lead while tracking to the left. I asked for this

8.9 and 8.10 Preparation for Flying Changes
Ruth alternates every few strides between true flexion and counter-flexion. While doing this she is careful to keep Mastermind's hind legs lined up directly behind his front legs so that his body stays straight and parallel to the long side.

counter-flexion at the poll by using an indirect rein as described in Book One, (Chapter Eight).

When I began the exercise, I knew that he would try to evade the "throughness" by swinging his hindquarters in the opposite direction from my indirect rein aid. So I made sure that his body didn't drift sideways when I asked for counter-flexion at the poll—by firmly supporting with my legs and the other rein. The "guarding" effect of my outside rein and outside leg were particularly important here. I knew if I let my outside hand go forward, he'd pop his shoulder to the outside. And if my outside leg didn't control his hindquarters, they would swing off the line we were on as well.

No matter where I was in the ring—circles, corners, long sides—I checked that I kept his legs exactly overlapping whatever line I was on.

We went around and around in counter-canter in this position until he felt comfortable. I could tell this was happening when I felt two things. First, I didn't have to work so hard to keep his body straight. I could relax the pressure of my "guarding" outside rein and leg, and he'd keep following the line we were on. And second, when I asked for counter-flexion, he'd answer my rein aid without stiffening against my hand.

Sometimes I rode around with him counter-flexed all the time. Other times, I alternated between counter-flexion and correct flexion every few strides (figs. 8.9 and 8.10). We did everything in this position—circles, serpentines, diagonals, and shallow loops. Over the course of the six weeks, this horse began to feel very soft on the outside of his body. I imagined that when he was "through," he felt like butter on that side. When I finally asked for the flying change, it was clean. Today this horse does beautiful flying changes, including one-tempi changes. But it took several weeks of patient reschooling to change his habitual response.

The second drastic measure that I took with this horse was to supple him in the canter as described in Chapter Eleven in Book One. However, in his case, I always suppled him away from the lead he was on (figs. 8.11 and 8.12). (I guess you could call this "counter-suppling" as opposed to counter-flexion!) In the beginning, I really had to pay attention that I used my "guarding" outside rein and leg to keep him straight. When he could finally bend his neck willingly while keeping the rest of his legs on the line of travel, I knew he was more "through" and was ready to attempt a flying change.

If you start the flying changes yourself rather than inheriting someone else's problem, you probably won't have to resort to such drastic measures. (By the way, if you're concerned about starting the flying changes yourself, get professional help. It's a lot easier to do them right in the beginning than to have to reschool a problem later.) But this is a good exercise to file away in your bag-of-tricks if you run into a reschooling problem with another horse.

In fact, you'll find that you can use it for much more than fixing late flying changes. For example, if you're trotting or cantering along and you feel your horse stiffen against your outside rein, counter-flex or "counter-supple" him until he feels softer. Or, if you're on a circle or corner, and you feel like your horse is becoming crooked because his shoulders are bulging or "popping" to the outside of the line you're on, counter-flex him at the poll to help make him **axis-straight**. When you counter-flex him, his shoulders will slide over to the inside so that they're back in front of his hips (figs. 8.13 and 8.14).

8.11 and 8.12
Counter-Suppling While
in Counter-Canter

8.11
Mastermind is in counter-
canter (on the right lead
while going to the left), and
Ruth is counter-suppling him
to put him "through" by
bending his neck away from
the lead he's on—to the left.

8.12
Once again Ruth is counter-
suppling her horse to put him
"through" the left side of his
body while he's in counter-
canter. But in this example,
she is increasing his relaxation by also riding him in a
deep frame.

8.13

Here, Mastermind has become a bit crooked. His shoulders are popping out toward the fence, and his hind feet do not follow directly in the tracks of his forefeet.

8.14

Ruth straightens Mastermind by counter-flexing him at the poll. By positioning him so that he looks very slightly toward the fence, his shoulders slide over so that his front feet are now directly lined up in front of his hind feet.

8.13 and 8.14 Using Counter-Flexion to Straighten the Horse

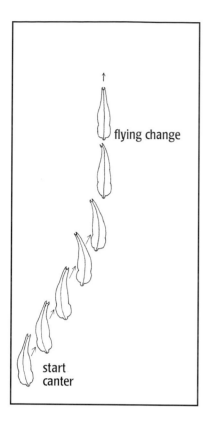

flying change

start
canter

8.15

A "throughness" exercise to
improve flying changes that are late
behind: start a canter half-pass to
the right, and gradually bend your
horse's neck to the left. When he
feels soft and doesn't resist the
action of your left rein, straighten
his neck, ride straight forward, and
ask for the flying change.

8.15 to 8.18
Exercises to Improve Flying
Changes That Are Late Behind

2. You can use a similar throughness exercise to help fix flying changes that are late behind. Start a canter half-pass to the right. Go sideways for a few strides, and then continue to move to the right but begin to bend your horse's neck to the left. When he feels soft on his left side and doesn't resist the action of your left rein, straighten his neck and ride straight forward. Be sure you straighten his neck completely before you ask for the flying change (fig. 8.15).

3. Another "throughness" exercise to help with late flying changes is to canter a serpentine of three or more loops. As you approach the center of the arena to start the second loop, slide your "new" (upcoming) inside leg forward on the girth. Once your leg is in this position, press with it and push your horse sideways for a stride or two toward your new outside rein. If your horse feels stiff in his rib cage and leans his barrel against your leg instead of moving away from it, don't continue onto the second loop of the serpentine. Instead, circle so that you stay on the first loop. Then, as you approach the center line again, push him away from your inside leg. You might have to do the first circle and ask him to move sideways several times before he softly bends around your new inside leg.

Don't be in a hurry to ask for the change. Your main concern should be that your horse "gives" in his barrel and feels like he's stepping sideways toward your new outside rein. When that happens, you can straighten his body, ask for the flying change, and work your way back onto the arc of the second loop of the serpentine. Go through the same process as you approach the centerline between the second and third loops of the serpentine (fig. 8.16).

4. Sometimes the cause of late changes isn't a lack of "throughness" but is the result of insufficient engagement of the inside hind leg–the leg that will become the new outside hind leg. So, if that's what you're running into, here are some "engagement-of-the-new-outside-hind-leg" exercises for you:

a. Do a half-pass in the canter to engage your horse's inside hind leg. Then, ride straight forward for a stride or two before you ask for the flying change. Since the old inside hind leg becomes the new outside hind leg (the strike-off leg) in a flying change, the more ready, eager and, therefore, engaged it is from the half-pass, the more likely you'll be to get a clean change (fig. 8.17).

b. Ride a haunches-in in the canter on a small circle until you feel your horse lower his hindquarters and "sit down" behind. When he does, straighten him, leave the circle by riding straight forward, and immediately ask for the flying change. If you wait too long before you ask, your horse has time to shift his center of gravity toward his front legs, and you'll lose the benefits of the exercise (fig. 8.18).

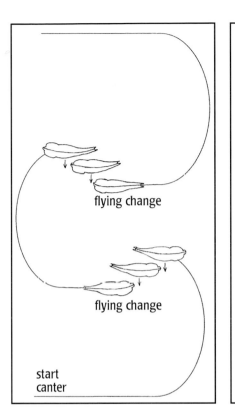

8.16

Canter a serpentine of three or more loops. As you approach the center to start the second loop, slide your "upcoming" inside leg forward on to the girth, press with it, and leg-yield your horse for a couple of strides into your new outside rein. Then ask for the flying change.

8.17

For late flying changes due to insufficient engagement, do a half-pass in canter, then ride straight forward for a stride or two before asking for the change.

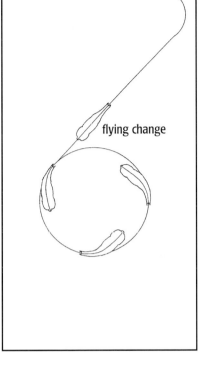

8.18

Ride a haunches-in in the canter on a small circle until you feel your horse "sit down" behind. When he does, straighten him, leave the circle by riding straight forward, and immediately ask for the flying change.

c. Ride three **preparatory half-halts** that are directed to your horse's inside hind leg–the leg that will become the new outside hind leg. These half-halts are yet another variation of the ones you're used to doing in that they are shorter than the usual half-halt that lasts for three seconds. Each "preparatory" half-halt consists of a momentary closure of seat, legs, and hand. You close your legs, push with your seat, and close your inside hand in a fist.

Do three of these half-halts very quickly in a row in sync with the rhythm of the canter. Since you want to engage the inside hind leg, give the half-halts when that leg is on the ground (during the second beat of the canter). That is the moment during which you can influence it so that it will be used more powerfully.

Then after three quick half-halts, ask for the flying change. It's even helpful to count out loud, "1-2-3- change," or, "now, now, now, change," each time the inside hind leg is on the ground, to get your timing. If you can't feel this moment, look at your horse's mane. It usually goes up during the second beat of the canter. Each time you count out loud, push with your seat, close your legs and quickly open and close your inside hand in a fist. Specifically, if you're changing from the right lead to the left lead, you'll be giving the half-halts on the right rein. At the fourth canter stride when you say the word "change," close your inside hand in a fist again at the same time that you bring your inside leg back to tell your horse to do the change.

d. If your "preparatory" half-halts don't engage your horse's new outside hind leg sufficiently, use the whip in a similar way. Ride around in canter and say "now, now, now" as you give three taps on the inside hind (the leg that will become the new outside hind). Tap as lightly or as vigorously as you need to get that leg active and "jumping." While tapping, imagine that the hind legs are so eager that they're begging to switch leads. If your horse's hind legs could talk, you'd hear them saying, "When? When? How about now?" with each tap of the whip. Do this several times and then finally go ahead and give the aid for the flying change—tap, tap, tap, change (fig. 8.19).

e. Here's another exercise to help to engage the horse's new outside hind leg.

Start by riding to the left about a yard inside the track in counter-canter (on the right lead). Bend your horse around your right leg and ask for haunches-out around that leg. This means that his forehand will remain a yard away from the track and his hindquarters will be moved toward the rail. He will be on three tracks, with his left hind leg lined up directly behind his right front leg (figs. 8.20 and 8.21).

Once your horse can do this haunches-out easily, keep his legs in the same position but straighten his neck by bringing it toward

8.19

To engage your horse's new outside hind leg (the "old" inside hind leg) sufficiently to prepare him for a flying change, ride around in canter and say, "Now, now, now," as you tap it three times with the whip. If the horse's inside hind leg could talk, you would hear it saying, "When? When? How about now?" You want it to be "begging" to switch the lead.

8.20

Here Lynda prepares Joffrey for the flying change by riding him a little off the track in haunches-out in the counter-canter. He appears to be nicely bent and flexed to the right, but her right leg could be more forward on the girth to help with the bend.

8.21

Lynda keeps Joffrey's legs and body in the haunches-out position as she straightens his neck with her left rein. Once he feels like he's pushed from her left leg into her right rein, she'll give the aid for the flying change.

8.20 and 8.21 Preparing for a Flying Change from Right Lead to Left Lead

the center of the ring. Then, close your left leg and feel like you're pushing his left hind leg toward your right hand. You should be able to go easily back and forth from haunches-out with bend, to straightening his neck. When he feels like he's stepping from your left leg into your right hand, ask for the flying change.

To insure the straightness and the engagement of the inside hind leg while on the new lead, continue cantering forward in a shoulder-fore position after the flying change. This should not be too difficult; because of the haunches-out exercise you did before the flying change, your horse's legs are already lined up to do a three-track shoulder-in. So, all you have to do is decrease the angle slightly to get a shoulder-fore on four tracks. Keep his shoulders 15 degrees from the rail and use your active inside leg to hold his hind legs in the track.

Changing Late in Front

I also see horses who change leads behind first but are late to change in front. This situation doesn't concern me as much as the horse who changes late behind, because at least I know that this horse is thinking about his hind legs. In fact, usually when a horse does this, it's because the rider has restricted him with her new inside rein rather than softening it. It's definitely a challenge in rider coordination to be able to give a firm half-halt on the new outside rein while you ease the tension on the new inside rein.

I often have a student practice this when she is on the ground. To change from right lead to left lead, she closes her right (outside) hand in a fist and softens her left (inside) hand an inch or so forward. Then, she changes back from left to right by closing the left hand and softening the right hand. In the beginning, I suggest that she even exaggerate the forward movement of the inside hand. In this way she develops some muscle memory, so that it becomes automatic for her to soften the inside rein forward, rather than hang or pull on it, at the same time that she's closing the outside hand in a fist.

Late to Answer the Aid

Sometimes, you'll find that the problem isn't that your horse is late behind or in front, but that he's late to answer your aid. You give the aid and one or two strides after you ask, your horse finally answers with a clean flying change. This frequently happens in one direction more so than the other. One solution is to mentally prepare your horse by giving your three "preparatory" half-halts before asking for the change as described earlier in 4c on page 171.

You can also change the timing of your aid ever so slightly. Give the aid a fraction of a second earlier than you normally would, in order to give your horse an extra moment to mentally compute and physically respond to the aid.

Sometimes a horse gives a delayed reaction to the aid because the tempo of his canter is too slow, and it takes him an extra moment to respond to the aid. If you suspect that tempo is the issue, work on teaching your horse to canter more crisply. Do some transitions to medium canter to quicken the tempo, and when you come back to collected canter again, maintain the faster tempo. Mark this quicker tempo by speeding up the forward and back motion of your seat rather than just following along at the speed your horse chooses.

Keeping Your Horse Straight

I frequently see horses who aren't straight when doing flying changes. This crookedness can be expressed in a variety of ways—I'll discuss three of them here.

A horse may swing his hindquarters to the inside in the direction of the new lead. Sometimes this is because the horse is trying to avoid the engagement of his new inside hind leg. More often than not, however, the problem is created by the rider. If a rider pulls on her new inside rein during the change, not only will she turn her horse's neck to the inside, but the backward action on the rein will block his hind leg from stepping under his body.

Since he can't come under his body with his inside hind leg, he has a few options, none of which are desirable: he can be late behind in the change; he can change cleanly, but take a short step behind; or because it's difficult to come under, he can take the path of least resistance and swing his hindquarters to the inside. The rider needs to remember to soften her new inside hand forward as described in *Changing Late in Front* on page 174.

If it becomes a habit for her horse to swing his hindquarters to the inside during the change, it'll be helpful for her to do two things. First, close her new outside hand in a fist as she would do normally. Then move that hand laterally in the direction of the new lead as if asking for shoulder-fore. This rein action helps place her horse's forehand in front of his new inside hind leg.

Another expression of crookedness is when a horse does a straight flying change in one direction, but in the other direction his entire body drifts or even jumps sideways. You can prevent this by using your new inside leg firmly on the girth. In this way you can make a physical barrier that blocks your horse from jumping sideways during the flying change.

Yet a third form of crookedness is shown when a horse stays straight during the flying change but becomes crooked by swinging his hindquarters to the inside on the very next stride afterwards. He does this to avoid bending the joints of his inside hind leg and carrying weight on it in the canter. In this case, ride the change and immediately step into shoulder-fore for a few strides. That is, after a flying change from right to left, do left shoulder-fore until the horse learns that he must keep his new inside hind leg engaged and underneath his body (fig. 8.22).

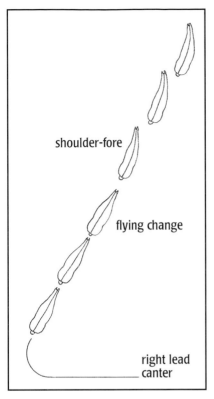

shoulder-fore

flying change

right lead canter

8.22

When your horse becomes crooked by swinging his hindquarters to the inside during and after a flying change, ride the change and immediately step into shoulder-fore for a few strides.

KEY POINTS

In order to do a flying change, the horse reorganizes his legs during the period of suspension in the canter. The hind leg that he places on the ground first determines the canter lead he will be on.

To prepare your horse to learn flying changes, work on simple changes of lead, self-carriage in the canter, and counter-canter.

In the initial stages, your priority is to get a "clean" flying change where the hind and front legs switch leads during the same canter stride. Later on, you'll systematically add in other ingredients such as relaxation, straightness, roundness, and the immediate reaction to the aid.

If you have a horse who changes late behind, focus either on "throughness" exercises or engaging his inside hind leg.

CHAPTER NINE

Typical Problems Solved by Using "Fancy Stuff"

These "typical" problems that I'm going to address in this chapter are not necessarily more complicated than the ones you might have been faced with earlier in your horse's training, but because you are further along in your education (your horse, too) and have more information at your disposal, you have more tools to deal with them.

When you run into trouble during schooling, the symptoms may vary, but the cause is almost always the same—something in **the Basics** has gone awry. So, rather than repeatedly drilling a movement or exercise, look for the answer in the Basics. Run through a checklist of the qualities that should be a constant theme throughout all of your work. Ask yourself if your horse is relaxed, moving freely forward, in a regular rhythm, and is straight. Check that he's responding to your half-halts so you can first connect him and later ask for self-carriage. Then, when the Basics are in order, try the movement again (the Basics are all covered in Book One).

I remember watching a clinic that Klaus Balkenhol (fig. 9.1), a member of the German dressage team that won the Olympic Gold Medal in 1992, was giving to the American riders who were aspiring to gain a slot on the 1996 Olympic team. All of these riders were very accomplished and the horses were trained to a very high level. Yet the message that Mr. Balkenhol repeatedly sent home was that if they were having a problem with any movement or exercise, it was always caused by a fault in the Basics.

He didn't want them to make adjustments or corrections during the actual movements. Instead, he had these top riders concentrate first and foremost on relaxation, rhythm, suppleness, contact, impulsion, and straightness. Invariably, with the Basics as a priority, the quality and correctness of the movements improved dramatically.

Olympic and World Champion Klaus Balkenhol, seen here with Goldstern, always goes back to "the Basics" every time he has a problem with any movement or exercise. Photo: Jan Gyllensten

9.2
Working your horse in a deep frame, as Ruth is doing here, is a great way to dissipate tension.

Decreasing Tension and Tightness

In Chapter Two, I talked about riding your horse in a **deep frame** at the beginning and end of your schooling session to warm him up and cool him down, as well as to help him stay connected if he was struggling to stay on the bit in a particular movement.

I also mentioned that working in a "deep" frame can be used to dissipate tension, and I'd like to explore that idea a bit more here. Understand that when you train a horse, you're dealing with an inseparable mind and body connection. If your horse is tense, excited, or inattentive you can effectively quiet his mind by relaxing him physically. This approach is often more productive than simply trying to calm his mood by speaking to him in soothing tones.

If a horse is tense or tight, he holds his back rigidly, and this blocks the connection from his hind legs to his forehand. However, when he's ridden deep, his back has to swing and as a result his whole body can become looser and freer. As his body relaxes, you can almost feel a horse take in a deep breath, exhale, and let go of his tension (fig. 9.2).

If your horse is a spooky type, deep is a great position for you to work him in. Take it from Holland's Anky van Grunsven, winner of the individual gold medal in the 1994 World Equestrian Games and 1995 World Cup, who relies on working deep with her timid and easily distracted Olympic Bonfire. She not only does a very lengthy warm-up in this frame, but she also does all of her advanced movements deep until just moments before she's ready to enter the competition arena. Even though you might not be headed for the World Championships or the Olympics, knowing how to put your horse deep can come in very handy in the many situations you encounter when he becomes frightened or defensive.

Generally, I start each schooling session with my horse deep. But, I'll also return to this frame when I'm introducing a new exercise that will stress him mentally as he tries to learn it. I'll alternate between the exercise itself and riding him deep on a circle until I can re-establish relaxation. Then I'll resume the exercise.

One of my students, Kathy, was having difficulty keeping her horse relaxed when she did a series of flying changes across the diagonal. Her horse was fine doing the flying changes on the long side of the arena, but as soon as she started across the diagonal line, he began to get worried. So we worked him deep as part of his relaxation program.

Kathy started across the diagonal on the right lead and asked for only one flying change to the left lead. Immediately after the flying change, she turned onto a 10-meter circle to the left and put her horse deep in the canter. She stayed on that circle several times around until he finally relaxed. Then she rebalanced him and continued across the diagonal, asked for the next flying change to the right lead, and immediately circled to the right and put him deep again. After about a week of riding the flying changes on the diagonal this way, her horse began to relax because he expected to do the comforting canter on the circle rather than anticipating the next flying change. Within a few weeks, she was able to ride flying changes in a sequence on a diagonal line with a calm and confident horse.

All Manner of Crookednesses

UNEVEN IN THE REIN

Riders frequently complain to me that their horses are hanging on one rein and won't take a contact with the other rein. This unevenness in the rein actually is a result of the horse's innate crookedness. On his stiff side, a horse steps into the rein and the contact can be quite firm. On his soft side, however, a horse avoids stepping into the rein, and the contact can be lighter, or even nonexistent. Your goal is to make your horse even in the reins so that you feel the same weight in both hands.

So what can you do to make your crooked horse straight so you feel the same amount of contact in each rein? Well, with a minor adjustment, the same half-halt that you learned in Chapters One and Two in order to **connect** your horse can also be used to make him even in the reins.

"Reversing" the Half-Halts

Let's say your horse is stiff to the right and soft to the left. When riding to the right, ride your usual half-halt where you drive the horse through your closed outside (left) hand. However, when riding to the left, you're going to reverse your half-halt. Send him forward through your closed inside hand—once again the left hand—and, if necessary, flex him a little to the outside (fig. 9.3 and 9.4). Your aids are essentially saying, "Step from behind into this light left rein and take a contact with my left hand...and stop hanging on the right rein."

Once your horse is consistently even in both reins, you can go back to riding normal half-halts through the outside rein in both directions. Horses change constantly during schooling. Always remember to ride the horse you have on any given day—not the one you were riding last month or even yesterday.

When I first got Eastwood he was stiff to the right and soft to the left as in the above example. So, when tracking left, I reversed my half-halt—sending him through my closed inside hand—for a month or so. Then gradually, I realized that his stiff and soft sides had changed in the course of training. So, temporarily I had to reverse my half-halt and drive him into my inside hand while riding to the right! Now, he's fairly even in my hands, but occasionally he'll collapse away from one rein so that the contact between it and my hand is too light, and he ends up hanging on the other rein. When he does this, I'll immediately give a half-halt through whichever is the light rein—the one he's not stepping into and taking a contact with—in order to remedy the situation.

RIDER CREATED CROOKEDNESS

Eastwood was a fairly short-term project as far as getting him straight and even in the reins. I do have a student, however, who had to ride her horse with "reversed" half-halts in both directions for a solid year. I had her do this because she was the cause of the problem. She made her horse crooked by being heavy-handed with her inside rein in both directions. In response to her inside hand, her horse was happy to overbend his neck to the inside, collapse away from whichever was the inside rein, and pop his shoulders to the outside. Because this is what she did habitually, this felt normal to her. She had lost her perception of what it felt like to have her horse **axis-straight.** (Remember, axis-straight means the horse's spine exactly overlaps his line of travel).

9.3

Dwight's soft side is his left side. It's obvious that he is uneven in the rein because there is a firm contact on the right rein and slack in the left rein.

9.4

Chris fixes the uneven contact by reversing his half-halt. He drives Dwight forward through his closed inside (left) hand and flexes him slightly to the outside. He has established a solid contact with the left rein here but, ideally, Dwight's nose should stretch more forward toward the bit.

I told her to reverse the half-halts so she could get the idea of keeping his shoulders in front of his hips. She needed to become familiar with this feeling of his spine being truly straight and the contact being equal in the two reins.

So, except for a canter depart when her horse needed to be flexed to the inside, she used half-halts through her closed inside hand for everything else that she did with him. It took a long time for her to learn the feeling of keeping her horse axis-straight, but now she is able to give normal half-halts through the outside rein. And, even though it took her awhile to learn the feeling of a straight horse, reversing the half-halt wasn't a big deal for either one of them.

USING HAUNCHES-IN TO STRAIGHTEN AND STRENGTHEN YOUR HORSE

Haunches-in can also be used as a straightening exercise for a horse who has one hind leg weaker than the other. I know it must seem like a contradiction to move a horse's hindquarters sideways in order to make him straight. But this displacement done on purpose by the rider is different from an evasion caused by a crooked horse. The crooked horse moves his hindquarters sideways, with no bend in his body, to avoid bending the joints of his weaker hind leg (figs. 9.5 to 9.7).

Do you remember the formula from our discussion of advanced lateral movements? Bend + Sideways = Engagement (Chapter Six). During haunches-in there's a bend through the horse's body, so as he goes sideways with a bend, he has no option but to engage this hind leg (fig. 9.8).

In addition, the leg that steps under his mass—the outside hind leg—has to "weight-lift." So the haunches-in becomes a strengthening exercise as well. As this weaker hind leg becomes stronger, the horse is able to use his hind legs more equally, and it's easier to make him straight.

If I have a horse who habitually carries his quarters to the right, I'll ride him with his hindquarters slightly to the left regardless of where I am in the ring. This means placing him in haunches-in when I ride to the left, and haunches-out when going to the right. I do this because the horse whose hindquarters are always to the right isn't carrying as much weight on that right hind leg and is letting his left hind leg do most of the work. I need to reverse this tendency by placing his right hind leg under his body. This way it has to carry weight until it becomes strong enough for the horse to be happy to use it willingly (figs. 9.9 and 9.10).

I remember a horse that I had in for training that was incredibly crooked in this way. As soon as I picked up a contact, his haunches would swing to the left. All horses have some tendency to be crooked, but this horse had developed very unevenly because his rider had never straightened him. So, it was physical therapy time!

9.5

A crooked horse: in this photo Galen is crooked. She has moved her hindquarters ever so slightly sideways to avoid bending the joints of her inside hind leg and carrying weight on it. Her hind feet do not follow directly in the tracks made by her front feet.

9.6

A "requested" very slight haunches-in: compare this photo to 9.5 where Galen also has her hindquarters to the inside. In this case, however, the sideways displacement is useful (in an engaging way) rather than harmful (in an "unloading weight," or evasive, way), because Galen is bent around Deb's inside leg. Notice the position of Deb's outside leg. It is behind the girth to help with the bend and to specifically ask Galen's hindquarters to move in off the track.

9.7

A true haunches-in: Deb has increased the angle that Galen's hindquarters are moved in off the track. She is still doing a good engagement exercise, because Galen maintains a uniform bend from poll to tail around Deb's inside leg.

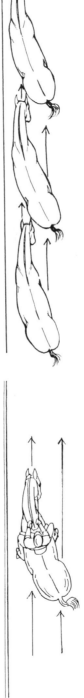

9.8

Correct haunches-in with uniform bend from poll to tail.

9.9

Given the choice, Mastermind would like to carry his hindquarters to the right all the time, and, therefore, avoid carrying weight with his right hind leg. To correct this tendency, Ruth always places his hindquarters a little bit to the left as a straightening and strengthening exercise. Here, as they go to the right she puts him in haunches-out.

9.10

When they change direction and go to the left, Ruth still wants to keep Mastermind's right hind leg underneath his body, so she rides him in haunches-in. She could even ask for less angle than we see in 9.9 and this photo and still get the job done. As long as his right hind leg is under his body and lifting his weight (even if she only moves it over an inch or two), it will get stronger.

9.9 and 9.10 Strengthening the Right Hind Leg While on the Rail

For three weeks, when riding to the right in the walk, trot, and canter, I rode him in a very subtle version of haunches-in on circles and straight lines—just enough positioning to put his left hind leg ever so slightly underneath his body. When riding to the left, I rode a slight haunches-out position in the walk and trot or a shoulder-fore position in walk, trot, and canter.

All of my efforts and every position I used were designed to keep his left hind leg under his body so that it had to carry weight. I knew that the left hind had become stronger when I picked up the reins one day and this horse adopted a slight, right haunches-in position on his own. His willingness to carry weight on his left hind leg proved to me that it was getting as strong as his right hind leg. At that point I abandoned those particular physical therapy exercises and began to school him more like a normal horse (fig. 9.11).

USING SHOULDER-IN TO MAINTAIN BALANCE AND IMPROVE EXTENSIONS

Use shoulder-in to help you when you ride movements during which your horse habitually loses his **self-carriage** and falls on his forehand. For instance, when you ride an extended trot or canter and then find it difficult to do the transition back to the collected gait because your horse's balance has shifted toward his front legs. Try riding shoulder-fore or shoulder-in to keep his shoulders "up" in the moment of the downward transition. For this exercise you don't need to extend for a whole long side. Ask for the extension for five or six strides. Then rather than using a half-halt to collect the pace, put him in a shoulder-in to engage him and keep his balance back toward his hindquarters for the downward transition. Then repeat the sequence again.

You can also use shoulder-in to develop your horse's medium and extended gaits and make them more expressive. Remember that the degree of extension that a horse can do is directly related to the degree of collection he has prior to the extension. Think of it this way. A spring that is only gently coiled won't have much thrust. But a tightly coiled spring will have more power when it's released.

So ride several steps of shoulder-in to coil the spring of your horse's hind legs. Then straighten him and ask for the extension.

CROOKEDNESS SHOWS UP MORE IN COLLECTED AND EXTENDED GAITS

Remember that it's important all through your training from the very beginning, to always ride your horse **axis-straight** in order to make the hind legs equally strong. If you don't, you'll end up having problems sooner rather than later, and certainly in the collected and extended gaits.

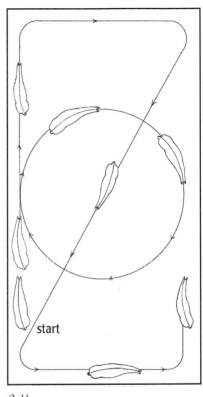

9.11

To strengthen your horse's left hind leg, move his hindquarters slightly to the right no matter where you are in the ring—going right, changing direction across the diagonal, circling, and even going left.

9.13
Lynda continues the circle to the right and brings her right leg back to place Joffrey in haunches-out, so he has to carry weight with his right hind leg. This leg steps directly in the track of his left front leg. This position helps his right hind leg become stronger.

9.12
By standing directly behind Joffrey, it's easy to see that he prefers to carry more of his weight with his left hind leg. While circling to the right, he is carrying his haunches slightly toward the inside of the circle so he can "unload" his right hind leg. You can see this because neither of his hind feet is going to step into the track of the corresponding front foot.

9.12 to 9.14 *Strengthening the Right Hind Leg While on a Circle*

9.14
To strengthen his right hind leg so that he's more willing to carry weight on it, Lynda places Joffrey in haunches-in when she tracks to the left. Once again, this position makes him "weight-lift" with his right hind leg.

Here's an example of the way a rider allows one hind leg to become weaker and the consequences of doing so. She keeps her horse axis-straight when she rides in one direction, but lets his haunches drift to the inside when she goes the other way. As a result, over time the hind leg that deviates toward the inside of the ring, as opposed to stepping directly under the horse's body, gets weaker because it's not carrying an equal amount of weight. This can seem fairly subtle in the beginning. But eventually, when the physical demands on that leg are increased as they are in a collected gait, the weaker hind leg can't cope with the added burden, so the horse becomes even more crooked by carrying his hindquarters off to one side.

Then when he's asked to do something like a trot extension, he shows his weakness. His stronger hind leg is more engaged, comes under his body correctly and has more pushing and carrying power than the weaker leg. As a result, he makes a greater effort with this stronger leg, making him look uneven behind.

You may have wondered all along if your horse has one hind leg weaker than the other. Well, the reality is that most horses do. You can probably assume that one side of your horse is stronger than the other, just as you're stronger on one side of your body than the other. This becomes quite apparent in the collected and extended gaits.

Have someone stand directly in front of, or behind, your horse as you walk, trot, and canter on both a straight line and on a circle. That person can tell you which direction your horse chooses to carry his hindquarters. If they drift to the left, he's unweighting the left hind leg because it's weaker. If he carries his hindquarters to the right, then the right hind leg is the weaker one (figs. 9.12 to 9.14).

If you have a horse that is noticeably stronger with one hind leg than the other, strengthen the muscles by using them. Insist that he carry the weaker hind leg under his body regardless of the direction he's going. If his left hind leg is weaker, ride a shoulder-fore or shoulder-in when you go to the left, and ride haunches-in or shoulder-out when you track to the right (fig. 9.15).

Doing these exercises as I've described places his left hind leg underneath his body all the time so it has to do some "weight lifting." You can do them as a series of exercises every day. Or you can do a very slight version of these exercises during your entire ride. For example, you

9.15

Kelly is working on strengthening Kousteau's left hind leg by placing him in left shoulder-in as he makes a circle to the left. Every step he makes with his left hind leg stepping under his body will help to make that leg stronger.

9.16

Use makes the muscle! Asking a hind leg to "weight lift" will make it stronger.

could always place his weaker left hind leg an inch or so to the inside of the left front leg no matter what line or figure you're on, or which direction you're traveling (fig. 9.16).

But understand that there's a fine line between strengthening muscles and straining them. Sometimes you don't know if you've gone over that line until it's too late. At that point your horse lets you know because he will become markedly resistant, or even sore. To avoid this scenario, work on making his muscles stronger *gradually* and *systematically* rather than suddenly demanding that your horse do the exercises for forty-five minutes.

Do a few the first day and, over the course of several days to a couple of weeks, build up to a series of exercises. Also, within each session, make sure you give your horse lots of breaks to a walk on a loose rein so he can relax his muscles. Plan to intersperse extra "play days" in between days of hard work. Keep in mind that with all "weight-lifting," muscles repair and get stronger when they're given an opportunity to recover—on rest days and play days.

Faulty Transitions to and from the Canter

Before I show you how to use some of the dressage exercises that you know for improving both the upward to, and the downward transition from, the canter, I want to make a point about the canter aid itself. It's important that you get into the habit of using your outside leg—the one that actually signals the depart—in a quick windshield wiper-like motion. If you haven't trained the aid in this way from the beginning, you can run into problems later on in schooling.

For example, let's say you want to start teaching your horse how to do a half-pass in the trot. So, you give the leg aids to initiate the half-pass and instead of going sideways, your horse hops into the canter because he thinks that's what you're asking for. You need to realize that the leg aids for a half-pass and the aids for a canter depart are very similar. There has to be a way for your horse to differentiate between them.

In both cases, your horse is flexed to the inside, your inside leg is on the girth, your weight is on your inside seat bone, and your outside hand is closed in a fist. So what's the difference? In a half-pass your outside leg stays behind the girth to help with the bend and to move him sideways, while in a canter depart, it swings back and forth once to give the signal to canter.

Also, if you get into the habit of holding your leg back and waiting for your horse to react to the canter aid, you're going to have difficulties if you ever decide to go further with his training and do flying changes in a sequence. When you do a series of flying changes, your legs have to move quickly. Your horse must respond immediately so you can do them on the fourth, third, second, or even every stride. You might as well train your horse with the correct canter aid from the beginning rather than have to reschool him later on.

IMPROVING THE UPWARD TRANSITION TO THE CANTER

In Book One, in Chapter Thirteen on problem solving, I gave you some ideas on how to help a horse who was picking up the wrong lead. Now that you have more tools in your arsenal, I can give you some other exercises to help with canter departs.

Sometimes you'll ride a horse who picks up the wrong lead because his outside hind leg isn't sufficiently engaged. So alert his outside hind to be ready to strike off into the canter by directing two or three quick **preparatory half-halts** to it as a call to attention. Your half-halts ask the question, "Are you ready, outside hind leg?"

In this case, rather than maintaining your half-halt for three full seconds, each preparatory half-halt lasts for only a moment. Start in either the walk or the trot. Then half-halt in the rhythm of the gait by pushing with your seat, closing your legs, and closing your outside hand in a fist each time you feel your horse's outside hind leg on the ground. (You'll be able to feel when it's on the ground because your outside seat bone will feel like it's being pushed forward or up.) Then on the next stride, after the three quick half-halts, ask for the canter depart.

To help with the timing of the aids, say out loud in the rhythm of whichever gait you're in prior to the depart, "1, 2, 3, canter" or "Half-halt, half-halt, half-halt, canter."

You can also do an "engagement of the outside hind leg" exercise by doing a few steps of shoulder-out, in the walk or the trot, on a circle or a straight line. Position your horse's hind legs one meter in from the original track of the circle or line, bend him around your outside leg, and lead his forehand toward the outside by bringing both of your hands in that direction. While you're doing this be sure to drive his "old" outside hind leg (this leg has now become the horse's "inside" leg since you've changed the bend) under his center with your active "old" outside leg. Then, straighten him by re-establishing the correct bend and quickly give the aid for the strike-off before you lose the engaging effects of the shoulder-out (see fig. 5.23).

You can even use haunches-in to help with the departs. You might wonder why this is okay to do since I've already said that horses like to be crooked in the canter by swinging their hindquarters to the inside. Well, there are two things to consider here. The first is that when a horse places his hindquarters to the inside to avoid bearing weight, he loses the bend through his body. As a result, he can avoid engagement because he doesn't have to bend the joints of his hind legs. But because he's asked to bend through his body in a haunches-in, he has to bend the joints of his hind legs and engage them.

In addition, I won't be asking you to maintain the haunches-in position during the actual moment of the depart. You just use the haunches-in prior to the depart to put your horse more "through" the inside of his body. Then, straighten him before the transition. For example, start in the walk in haunches-in on a straight line; arc onto a circle and go back to a line—all in haunches-in while walking. When your horse feels very soft, straighten him, and immediately ask for the canter.

IMPROVING THE DOWNWARD TRANSITION FROM THE CANTER

Now let's look at how you can use some dressage exercises to improve the downward transition from the canter to the trot.

One of the most common problems I see with a horse learning to do downward transitions from the canter to the trot is the horse who rushes off rather than ending up in a balanced trot. Your instinct will probably be to pull on the reins to slow him down. As I've discussed before, this may well decrease your horse's speed but, unfortunately, it'll also stop his hind legs from coming forward. As you know, once his hind legs stop coming under his body, his back goes down, and his head and neck come up. So you might manage to keep your horse from running off, but he'll no longer be connected!

There's an exercise to teach your horse to keep his hind legs underneath him during the downward transition from the canter. Go on a circle in the canter. Then, ask for the transition to the trot. During the first stride after the transition, ask for shoulder-in on the circle. By doing a good shoulder-in and engaging his inside hind leg, he won't be able to rush off. As soon as you're at a manageable speed going sideways, you can go straight forward again.

Sometimes you'll find yourself asking for a downward transition from the canter, and you feel like you're being totally ignored. Your horse just won't listen to your **stilled seat**, and he keeps cantering merrily along.

Once again, don't resort to pulling on the reins. Instead, send him steeply sideways in the canter by pushing his hindquarters away from the lead you are on (If you're on the right lead in the canter, push his hindquarters to the left with your right leg.). If he's leg-yielding at a 35 degree angle, your horse will find it impossible to stay in canter and he'll eventually fall into the trot. Then you can praise him, go back to the canter, and ask for the downward transition again. Ride the leg-yield at the same time that you still your seat until you can use your seat alone to get the downward transition.

Combining Two Sets of Aids to Improve Balance

At this point you've learned how to ride many movements. In addition, you know how to give half-halts not only to put your horse on the bit but also to increase his self-carriage. The next step for you is to do both of these things at once. (Don't panic. It is possible!) By combining two sets of aids, you can ride the movements and maintain good balance at the same time.

In the beginning you might feel uncoordinated. You know the feeling—like you're trying to pat your head and rub your stomach at the same time. But eventually you'll rely on this blending together of two sets of aids because you'll discover how much easier it is to *maintain* your horse's balance rather than to have to *correct* him every time you do something different.

The half-halt and the movements themselves should become dependent on each other. The half-halt improves the quality of the movements and the movements themselves make your horse more athletic.

For instance, you normally use a certain amount of seat, leg and hand to ask a horse to come on the bit in the working gaits. If you use a greater degree of those three elements, you ask for more self-carriage. And, if you want an extension, use more driving seat and legs—compared to the amount of restraining outside hand—than you would to do a **connecting half-halt**. When you want to do a downward transition at the end of this extension, apply your legs as usual, but still your seat, and use more outside rein to collect the gait.

As far as all the lateral movements are concerned, you first produce "connection," then "direction." Begin each movement with a half-halt that produces balance and roundness, then emphasize whichever aids within the half-halt you need to send your horse in the direction you want. For instance, more inside leg pressure moves him into shoulder-in, while more outside leg pressure moves him into a half-pass.

You want to become adept at doing this because it's reasonable to expect your horse to lose his balance every time you do any kind of a transition. Simply put, anytime there's any sort of a change, there's a potential loss of balance. When you change from one pace to another, lengthen and shorten, go from a single track to a two-track exercise and back to a single track, or change from one bend to the other, you can assume your horse might lose his balance. This loss of balance can express itself in a variety of ways. Your horse can drop his back and become hollow. Or, he might fall on the forehand, rush off, or lean on one or both reins. Any loss of balance should trigger you to give a half-halt.

9.17

Woody and I are in trot here and I'm about to ask him to do a transition to the right lead canter. Because he's not properly connected in the trot, it will be impossible for him to do a canter depart on the bit. Note the inactive hind legs, the concave-looking back, the high neck, and the stiff poll and jaw.

9.18

Woody's balance, frame, and connection during the first stride of canter can be no better than they are in the steps just before the transition. Because I failed to connect him with a half-halt while we were still in the trot, he's hollow and disconnected in the canter.

9.17 to 9.20 Trot to Canter Transition

Think of every situation where there's a potential loss of balance, and **blend** or "superimpose" a half-halt on top of those critical moments. Rather than waiting to correct your horse after the fact, prepare him for what's coming up by riding a half-halt a little bit before, during, and for a step or two after you begin each new movement. Obviously, to do this, your half-halt will last longer than the standard three seconds I described in Chapter One. In fact, it's not unreasonable for this half-halt to last five or six seconds.

Here are some examples of how to blend two sets of aids at once.

TRANSITIONS FROM ONE PACE TO ANOTHER

Let's first have a look at transitions from one pace to another. To maximize the physical benefits of a transition and to make your horse more comfortable for you to ride, the transition should be done on the bit.

9.19

Compare Woody's shape and balance in these next two photos with the two previous ones. We're in the trot preparing to step into the right lead canter. Woody is nicely on the bit and I want to keep him there during the transition to the canter. To do that I have to blend a connecting half-halt into the aids for the canter. So I start the half-halt by closing my legs, pushing with my seat, closing my left hand in a fist, and using my right hand to keep him softly flexed to the right.

9.20

I maintain the connecting half-halt and ask for the canter depart by bringing my left leg behind the girth at the same time. By giving both sets of aids at once, I'm telling Woody to stay on the bit as he does the transition to the canter.

Think about what your signals say to the horse. Your transition aids just tell your horse to change from walk to trot, or canter to walk, for example. They don't tell him to stay connected or in good balance. It's not the transition aid's responsibility.

Staying connected is the half-halt's job. So, if you're having difficulty keeping your horse on the bit during a transition, you need to do two things at once: a half-halt and the transition aid. The half-halt says "stay on the bit" and the transition aid tells your horse to change from trot to canter, for instance. When both sets of aids are applied at the same time, you're telling your horse to "do a transition on the bit." Start the half-halt first, and somewhere during those three seconds increase your legs for an upward transition or tighten your stomach muscles and still your seat for a downward transition (figs. 9.17 to 9.20).

Remember that your horse's balance and connection during a transition can be no better than it was during the steps just before the transition. So if he's hollow, on the forehand, stiff, or leaning, first use a preliminary, three-second half-halt to rebalance him. Then give another longer half-halt, which you'll blend into the aid for the transition to keep him balanced throughout.

Make sure your horse doesn't anticipate the transition and do it when you start the half-halt. He has to wait for the actual aid. For instance, let's say your goal is to go from canter to trot with your horse on the bit. You start the half-halt and before you get a chance to blend it into the aid for the downward transition, your horse breaks to the trot on his own. If this happens, you need to tell him he's wrong. Otherwise, he'll start to make his own decisions. For example, you might be in the canter, and you give a normal three-second half-halt for the purpose of making him rounder. Before you know it, your horse slips into the trot on his own!

This miscommunication can be particularly inconvenient in competition. Maybe you know the feeling. Even though you'd like to make an adjustment to improve your horse's balance in the canter, you don't dare disturb the status quo because you're afraid he'll anticipate, or misinterpret, your signal and make a costly mistake by falling into the trot.

To correct this in training, give some three-second half-halts while cantering and touch him with the whip to remind him to keep coming from behind in the canter rather than trotting. Do a few half-halts without a transition. Then when you know he's listening and waiting, give a half-halt and blend it into the aid for the downward transition. Then go back to the canter and do a few half-halts without a transition. Keep alternating until you trust that he's really paying attention to you.

What if your problem with downward transitions is even more basic than the maintenance of connection and balance? Maybe the bottom line is that your horse is not paying attention to you. If that's the case, you need to give short preparatory half-halts rather than blending a long, connecting half-halt into the aid for the transition. In the section on faulty canter departs, (page 191) I explained how to engage the outside hind leg—the strike-off leg—for the canter depart by giving three quick preparatory half-halts when that leg is on the ground. You can also use quick preparatory half-halts to set your horse up for downward transitions.

For all downward transitions, you need to direct your quick half-halts to the *inside* hind leg because that is the leg that has to work harder, and engage more, on circles and corners. Close your eyes and feel when the inside hind leg is on the ground, by noticing when your inside seat bone is being pushed forward. (It might feel to you as if it's being pushed up, rather than forward).

This is the moment when you give your preparatory half-halts by pushing with your seat, pressing with your legs, and closing the fingers of both hands. Each time you apply this quick half-halt, say out loud "now, now, now," or "one, two, three." Then on the fourth step, close your legs and hands again but still your seat to ask for the downward transition.

If you want to go from canter to trot, direct your half-halts to the inside hind leg. When that leg is on the ground, half-halt three times in the rhythm of the canter, and say "now, now, now, trot." Do the same for other downward transitions. For example, when you want to go from trot to walk, direct your half-halts to the inside hind leg, and in the rhythm of the trot say, "now, now, now, walk." When you want to go from the walk to halt, direct your half-halts to the inside hind leg, and in the rhythm of the walk, say "now, now, now, halt."

TRANSITIONS FROM A SINGLE TRACK TO TWO TRACKS

Now, let's have a look at how you can combine two sets of aids to keep your horse on the bit as you start a lateral movement. Let's say you're riding to the right and you want to do a leg-yield to the left with your horse on the bit. First, insure the connection over your horse's back by giving a half-halt while you're still on a single track. Close your legs, close your left hand in a fist and, if necessary, vibrate the right rein. Then continue to give the half-halt as you add in the aids for leg-yielding to the left. Keep your weight centered and your left leg on the girth, but slide your right leg slightly behind the girth. Your left hand is supporting and remains closed in a fist while your right hand continues to vibrate to ask for a little flexion.

CHANGES OF BEND

Suppose you want to do a figure-eight. Each time you go from one circle of the figure-eight to the other, you have to change your horse's bend. Because of this change, there's a risk of upsetting his balance.

To avoid any stiffening, losing the connection over his back, or falling on the forehand, superimpose your half-halt over the change of bend in the following way. Two or three strides before you change direction, close your legs (your inside leg is on the girth and your outside leg is behind the girth), close your "old" outside hand in a fist and ask for flexion by vibrating with the "old" inside hand. At the point where the two circles are tangent, keep your legs on but switch their positions so that your "new" inside leg is on the girth and your "new" outside leg is behind the girth. You'll also need to change the action of your hands. As your old inside hand becomes your new outside hand, close it in a fist.

As your old outside hand becomes your new inside hand, ask for flexion by vibrating this rein. Once the change of bend is completed, relax the aids.

You can use this same technique for changes of bend between each loop of a serpentine. Start your half-halt a little before you ask for the change of bend and continue to apply it until a stride or so after the change of bend is completed.

KEY POINTS

You now have more tools in your "bag of tricks" that you can use to help solve some common training problems. For example, you can:

🐎 Help your horse relax by working him in a deep frame.

🐎 Make your horse take an even contact with both reins by reversing the half-halt and asking him to step into the light rein.

🐎 Straighten your horse and strengthen his weaker hind leg by using shoulder-in and haunches-in.

🐎 Improve canter departs with engagement exercises such as preparatory half-halts, shoulder-out, and haunches-in.

🐎 Improve the downward transitions from canter to trot with shoulder-in and leg yielding.

🐎 Maintain good balance by blending half-halts into the aids for different movements.

CHAPTER TEN

Putting It All Together:
How to Organize a Logical,
Systematic, Daily Work Session

In Book One, I gave you a sample schooling session that you could do with your horse once he is well-grounded in the Basics (Book One, Chapter Twelve). If you have been working along with me for part, or all, of Book Two, it's time for me to give you some examples of how to incorporate what you've learned in your work in a logical, organized way that is conducive to the development of your horse's physical well-being and his ability to carry out what's asked of him.

It's not, for instance, very sensible to start working your horse in shoulder-in and half-pass and then finish up with leg-yielding! Leg-yielding helps to loosen, stretch and relax your horse's muscles, so it belongs in the warm-up to prepare him for the more advanced work. Shoulder-in, haunches-in, and half-pass are exercises that collect the gaits and should only be done *after* your horse is thoroughly warmed up.

Think of each of your daily schooling sessions, as a story unfolding. Like any good story, there should be a beginning, a middle, and an end.

The way you warm up your horse at the beginning of your ride is important because it sets the tone for everything that follows. You really can't continue productively with your work if your horse's body is tight or he's tense and inattentive.

The middle of the session starts with a review and refinement of established work as well as occasionally introducing new ideas. You should always have a plan before you start, but be flexible enough to modify your program depending on what surprises come at you on any given

10.1

Think of each of your daily schooling sessions, as a story unfolding. Like any good story, there should be a beginning, a middle, and an end.

day. You know the kind of day I'm talking about: rollerbladers in fluorescent tights are zipping down the road by the ring, and all the horses are bouncing around like bumper cars. This is probably not a great day to start flying changes!

And, of course, you should carefully cool your horse's muscles down at the end of your ride. A good finish insures that you won't have to deal with a stiff or sore body the next day. Plus, psychologically, ending up on a good note leaves everyone satisfied and with a positive "to be continued" feeling.

The Beginning: Warm-Up

Students often ask me how long a warm-up should last and what work is appropriate during this period. The answer to the first question is "as long as it takes." The main goal of the warm-up is to loosen and supple your horse's body and make him calm and attentive. If your horse starts out stiff, tight, or tense, you'll have to do a lengthy warm-up. If he's relaxed, supple, and agreeable, the warm-up can be as brief as five or ten minutes.

THE WARM-UP FRAME

Spend the first five to ten minutes of your ride walking energetically around on a loose rein. At this point your horse can carry himself in any frame he chooses. This is simply the time for him to begin to adjust to your weight. Since he may have been standing around in the stable for hours, these few minutes give him the opportunity to move freely forward.

Once you pick up contact, however, you should **connect** him. I'm not saying **collect** him, mind you—merely put him on the bit, with his hind legs stepping well under his body, his back raised, and his head and neck stretching toward your hand. Your horse's center of gravity will be toward the forehand, and you should ride him in the deep frame that I described in detail in Chapter Two. (See photo 2.21. on page 47). This frame accomplishes two things at once. You'll warm up his cardiovascular system as well as stretch the muscles over his back and top of his neck to the maximum, so it'll be easier to school him in a round frame.

I recommend this deep frame during the warm-up because generally I think it's a mistake to do your first trot and canter on a loose rein. Riders who do this believe they're giving their horses a chance to limber up before serious work. I agree that you'll be warming up your horse's cardiovascular system, but you won't be loosening up his muscles correctly for the frame he'll eventually be working in.

Warming up on a loose rein is akin to you preparing yourself to touch your toes by walking around for ten minutes with your back arched. All your back muscles become shortened and contracted, and you'll find it difficult to stretch them enough to comfortably reach your toes on the first effort.

WARM-UP EXERCISES

So now you know what frame to put your horse in during the warm-up, but you also need to know what you should do for work. At the beginning of the warm-up, check that your horse is forward, straight, and moving in a regular rhythm in all three paces. After these prerequisites are established, make sure that your horse is listening and responding to your half-halts since that's the key to dealing with all his balance issues—both mental and physical. Be sure to do this check not just once but throughout the entire warm-up.

In the sample training session that I gave you in Book One, school figures, leg-yields, and lengthenings made up the "heart" of your story or the middle of your session. But now that your horse is more educated, these movements are incorporated into the warm-up.

Mix and match these movements so your warm-up doesn't take any longer than necessary. For example, you can ride a serpentine of three loops in the trot and lengthen the strides around the middle loop. Or you might start on a very large circle, decrease the size of the circle by spiraling in on a gradually decreasing arc, and go sideways in a leg-yield back out to the original circle. Then when you're back on the larger circle, lengthen and shorten for a few strides.

School Figures

Let's talk first about school figures in the warm-up. They help your horse to become more flexible by bending him laterally. (He's already bent longitudinally because you've warmed him up in a deep frame.) So practice circles, serpentines, shallow loops, and figure eights. All these figures should be large enough for your horse to do them comfortably, because it's too early in your ride to ask him to cope with doing small circles.

Make sure your horse is bending equally in both directions. Compensate for any one-sidedness by bending him on his stiff side and not letting him bend too much on his soft side.

The other important thing to remember when riding school figures is to be sure you're absolutely accurate. You may ask why you need to be so precise if you're not going into a dressage arena to be judged. Well, there are actually several reasons.

First, you want to develop your horse's ability to stretch or shorten the muscles on both sides of his body equally well. Horses tend to make circles and loops larger when they are circling with their stiff sides on the inside. They do this because it's difficult to elongate the shortened muscles on the outside of their bodies.

Second, you also want to encourage your horse to use his hind leg on his soft side better so that it becomes as strong as his other hind leg. When horses circle with their soft sides on the inside, they "cut in" on the circle to avoid carrying weight on their weaker inside hind leg.

Third, any strides the horse takes that bulge out from the line of the circle, or follow a straight line for more than one step, allow him to lose the bend and the engagement of the inside hind leg.

Last, when your horse cheats on circles in any of the ways just described, he's being mildly disobedient. By allowing him to do so, you're setting a precedent for him to make other decisions on how to evade the difficulty of work.

So, use reference points to make sure that you're riding accurate school figures. At the end of this chapter, I'll give detailed instructions on how to ride school figures with precision.

Tuesdayish

Leg-Yielding

Although I don't recommend doing advanced lateral exercises in the warm-up, it can be very useful to do some leg-yielding for a few minutes. Remember, leg-yields differ from the rest of the lateral work like shoulder-in, haunches-in, and half-pass in that there isn't any bend through the horse's body—just flexion at the poll away from the direction of movement.

Leg-yielding allows your horse to stretch and loosen muscles physically, as well as mentally answer some obedience questions. As you alternate between having your leg on the girth to placing it slightly behind the girth, you're asking some important questions. "Are you paying attention?" "Will you go forward when my leg is placed on the girth and immediately sideways when my leg is moved behind the girth?"

I find leg-yielding particularly useful for my older horses after they've had a day off. I know from experience that "rigor-mortis" has probably set in after their rest day! (Since most of our horses have Monday off, when they're stiff we say that our horses are feeling "Tuesdayish" even if it happens to fall on a Friday.) So, I'll almost always do some leg-yielding in the walk to get rid of the "Tuesdayish" feeling before I even do my first posting trot. As I ask my horse to go sideways, I visualize his muscles stretching, loosening, and elongating so that by the time I trot, he feels buoyant and supple (fig. 10.2).

Lengthening and Shortening

Lengthening and shortening the stride in working trot and canter also supple the horse physically and mentally. Physically, these exercises develop the "rubber band effect." Can your horse stretch and compress his body smoothly and easily? Mentally, they ask vital questions like "Are you hot off my leg and willing to go forward?" and "Are you attentive to my rein and back and willing to slow down?"

As I explained in Book One (Chapter Twelve), if you're riding a young horse (five years old or less), the warm-up is pretty much all you'll do in an entire session. The session itself can be as brief as twenty or thirty minutes. Young horses need to develop their ability to concentrate as

10.2

When my horse feels "Tuesdayish" after a day off, I leg-yield and visualize his muscles stretching, loosening, and elongating in the walk, so by the time I trot, he feels buoyant and supple.

much as anything else. So it's desirable to do short periods of work with frequent breaks. You want to bring your horse back to the barn as fresh and eager as he was when he came out.

Also, if your goal for the day is simply to exercise your horse, just do the warm-up and then go for a hack. Remember how important those "play-days" are to your horse's emotional and physical well-being.

But if this is a normal work day, warm up your horse until his body is loose and supple and he is concentrating on you. Then, you'll be ready to review and confirm established work as well as perhaps introduce something new.

Organizing the Middle of Your Session

REFINING OLD WORK
AND INTRODUCING NEW EXERCISES

Most of your schooling session will be about confirming, refining, and improving balance in established work. I probably spend ten minutes or so reviewing work from the day before, and then I strive over the next fifteen to twenty minutes to get "a little bit more" **self-carriage** in all my established work through half-halts. If all is going well, I'll spend the last few minutes before my cool-down introducing something new.

I don't try to teach my horse anything new when the work isn't going well. When I do start something new, I don't expect him to do it perfectly. As long as he makes an effort, that's good enough. I reward him and finish the session. I always want to end on a good note, even if it means I have to go back to doing something very simple like leg-yielding or a lengthening. That way we go back to the barn feeling satisfied and start the next day with a positive outlook.

On the one hand, you should always have a plan when you work your horse so you can go a little further with your training every session. But you should also be willing to abandon your program in favor of a simpler agenda if your horse is distracted, bewildered, or tense.

THE MAIN GOAL—
HOW TO IMPROVE SELF-CARRIAGE

If you've read this book from the beginning, you'll know by now that when I talk about self-carriage I'm referring to the loading of the hind legs—the change in balance caused by the lowering of the hindquarters and the resulting raising, lightening, and freeing of the forehand.

So, what can you do to improve self-carriage? Riding smaller school figures than you did in the warm-up, doing lots of transitions, and practicing lateral movements with bend are all exercises that will help you to improve your horse's balance. Remember that these self-carriage exercises belong in the "middle of your story" rather than at the beginning in the warm-up where you must be careful not too ask your horse for too much before he's ready.

Ride smaller circles and serpentines with several loops making sure your horse doesn't evade the bend by swinging his hindquarters in or out, or by leaning in on your inside leg. The tighter arcs will change your horse's balance and promote self-carriage because they demand an increase in the bending of the joints of his inside hind leg.

If you're riding a horse that's just beginning to develop collected gaits, reduce your large 20-meter circles to 15-meter circles. Once your horse can cope with the demands of 15-meter circles, gradually (over the course of several months), decrease your circles to 12 meters and then 10 meters. If you ask your horse to do smaller circles than he's ready for, he'll find some sort of escape route. You're better off doing larger figures correctly than smaller ones incorrectly. If your horse has to cheat on small circles because he hasn't been systematically developed to the point that he can deal with the greater demands of bend through his body and engagement of his hind legs, doing smaller circles is counterproductive.

Frequent transitions from pace to pace as well as within the pace also contribute to self-carriage. The key word here is frequent. By riding many transitions, particularly those where you skip a pace, such as walk to canter and canter to walk or trot to halt and back to trot, you'll shift your horse's center of gravity more toward the hindquarters.

With the exception of leg-yielding, which has no bend, all lateral work with a bend will help you work toward self-carriage, as these lateral movements demand an increased bending of the joints of the hind legs. Be sure to pick exercises that are appropriate for your horse's level of training, or you'll run into the same difficulties that you'd encounter by prematurely asking for very small circles.

Remember to give frequent half-halts to maintain or restore balance— either before, during, or after any of these exercises that you're doing to promote self-carriage. With every half-halt, you'll *add* hind legs up to a restraining outside hand. Your driving aids send the hind legs further under the body while your closed outside hand captures that energy. Because the "door is closed" in front, there's an increased bending of the joints of the hind legs. As a result, the horse changes his shape and balance as his hindquarters lower and his center of gravity shifts more toward his hind legs.

PROGRESSIVE LEVELS OF TRAINING

If you're still confused as to what kind of work to do in the middle of your session, take a look at the dressage tests. They offer a guideline for training that is systematic and progressive.

10.3

Dressage tests are designed with the systematic development of the horse in mind, and can, therefore, be used as guidelines to training.

FOURTH LEVEL

Canter serpentine with flying changes when crossing center line

8m circles in canter

Changes of lead every fourth and third stride

Counter-change of hand in trot

Half-pirouettes in canter

Walk pirouettes

THIRD LEVEL

Collected and extended walk

Collected, medium, extended trot and canter

Half-pass in trot and canter

Half-turn on the haunches

Single flying changes

8m circles in trot

Überstreichen (2 hands) in medium canter

SECOND LEVEL

Collected and medium trot and canter

Medium walk

Shoulder-in

Travers

Counter-canter

Three loop serpentine in canter–width of arena–no lead change

Half-turn on the haunches

Walk to canter transitions

Simple change of lead (through the walk)

10m circles in trot

Rein back

Überstreichen (1 hand) in the canter

FIRST LEVEL

Lengthenings in trot and canter

15m and 10m circles in trot

15m circles in canter

Shallow serpentine in canter (no lead change)

Leg-yields

Change of lead through the trot

Let horse take reins out of hands in trot

TRAINING LEVEL

Medium Walk

Working trot and canter

20m circles in trot and canter

Transitions from pace to pace

Let horse take reins out of hands in trot

BASED ON 1995 AHSA DRESSAGE TESTS

In dressage in the United States, all the levels starting at Training level and progressing through First, Second, Third, Fourth, and Fifth Level as well as the International Levels of Prix St. Georges, Intermediare I, Intermediare II and Grand Prix are designed to show a progressive development of strength and self-carriage. Although this book focuses on the work required through Third Level, I think it's interesting to take a moment to look at all the levels in order to get a feeling for the big picture (fig. 10.3).

In the United Kingdom the levels have different names: they start at preliminary, go through novice, elementary, medium, advanced medium, advanced, and then on to the International Levels described above. This book covers the movements required through advanced medium level.

Depending on your horse's talent, physique, gymnastic ability, and attitude, you can reasonably expect to advance from one level to the next

10.4

The Training Level horse's muscles are supple and loose, and he accepts a contact with his rider's hand. He carries about 60% of his weight on his forehand. This horizontal balance is apparent because his withers and croup are basically level.

10.4 to 10.9

In this series of photos, Woody shows the progressive change of a horse's balance as he goes up through the levels.

in approximately six months to a year. You might get "stuck" at one level longer than another; just watch your horse's progress. You'll be able to tell when he's ready to go on by the ease with which he performs the requirements at each level. In the long run, training progresses more quickly and smoothly if you don't force your horse to conform to some preconceived timetable. One of my students bought a six-year-old who had not been started correctly, so she had to spend over a year and a half working at First Level to establish and confirm his basics. But then once her horse had a solid foundation, he easily learned everything in Second through Fourth Levels over the next year!

So let's have a look at how each successive level builds upon the work from the previous level (figs. 10.4 to 10.9). The purpose of the tests at

10.4 to 10.9 con't.

10.5

At Training Level, the horse should "take the reins out of your hands" in the trot as he seeks the contact forward and down to the ground. The rider determines just how much her horse can stretch by the amount of rein she feeds out to him. Be sure not to offer him more than he will take, because you always want to maintain a contact with his mouth rather than letting the reins get slack.

the lowest level, Training Level, is to establish that the horse's muscles are supple and loose, and that he moves freely forward in a distinct and steady rhythm, accepting contact with his rider's hand. At Training Level you are only required to show that your horse accepts a contact with your hand—he doesn't necessarily have to be on the bit; you're asked to show medium walk, working trot, and working canter as well as the transitions in between each pace. You'll ride some large curved lines like 20 meter circles and shallow loops.

You are also asked to show that your horse will "take the reins out of your hands" in the trot as he seeks the contact forward and down to the

10.6

At First Level, the horse shows greater thrust from behind than he does at Training Level. His frame is shorter, he is connected over his back, his balance is more toward his hindquarters, and his neck is slightly raised and arched.

ground while maintaining balance and regular rhythm. This movement proves that the horse is relaxed and is moving forward into the rider's hand rather than being forced into a frame by being pulled in from front to back.

At First Level, the tests are designed to show that in addition to the requirements of Training Level, the horse has developed **thrust** from behind (pushing power) and is connected over his back (**throughness**), as well as showing the beginnings of a shift in his center of gravity toward his hindquarters (self-carriage).

These changes are achieved by connection, or expressed another way,

10.4 to 10.9 con't.

10.7

At Second Level, a horse clearly accepts more weight on his hindquarters and accordingly his neck is raised and arched to a greater degree than a First Level horse.

putting your horse on the bit. Your trot circles progressively become as small as 10 meters and you're asked to do 15 meter circles in the canter. You are also required to show lengthenings in the trot and canter, leg-yielding in the trot, and a gentle loop in counter-canter.

The purpose of the Second Level tests is to confirm that the horse, having demonstrated that he has achieved the thrust required in First Level, now shows that through additional training he accepts more of his weight on his hindquarters and shows the power required at the medium gaits. At this level he should be reliably on the bit. A greater degree of straightness, bending, suppleness, throughness and self-carriage is required than at First Level.

10.8

*Relaxing the inside rein on a circle at the canter (doing a one-handed überstreichen), demon-
strates the balance of the Second Level horse. Woody has obviously maintained his self-carriage
and the quality of the canter.*

This is the first time you'll be asked to show real self-carriage by being
required to do a collected as well as a medium trot and canter. Your
canter circles are reduced to 10 meters and counter-canter loops are
tighter, demanding greater engagement. New movements include
shoulder-in and haunches-in at the trot and a turn on the haunches at
the walk. Up until this point, changes of canter leads have been done
through the trot. But now you'll be asked to show simple changes of lead
going from one canter lead directly to the walk and then after three steps
immediately to the other lead.

You are also asked to do a one-handed **überstreichen** on a canter
circle to demonstrate your horse's self-carriage. Let me explain this

10.4 to 10.9 con't.

10.9

The horse in Third Level balance is accepting even more weight on his hindquarters and as a result his forehand is raised. You can also see that he is a more compact "package" from poll to tail.

German expression: you'll extend your inside hand forward up the horse's neck for three to four strides while maintaining contact on the outside rein. During this exercise, your horse should maintain his self-carriage, rhythm, bend, and quality of his canter. Done correctly, this movement demonstrates that your horse is truly connected with a half-halt and, therefore, steps from behind through your outside hand.

Both "überstreichen" and "taking the reins out of your hands" are part of the tests that I told you to use to check the honesty of the half-halt (see page 40). Since the half-halt is so much a part of my students' training programs, they always get the highest points possible on those movements!

At Third Level, the horse must show rhythm, suppleness, acceptance of the bit, throughness, impulsion, straightness, and self-carriage in each movement. This is particularly important during the transitions to and from the movements as well as in the medium and extended gaits themselves. There must be a clear distinction between these gaits. This is the first time you'll be asked to show three clear "gears" in the trot and the canter—collected, medium, and extended. Although it's interesting to note that even at this level only medium and extended walk is shown. The committee that created these tests is only too aware of how easily the walk can be ruined, so they take great care not to introduce the collected walk too early.

New movements include half-passes at the trot and the canter and a flying change in each direction. The rider is also asked to show that her horse is in self-carriage in medium canter by doing a two-handed "überstreichen." The rider extends both her hands up the crest of the neck toward her horse's ears. If the horse is carrying himself and not relying on the rider's hand, his frame and balance stay the same as she does this.

Although Fourth Level is beyond the scope of these two books, you will probably be interested to know that the tests are designed to confirm that the horse has acquired a high degree of suppleness, impulsion, throughness, balance and self-carriage while always remaining reliably on the bit. His movements are straight, lively, and cadenced (a steady tempo with marked accentuation of the rhythm and emphasized springiness), and the transitions precise and fluid.

At this level the horse is also asked to show all three gears—collected, medium, and extended—in trot and canter. Circles are reduced to 8 meters. New movements include walk pirouettes, half-pirouettes in the canter, and flying changes of lead every fourth stride and every third stride.

If you compare horses at the successive levels in terms of their progressively changing balance, you'll see that even though the First Level tests do not specifically ask for collected gaits, the horse at this level is carrying himself somewhat more than the Training Level horse. And the Second Level horse is more in self-carriage than the First Level horse.

Not only is self-carriage a goal for dressage horses, but it also helps horses in other fields do their jobs successfully. For example, to avoid fatigue and wear and tear on their limbs over long distances, endurance champion Becky Hart asks her horses to work in a Second or Third Level balance. Before Dennis Reis even starts to ask his horses to perform roll backs, he insures success by asking for the balance required at Third Level. And, I can guarantee you that Anne Kursinski's jumpers are rocked well back onto their hindquarters at a Fourth Level balance to have the power and thrust necessary to propel themselves over the obstacles on a Grand Prix jumper course.

10.10

*Before you let your horse "relax,"
allow him to stretch and loosen
his body in a deep frame. Then,
walk him on a loose rein before
you take him home.*

The Conclusion: the Cool-Down

You'll finish your ride with a cooling-down period. This is as important as your warm-up. You certainly wouldn't jog five miles and then immediately sit in an easy chair even though you'd probably love to do just that! If you did, your muscles would contract, and you'd probably feel pretty stiff and sore the next day. The same common sense applies to schooling your horse. Allow him to stretch and loosen his body in the same deep frame you used for the warm-up. He should trot or canter around with a feeling of harmony for awhile and then walk on a loose rein before he returns to the stable feeling relaxed and satisfied with himself (fig. 10.10).

I say he should stretch "for awhile" because the length of time is going to vary, depending on what's happened during your session. On a normal day, a couple of minutes of working him deep is going to be plenty. Not only is this good for your horse's muscles but once he learns that this final stretch means he's finished for the day, you can use this routine to dissipate any tension that might have crept in while you were teaching him something new.

For example, when I start anything new with Woody, it's a given that he'll get worried and I'll have to ride him deep for longer than normal. I know that this is just his personality and that once he understands and becomes adept at the new exercise, he becomes calm and even proud of his new accomplishment. So I always wait until the very end of my session before I start new work. Then, after practicing the new movement briefly, I go right into the deep frame in the posting trot. This way Woody knows we're done and his tension doesn't escalate.

Another example of when "awhile" may have to last more than a couple of minutes happened when one of my students, Nikki, started flying changes with her very sensitive Thoroughbred, Rupert. When Nikki gave her horse the aid to change, she applied it a little too strongly. Rupert did, in fact, do the flying change, but he thought it was so exciting that he took off afterwards, bucking exuberantly. Needless to say, Nikki "bought some real estate" (although she was quick to reassure me that it was the softest landing she ever had!), and that startled her horse even more. So, after she remounted, she cantered him in a deep frame until he was thoroughly relaxed. We wanted to be sure there wouldn't be any skeletons in his closet the next time we worked on the flying changes. (By the way, he does lovely, relaxed flying changes now.)

Two Sample Schooling Sessions

I'll give you a couple of sample schooling sessions—one for the horse working at First Level (Novice in the UK) and one for the horse at Third Level (Medium in the UK). In between each new exercise, always give your horse a short break by walking on a loose rein. Remember, these are merely examples of how to put things together in a logical sequence. They are not "the Gospel"! Some horses get bored if you don't challenge them with new work, while others take comfort in the familiarity of a routine.

For the First Level horse:

5-10 minutes: free walk on a loose rein.

5-10 minutes: medium walk, working trot posting, and working canter in both directions in a deep frame on straight lines and 20-meter circles.

15-25 minutes: trot work including 15- and 10-meter circles, serpentines, lengthenings, and leg-yields. Canter work including 15-meter circles, changes of lead through the trot, lengthenings, and shallow loops that require a little counter-canter.

5 minutes: introduction of shoulder-in.

2 minutes: working trot in a deep frame to stretch and relax.

5-10 minutes: free walk on a loose rein.

Third Level Horse:

5-10 minutes: free walk on a loose rein.

5-10 minutes: medium walk, working trot posting, and working canter in both directions in a deep frame on straight lines and 20-meter circles. Then shorten the reins a bit and add in leg-yields in the trot and lengthenings in the trot and the canter.

15-25 minutes: use half-halts, 10-meter circles, lateral work in the trot (shoulder-in, haunches-in, and half-pass) in both directions, and transitions within the trot (collected, medium, extended) to increase self-carriage and collect the trot. Use half-halts, half-passes, counter-canter, and transitions within the canter to increase self-carriage and collect the canter.

5 minutes: introduction of flying changes.

2 minutes: working trot or canter in a deep frame to stretch and relax.

5-10 minutes: free walk on a loose rein.

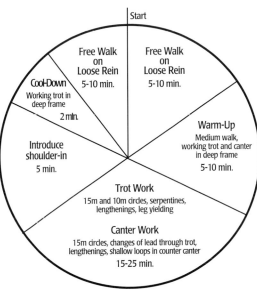

Sample Schooling Session - First Level

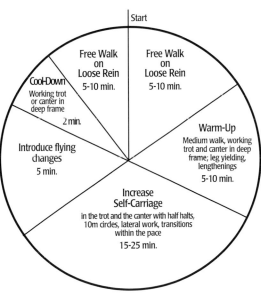

Sample Schooling Session - Third Level

10.11
Arenas for dressage:
Standard and Small

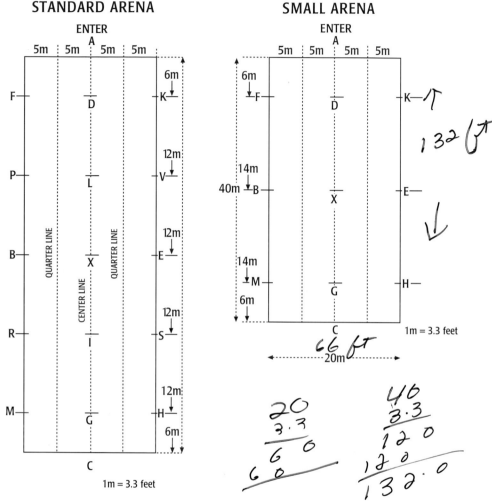

STANDARD ARENA

SMALL ARENA

1m = 3.3 feet

Riding Accurate School Figures

I stressed earlier how important it is to ride precise school figures. To get a feeling for the correct size and shape of these figures, we'll go into both a small and a large dressage arena where we have specific dimensions and designated placement of letters. Once you have a feeling for the dimensions and flow of a truly round circle by riding it in a prescribed area, it's a lot easier to recreate this feeling in an open space.

If you don't have access to a regulation dressage arena, measure the distances out in a field and put some markers where the letters should be. Mark off the perimeter with fence poles or simply mow the grass shorter to form a rectangle. You don't need expensively made letters, either. Buy some traffic cones at a sporting goods store or fill some plastic gallon containers with sand so they don't blow away, then mark them.

The key to riding school figures accurately is to have very specific reference points and to always look two points ahead. As you approach one reference point, look over to the next one, and as you approach that point, look toward the next one. Pretend you're playing the child's game of "connect-the-dots." See all the reference points in your mind and then connect them while maintaining correct bend.

If you have trouble seeing distances, get out on the arena on foot and pace them off until you develop an eye for them.

THE SMALL ARENA

A small arena is 20-meters wide and 40-meters long—twice as long as it is wide. The arena is divided in half lengthwise by the centerline. Each of these halves is again divided lengthwise by the quarterlines. Since the arena is 20-meters wide, each of these sections is 5-meters wide. The two quarterlines are 10 meters apart. The centerline is 10 meters from either long side. Each quarterline is 5 meters from one long side and 15 meters from the other long side.

The middles of the long sides are marked by the letters B and E. The middles of the short sides are marked by A and C. The corner letters are all 6 meters from the corner. (That's right! I said 6 meters—not 10. No wonder your 20-meter circles always look like eggs. You've been aiming for the corner letter all this time!). See fig. 10.11

The four reference points for a 20-meter circle at the end of the small arena are: 1) A or C; 2 & 3) 4 meters past the corner letters (so that you are 10 meters from the corner when you touch the long side); and 4) X (which is located on the centerline between B and E). See fig. 10.12.

The four reference points for a 20-meter circle at B or E (in the middle of the small arena) are: 1) B or E; 2) the centerline 4 meters above D (10 meters from A); 3) B or E; 4) the centerline 4 meters above G (10 meters from C). See fig. 10.13.

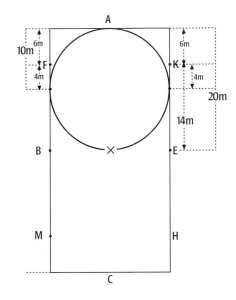

SMALL ARENA

10.12

Small arena: correct 20-meter circle at A.

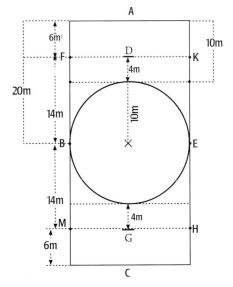

10.13

Small arena: correct 20-meter circle between B and E.

SMALL ARENA

10.14

Small arena: correct 15-meter circle at A.

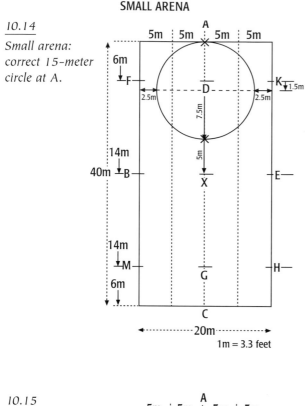

1m = 3.3 feet

10.15

Small arena: correct 15-meter circle at B.

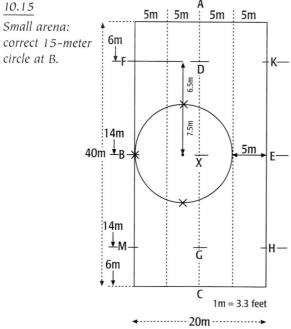

1m = 3.3 feet

The four reference points for a 15-meter circle starting at A or C are: 1) A or C; 2) 2.5 meters in from the rail and 1.5 meters above the corner letter (so you are 7.5 meters from the corner); 3) 5 meters from X; 4) 2.5 meters in from the rail and 1.5 meters above the corner letter (so you are 7.5 meters from the corner). See fig. 10.14.

The four reference points for a 15-meter circle starting at B or E are: 1) B or E; 2) 7.5 meters above an imaginary line connecting B and E (hit this point when you are 2.5 meters past the first quarterline); 3) the far quarterline across from B or E; 4) 7.5 meters below an imaginary line connecting B and E (hit this point when you are 2.5 meters before the first quarterline also). See fig. 10.15.

THE STANDARD ARENA

A large or standard arena is 20-meters wide and 60-meters long (see fig. 10.11). Since the width of the small and large arena is the same, the same distances for the centerline and the two quarterlines apply. In addition, the corner letters are still 6 meters from the corners, the middles of the long sides are marked by B and E, and the middles of the short sides are marked by A and C. The main difference is that all the other letters are twice that distance, or 12 meters, apart. Therefore, an imaginary line drawn from M to H is 6 meters from the short side and an imaginary line from R to S is 18 meters from the short side.

Because the large arena is three times as long as it is wide, you can fit three 20-meter circles end to end in it.

The four reference points for a 20-meter circle that begins at C are: 1) C; 2) 4 meters past M (so that you're 10 meters from the corner); 3) 2 meters past the R to S line; and 4) 4 meters above H (so that you're 10 meters from the corner). Remember, always look two points ahead and then "connect the dots." See fig. 10.16.

STANDARD ARENA

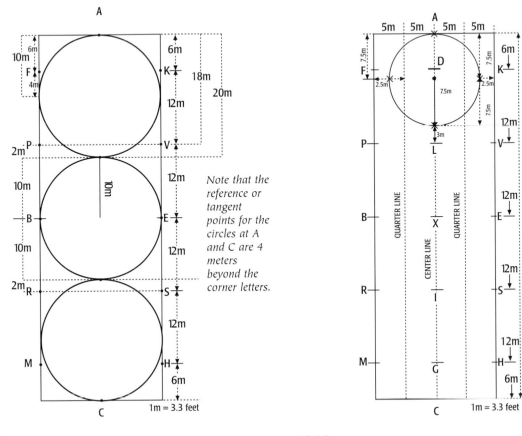

10.16

Standard arena: correct placement of 20-meter circles.

10.17

Standard arena: correct 15-meter circle at A.

The four reference points for a 20-meter circle in the middle of the standard arena are: 1) B; 2) 2 meters shy of the P to V line; 3) E; and 4) 2 meters shy of the S to R line. See fig. 10.16.

The four reference points for a 20-meter circle at A are: 1) A; 2) 4 meters past K; 3) 2 meters past the P to V line; and 4) 4 meters above F (so that you're 10 meters from the corner). See fig. 10.16.

For a 15-meter circle at A in a large arena, your reference points are: 1) A; 2) 2.5 meters in from the rail and 1.5 meters above the corner letter (so you are 7.5 meters from the corner); 3) 3 meters shy of the P to V line; 4) 2.5 meters in from the rail and 1.5 meters above the corner letter (so you are 7.5 meters from the corner). See fig. 10.17.

STANDARD ARENA

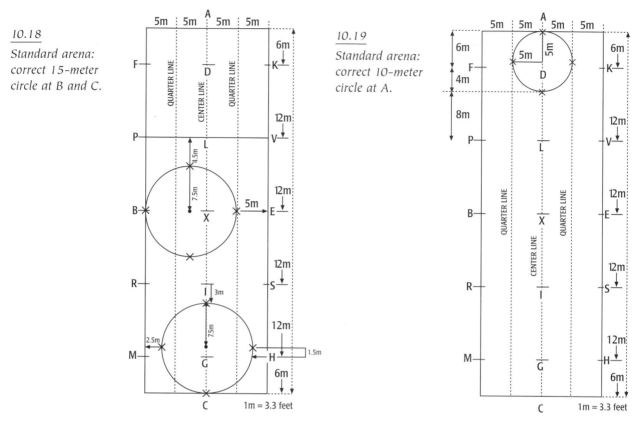

10.18

Standard arena: correct 15-meter circle at B and C.

10.19

Standard arena: correct 10-meter circle at A.

1m = 3.3 feet

For a 15-meter circle at B in a large arena, your reference points are: 1) B; 2) 4.5 meters shy of the P to V line; 3) the far quarterline; and 4) 4.5 meters shy of the R to S line. See fig. 10.18.

For a 10-meter circle at A in a large arena, your reference points are: 1) A; 2) the quarterline (aim for a point one meter before the corner letter so you hit that point when you are 5 meters from the short side); 3) 4 meters above D; 4) the quarterline (once again, aim for a point one meter before the corner letter so you touch that point when you are 5 meters from the short side). See fig. 10.19.

For a 10-meter circle at B in a large arena, your reference points are: 1) B; 2) 5 meters above the B to E line; 3) the centerline at X; and 4) 5 meters above the B to E line. Riders often make offset 10-meter circles

STANDARD ARENA

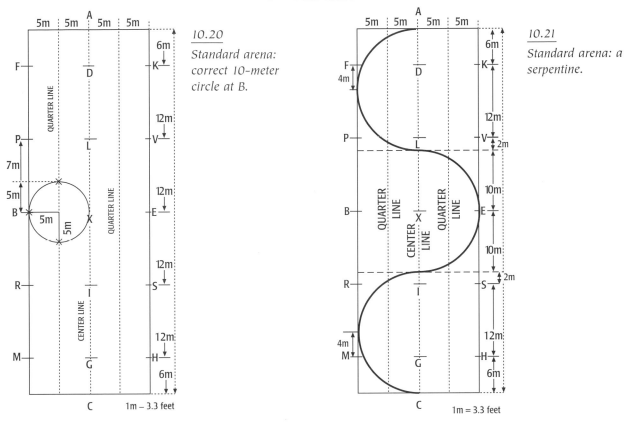

10.20

Standard arena: correct 10-meter circle at B.

10.21

Standard arena: a serpentine.

in competition and lose points. Their 10-meter circles are round, but the circles are displaced toward one end of the arena. See fig. 10.20.

A three-loop serpentine in the large arena consists of three 20-meter half-circles. Remember that circles and serpentines don't go into the corners. The serpentine itself begins and ends at A or C. If you begin at A, go into the corner before A and after you finish the serpentine at C. But as soon as you come to the beginning point (A or C), arc off the track and aim for your next reference point.

Follow the reference points for a 20-meter circle at A, and when you get to the centerline, switch direction and follow the reference points for the 20-meter circle in the middle of the arena. Once again when you reach the centerline, switch direction and follow the points for the 20-meter circle at C. In each case, change the bend before you change direction. See fig. 10.21.

KEY POINTS

🐎 The length of time it takes to warm up your horse will vary depending on a number of factors. The bottom line is that the warm-up should last as long as it takes to loosen and supple your horse's body and make him calm and attentive.

🐎 Ideally, the warm-up should be done in a deep frame so that there is a solid connection from back to front and the right muscles are being worked.

🐎 Exercises that belong in your warm-up include school figures, leg-yields, and lengthenings.

🐎 The heart of your session will be used to review and refine old work with the goal of increasing self-carriage in all of the gaits and movements.

🐎 Improve self-carriage with collecting half-halts, frequent transitions, smaller circles, and lateral movements that have a bend.

🐎 Always finish your session by doing something your horse enjoys and does well so that you end on a satisfying note.

🐎 The cooling-down period should also be ridden in a deep frame so that the horse's muscles are stretched and loosened and he won't be stiff and sore the next day.

🐎 As you progress through the levels of training, think of your goal as the systematic development of self-carriage, so that your horse can do his job more athletically and be more of a pleasure to ride.

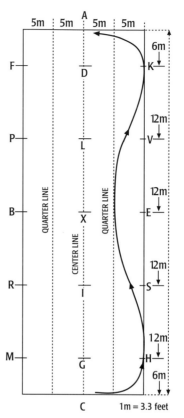

10.22
Standard arena: a shallow loop.

Along the same lines, you can ride a shallow loop down the long side. In this case, your reference points are: 1) H; 2) the quarterline across from E; and 3) K. If you're tracking left, arc off the wall at H with left bend. When you're midway between H and the quarterline across from E, begin to bend your horse to the right. When you are midway from the quarterline to K, smoothly change the bend back to the left. Don't allow the horse to be drawn back to the wall before the letter. Ride precisely to each point. See fig. 10.22.

Afterword

My horse, Eastwood (Woody), was six years old when I purchased him. The kindest way to describe him was that his body had an odd shape. In fact, Woody has the longest back I have ever seen on a horse! This peculiarity gave him a strange, overly rectangular look. In addition, he didn't have much muscle on his big, rangy frame, and this lack of development exaggerated his unique conformation and awkwardness.

Poor Woody! He suffered a lot of "verbal abuse" in the beginning. We heard all kinds of remarks, from the subtle comment of one of my peers who saw him and murmured, "Hmmm...interesting conformation," to the not so discreet gibes of my stable colleagues who said that in addition to my halter plate sporting the name "Eastwood," I needed a sign for his hindquarters that said "Westwood!" My own trainer took one look at him, sighed and said, "Well, I suppose when we get some muscle on him he won't look so terribly disgusting."

A year later, lots of spectators and competitors alike came up to me to say that they thought my new horse was just beautiful. Ah, revenge is sweet! Dressage allowed my ugly duckling to become a beautiful swan.

I hope that you have fun cross-training your own "duckling" with dressage. I'm convinced you'll find that not only can you mold and strengthen his body, but you'll also build a stronger bond and level of communication with your equine best friend.

Your goal in all your work with your horse is for him to move in a regular rhythm in all three paces, go forward with energy, travel straight, and accept a contact with your hands—the subject of Book One, *Cross-Train Your Horse: Simple Dressage for Every Horse, Every Sport.*

Once those Basics are solidly in place, most of your training will revolve around connection and collection—the material I've covered in this book.

Glossary

AHSA. The American Horse Shows Association: the national equestrian federation of the United States.

axis-straight. Refers to the straight horse's spine, which should overlap his line of travel. *See* **Straight.**

Basics, the. Rhythm, forward, and straightness. The Basics are the foundation for all correct work.

behind the leg. The horse doesn't respond promptly to light leg aids.

blend (half-halt). Combining the half-halt with another aid in order to keep the horse **on the bit** and maintain good balance during an exercise or movement.

Book One. *Cross-Train Your Horse: Simple Dressage for Every Horse, Every Sport* by Jane Savoie.

bridge. The connection over the horse's back that allows the unrestricted flow of energy from back to front.

cadence. A steady **tempo** showing marked accentuation of the rhythm and emphasized springiness.

change of lead through the trot. A downward transition from one canter lead into a few steps of trot followed immediately by an upward transition to the other canter lead.

collect. To gather your horse together so that he carries himself in a balanced way. A horse is collected when his center of gravity shifts more toward his hind legs and this is because he has engaged his hindquarters. This causes the hindquarters to lower and carry more weight so that the forehand lightens and appears higher than the hindquarters.

collected gaits. A walk, trot , and canter that show the horse **on the bit,** with the hind legs engaged and clearly in **self-carriage.** He covers less ground with each step than he does in the **medium** gaits, but his hind legs arc higher off the ground because the joints bend more markedly.

collecting half-halt. A short, simultaneous action of seat, legs, and hands that is used to improve the **self-carriage** of the horse. The collecting half-halt is only effective when a horse has first been put **on the bit** through the use of a **connecting half-halt**.

connect/connection. On the bit; when a horse is connected from back to front, energy can travel from the hind legs, over the back, through the neck, into the rider's hands and then be recycled back to the hind legs.

connecting half-halt. The primary three-second half-halt that is used to put your horse **on the bit**. Apply the driving aids, close the outside hand in a fist and (if necessary to keep the neck straight) vibrate the inside rein for three seconds. All other half-halts are variations of this basic one. *See* **collecting half-halt, increasing half-halt, preparatory half-halt, reversed half-halt.**

contact. When the horse stretches forward into the bit and accepts the taut rein as a means of communication with the rider.

counter-flexion. Flexion at the poll to the **outside.**

counter-suppling. An exercise that puts the horse "through" the **outside** of his body. The rider quickly but smoothly bends the horse's neck to the outside as she closes her outside leg while supporting with her **inside** rein and leg.

deep/deep frame. A horse whose silhouette shows the hind legs coming under the body, a raised back, a long neck, a low poll, and the nose ever so slightly behind the vertical but looking as if it is stretching toward the **contact**. A good position for warming up, cooling down, and teaching the horse to stay **connected** if he tends to come above the bit in an exercise.

engage/engaging. The bending and flexing of the joints of the hindquarters so that the angle between the bones is decreased. As a result, the croup lowers and the hindquarters bear more weight.

extended gait. At the trot and canter, a pace in which the horse, maintaining his **rhythm** and an **uphill balance**, lengthens his frame and covers as much ground as possible with each stride. At the walk, a pace that covers as much ground as possible without hurrying, showing greatest push from behind and maximum reach so that the hind feet touch the ground clearly in front of the footprints of the forefeet. The rider allows the horse to stretch out his head and neck but keeps a **contact** with his mouth.

extensions. *See* **Extended gaits.**

flexibility. The horse's ability to bend through his side equally easily to the left and to the right; the ability to move joints freely.

flying change. A change from one canter lead directly to the other canter lead; the flying change takes place during the period of suspension in the canter.

forward. One of **the Basics.** The direction the horse moves over the ground (i.e. forward as opposed to sideways).

frame. The outline or silhouette of the horse's body, showing his posture.

front to back. The *wrong* way to ride your horse; trying to force or manipulate the horse into a round frame by overuse of the hands.

half-halt. A hardly visible, almost simultaneous, coordinated action of seat, legs and hands that increases attention and improves balance and harmony. *See* **collecting half-halt, connecting half-halt, increasing half-halt, preparatory half-halt, reversed half-halt.**

half-pass. Haunches-in on a diagonal line; the horse is slightly bent around the **inside** leg, his body is parallel to the rail with his forehand slightly ahead of his hindquarters. The outside legs pass and cross in front of the inside legs and he looks in the direction of movement.

haunches-in (travers). The horse is slightly bent around the rider's inside leg. His front legs stay on the original track of the long side and his hindquarters are brought in off the track toward the center of the ring at about a 30-degree angle to the rail. His outside legs pass and cross in front of his inside legs and he looks in the direction he's moving.

haunches-out (renvers). This is the inverse movement of the haunches-in, with the tail to the wall instead of the head. Otherwise the same principles and conditions are applicable as in **haunches-in**.

horizontal balance. The horse's natural state of balance, with the center of gravity toward the forehand. He carries approximately 60% of his weight on his front legs and 40% of his weight on his hind legs. In horizontal balance, the withers and croup are basically the same height and the topline is parallel to the ground.

hot off the leg. The horse reacts promptly and enthusiastically to light leg aids; in front of the leg.

impulsion. Thrust. The horse gives the impression of carrying himself forward and springing off the ground. The elastic springing off the ground begins in the haunches with a bending of the joints of the hindquarters and culminates in very energetic gaits.

in front of the leg. *See* **hot off the leg.**

increasing half-halt. A modification of the basic **connecting half-halt**. It is used when the horse is either ignoring the half-halt or stiffening against the **outside** rein during the half-halt. Start with a light connecting half halt and increase the pressure of all the aids over the course of three seconds. *See* **connecting half-halt.**

inside. The direction or side toward which the horse is bent and/or flexed.

leg-straight. The hind feet follow in the exact same tracks as those made by the front feet. *See* **straightness.**

lengthenings. An exercise preliminary to extension. The horse lengthens his stride and frame while maintaining **rhythm**, **tempo,** and balance.

medium gaits. At the trot and canter, a pace at which the horse shows a length of stride and frame between that of **collection** and **extension.** He shows a more **uphill balance**, more forward and upward thrust, and more reaching than in the **working** gaits. The movement is rounder than that of an extended gait. At the walk, a free, regular, energetic yet calm walk of moderate lengthening. The hind feet touch the ground in front of the footprints of the forefeet.

moving from the hind legs into the hands. Connected; on the bit; correctly ridden from back to front so that the **frame** is round.

on the bit. The horse moves actively from behind through a **supple** back and accepts a light **contact** of the rein with no resistance. He yields in the jaw and poll to the rider's hand, has a **round** outline, and willingly responds to the rider's aids. *See* **connection, round.**

outside. The side of the horse's body opposite from the direction toward which he is bent and/or flexed.

over the back. *See* **through the back.**

packaged. Connected, on the bit, in a **round** shape.

preparatory half-halt. A quick, simultaneous action of seat, legs, and hands that is done to prepare the horse for a transition. The half-halt is timed so that it is given when the hind leg you want to engage is on the ground—that is, the **inside** hind leg for a downward transition and the **outside** hind leg for a canter depart.

putting on the bit. Using a three-second **connecting half-halt** to make your horse round.

rein of opposition. The outside rein.

renvers. *See* **haunches-in.**

reversed half-halt. A three-second half-halt that is used to correct the horse that is too light on the **inside** rein and too heavy on the **outside** rein, so that he takes an even **contact** with both hands. The legs and seat are used in the same way as they are in the basic **connecting half-halt**, but the inside hand closes in a fist and the outside hand vibrates to ask for a little **counter-flexion.**

rhythm. One of **the Basics**. The order of the footfalls or the "beat" of the pace (walk: 4-beat; trot: 2-beat; canter: 3-beat).

round/roundness/round outline, shape, or frame. The shape of the horse's outline or silhouette when the hind legs step well under the body, the back is raised, supple and looks convex, the neck is long and arched, and the horse stretches toward the **contact**. *See* **connection; on the bit.**

safe walk. A walk that always stays active and absolutely regular in **rhythm**.

self-carriage. The horse carries himself without balancing on the rider's hands. *See* **collection.**

shoulder-fore. A lateral movement that can be used as a **straightening** exercise. The horse is slightly bent around the **inside** leg and the forehand is brought in off the rail so that the inside hind leg steps in between the tracks of the front legs.

shoulder-in. A lateral movement that can be used as a **straightening, suppling** and **collecting** exercise. The horse is flexed to the **inside** and slightly bent around the inside leg. The forehand is brought in off the rail at approximately a 30 degree angle so that the inside hind leg is lined up directly behind the outside foreleg. The inside foreleg passes and crosses in front of the outside foreleg; the inside hind leg is placed in front of the outside hindleg. The horse looks away from the direction in which he is moving.

shoulder-out. A schooling exercise that is the mirror-image of **shoulder-in.** The horse is ridden on a line that is slightly to the inside of the rail. He is bent and flexed toward the rail and his forehand is brought closer to the rail. All of the same principles of shoulder-in apply.

simple change of lead. A downward transition from one canter lead directly into a few, clear steps of walk, followed by an upward transition to the other canter lead.

single track. *See* **work on a single track**

stilled seat. The aid that is used to signal the horse to slow his **tempo,** steady his **rhythm,** decrease his length of stride or do a downward transition. It is done by stretching up and tightening the abdominal muscles so that the seat stops following along with the horse's motion.

straight. One of **the Basics.** A straight horse is straight on lines and bent along the arc of curves, with his spine overlapping the line of travel and his hind feet stepping into the tracks of the front feet.

supple/suppleness. Pliability; free from stiffness or resistance; the ability to smoothly adjust carriage (longitudinally) and bend (laterally) without loss of flow of movement or balance.

suppling. An exercise used to reduce tension, loosen stiffness, teach acceptance of the rein, improve bending, or enhance connection.

tempo. The rate of repetition of the **rhythm.**

through the back. Over the back; a horse can only be through his back when he is **on the bit.** The back swings and looks convex rather than tight and hollow. See **throughness.**

through the horse's neck. A horse can only be "through his neck" when he is **on the bit.** The neck looks long and gracefully arched. *See* **throughness.**

throughness. The quality of being **on the bit, connected,** and having a **round frame;** the **supple,** elastic, unblocked, **connected** state of the horse's musculature that allows unrestricted flow of energy from back to front as well as the recycling of that energy back to the hind legs.

thrust. *See* **impulsion.**

travers. *See* **haunches-in.**

two tracks. *See* **work on two tracks.**

turn on the haunches. A 180 degree turn done at the walk. The horse bends in the direction of the turn and his forehand moves around his hindquarters. His forefeet and his outside hind foot move around his inside hind foot, which is picked up and put down slightly in front of the spot where it left the ground.

überstreichen. A clear release of contact, where the horse maintains **self-carriage, rhythm, tempo, straightness,** and the quality of the pace. In a one-handed überstreichen, the rider extends her inside hand forward up the horse's neck for three to four strides while keeping the **contact** on the outside rein. In a two-handed ubersteichen, the rider extends both of her hands up the crest of the neck toward her horse's ears.

uphill balance. The balance created by increased **engagement** (bending of joints) of the hind legs. The bending of the joints of the hind legs causes the hindquarters to lower. As the hindquarters lower, the forehand lightens and the horse's silhouette gives the appearance of an airplane taking off. The **self-carriage** shown by a horse in **collected, medium,** and **extended gaits.**

work on a single track. Work done going straight forward with the hind feet following in the tracks of the front feet, such as straight lines, school figures (circles, serpentines, figure eights, shallow loops), and transitions.

work on two tracks. Work done with the horse going forward and sideways at the same time such as **shoulder-fore, shoulder-in, shoulder-out, haunches-in, haunches-out,** and **half-pass.**

working gait. The trot or canter in which the young or uneducated horse shows good balance. In the trot, the horse moves energetically in a regular 2-beat **rhythm** and his hind feet step into the tracks made by the front feet. In the canter, he moves energetically in a regular 3-beat rhythm and his **inside** hind leg reaches well under his body.

Suggested Reading

The Achievement Zone, Shane Murphy, Putnam, 1996.

Advanced Dressage, Anthony Crossley, Trafalgar Square Publishing, 1996 (US)/ Swan Hill Press, 1995 (UK).

The Athletic Development of the Dressage Horse, Charles de Kunffy, Howell Book House, 1992 (US)/ Simon & Schuster UK, 1992 (UK).

Carriage Driving: A Logical Approach Through Dressage Training, Heike Bean, Howell Book House, 1992 (US)/ Prentice Hall UK, 1992 (UK).

Centered Riding, Sally Swift, Trafalgar Square Publishing, 1985 (US)/ Ebury Press, 1998 (UK).

The Classical Rider: Being at One with Your Horse, Sylvia Loch, Trafalgar Square Publishing, 1997 (US)/ J.A. Allen, 1997 (UK).

The Competitive Edge, Max Gahwyler, Half Halt Press, 1995.

Drawing on the Right Side of the Brain, Betty Edwards, Putnam, 1989 (US)/ Grafton Books, 1993 (UK).

Feel the Fear and Do It Anyway, Susan Jeffers, Fawcett, 1988 (US)/ Rider, 1991 (UK).

The Glossary of Dressage Judging Terms, United States Dressage Federation, 1993.

Heads Up!, Janet Edgette, Doubleday, 1996.

Horse Gaits, Balance and Movement, Susan E. Harris, Howell Book House, 1993 (US)/ Simon & Schuster UK, 1993 (UK).

Learn to Ride Using Sports Psychology, Petra and Wolfgang Hölzel, Trafalgar Square Publishing, 1996 (US)/ Kenilworth Press, 1996 (UK).

Lungeing and Long Reining, Jennie Loriston-Clarke, Half Halt Press, 1994 (US)/ Kenilworth Press, 1993 (UK).

My Horses, My Teachers, Alois Podhajsky, Trafalgar Square Publishing, 1997 (US)/ J.A. Allen, 1997 (UK).

The New Toughness Training For Sport, James Loehr, Dutton, 1995 (US)/ Atlantic Books, 1994 (UK).

1998-99 Dressage Division Rule Book, American Horse Shows Association, 1997.

101 Arena Exercises, Cherry Hill, Storey Communications, 1995.

Practical Dressage, Jane Kidd, Howell Book House, 1990 (US)/ Prentice Hall UK, 1994 (UK).

Practical Dressage Manual, Bengt Ljungquist, Half Halt Press, 1983 (US)/ Kenilworth Press, 1995 (UK).

Psychocybernetics, Maxwell Maltz, Wilshire, 1973.

The Psychology of Winning, Denis Waitley, Berkeley, 1986 (US)/ Simon & Schuster UK, 1989 (UK).

Ride With Your Mind: An Illustrated Masterclass in Right Brain Riding, Mary Wanless, Trafalgar Square Publishing, 1991 (US)/ Kenilworth Press, 1995 (UK).

Riding for the Rest of Us, Jessica Jahiel, Howell Book House, 1996 (US)/ Prentice Hall UK, 1996 (UK).

Riding Logic, Wilhelm Müseler, Simon & Schuster, 1985.

See You at the Top, Zig Ziglar, Pelican, 1994.

Seeds of Greatness: The Best Kept Secrets of Total Success, Denis Waitley, Revell, 1984 (US)/ Cedar, 1987 (UK).

That Winning Feeling!: Program Your Mind for Peak Performance, Jane Savoie, Trafalgar Square Publishing, 1992 (US)/ J.A. Allen, 1992 (UK).

Training Strategies for Dressage Riders, Charles de Kunffy, Howell Book House, 1994 (US)/ Simon & Schuster UK, 1994 (UK).

Training the Young Horse, Anthony Crossley, Trafalgar Square Publishing, 1994 (US)/ Stanley Paul, 1993 (UK).

What to Say When You Talk to Yourself, Shad Helmstetter, Grindle Press, 1986 (US)/ HarperCollins, 1991 (UK).

Index

Page numbers in *italic* indicate illustrations

Advanced Medium Level (UK), *206,* 213
Aids
    for bending, 5, 9-10
    blending, 145, 151-152, 193-198, *194-195,* 225
    for collecting half-half, 77, *78-80,* 226
    for connecting half-halt, 37-39, 226
    driving, 5, 9-10, 77, 80, *80*
    for flying change of lead, 161, 164-165, 174-175, 227
    for half-halt, 5-7, *6,* 9-10, 195, 227
    for half-pass, 117-118, 227
    for haunches-in, 108-109, 227
    for haunches-out, 113, *113,* 227
    for medium and extended gaits, 144, 228
    for shoulder-in, 95-96, *95-96, 97,* 229
    for shoulder-out, 104-105, *104-105, 229*
    for turn on the haunches, 128-130, 230
    See also Contact; Rein aids; Seat
"Air time," 159, *159,* 165
American Horse Shows Association (AHSA)
    on collected gaits, 71-72, 225
    on dressage tests, 206
    on extended medium and extended walk, 137-138
Axis-straightness, 167, 181, 182, 187, 225
"Back to front" riding, 5-6, 38
Balance
    and blending aids, 193-198, *194-195*
    connecting half-halt for, 193
    and extensions, 187
    horizontal, 30-33, *30-33, 60,* 66, 227
    uphill, 137, 149-150, 160, 230
Balkenhol, Klaus, 177, *178*
Basics of dressage
    defined, 4-5, 225
    for problem solving, 37, 177, *178*
    before self-carriage, 66
    for turn on the haunches, 131
    See also Contact; Forward movement; Rhythm; Straightness
Bean, Heike, *37*
"Behind the leg," 82, 225
Bending
    aids for, 5, 9-10
    and half-pass, maintaining during, 120-121, *121*
    and haunches-in, maintaining during, 109-111, *111*

    lateral movements and, 86-89, *87-88*
    and shoulder-in, maintaining during, 97-99, *98-99*
    troubleshooting, 197-198
    and turn on the haunches, maintaining during, 132-133
Blending aids
    for balance, 193-198, *194-195*
    into upward transitions, 145, 151-152
"Bridge" (back) of horse, 86, 225
"Bringing-to-attention." *See* Half-halt
Cameron, Lynda, *173, 188*
Canter
    collected, *71,* 71-72, *73*
    disunited, 162
    and haunches-in, 112, *112,* 191-192
    leads and shoulder-out, 104-105
    and leg-yielding, 192
    medium and extended, 142-143, *142-143,* 150, *151,* 211, *211*
    and shoulder-in, 192
    and shoulder-out, 191
    for Third Level, 213
    transitions, faulty, 190-193
    "unload" at, 150, *151*
    See also Counter-canter; Flying change of lead; Simple change of lead
Cellulosa, 34-36, *35*
Center of gravity (self-carriage), *58,* 58-59
"Chew the reins out of the hands," 40, *41,* 49
"Closed" hind leg, 46, *46-48*
"Coil the springs," 144
Collected gaits
    canter, *71,* 71-72, *73*
    described, *71-74,* 71-75, 225
    and driving aids, 77, 80, *80*
    and lengthenings, 81
    using rein-backs (backing up), 83
    rhythm and tempo, maintaining, 77, 80-81
    using school figures to develop, 81
    using transitions for, 81-83
    trot, 71, *71, 73, 140,* 211
    troubleshooting, 187-190, *188-190*
    visualization for, 82
    walk, 71, *71-72,* 138
    See also Lateral movements; Medium and extended gaits;

Self-carriage
Collecting half-halt, 25, 75-77, *76, 78-80,* 226
Combined-training, 36, *36,* 158
Combining aids. *See* Blending aids
Connecting half-halt, 25, 37-39, 75, 77, 193, 226
Connection
    appearance of, 28-33, *29-33*
    back to front riding, 5-6, 38
    and "behind the bit," 39, 50, *50*
    benefits for, 34-37, *35-37*
    "chew the reins out of the hands," 40, *41,* 49
    connecting half-halt, 25, 37-39, 75, 77, 193, 226
    and deep frames, 46-50, *46-50*
    described, 27-28, *28,* 226
    feeling of, 34
    for First Level, *209,* 209-210
    half-halt for, 10-13, *12-13*
    and horizontal balance, 30-33, *30-33*
    and lengthenings, 40
    muscling and, 39, *39*
    and self-carriage, *59,* 59-60, 65
    testing correctness of, *39-45,* 39-46
    "uphill" look of, *31*
    during warm-ups, 201
    See also Aids; Contact; Half-halt
Contact, 5, 208, *208,* 226
    See also Aids
Counter-canter
    for changing late behind, 165, 167, 172-174, *173*
    preparation for flying lead change, 160-161, *162*
Counter-suppling, 165-167, *166, 168-169,* 226
"Covering more ground," 135
    See also Lengthenings; Medium and extended gaits
"Cracks" legs, 149
Crookedness, 106, *107,* 150, 175, *175*
Cross-training with dressage. *See* Aids; Basics of dressage;
    Collected gaits; Connection; Lateral movements;
    Troubleshooting; Visualizations; Work sessions
*Cross-Train Your Horse: Simple Dressage for Every Horse,
    Every Sport* (Savoie), 4, 66, 85-86, 96, 135, 152, 155, 166,
    167, 199, 203, 223
Cutting horses and self-carriage, 55
"Dance," 115
Dean-Smith, Deb, *20-21, 32, 59, 93-94, 107, 127-130, 184-
    185*
Deep frames
    for connection, 46-50, *46-50,* 226
    for cooling-down, 201, 214
    for flying change of lead, 163, *163,* 164
    for troubleshooting, *179,* 179-180
    for warming-up, 201
De Puy, Mara, *56*
Direction, concept of, 89
"Door is closed," 205
Dover, Robert, 3, 10
Downward transitions
    for collected gaits, 82
    and flying change of lead, 159
    for medium and extended gaits, 152-153
    and shoulder-in, 103-104

Dressage
    arenas, 216-222, *216-222*
    for disciplines, other, 34, 36, *36,* 55, *56-57,* 158, 213
    tests, 205-213, *206-212*
    See also Aids; Basics of dressage; Collected gaits; Connec-
    tion; Lateral movements; Self-carriage; Troubleshooting;
    Visualizations; Work sessions
Driving aids, 5, 9-10, 77, 80, *80*
Dwight, *116-117, 122-124, 140-141, 156-158, 182*
Eastwood (Woody), *12-13, 23-24, 31,* 34-36, *35, 40, 40-45,
    62-64, 72-73, 78-80, 138-139, 142-143,* 164, 181, *194-
    195, 207-212,* 214, 223
Elementary Level (UK), 67, *206, 210-211,* 210-212
Elevating the forehand. *See* Self-carriage
"Embracing" horse's barrel, 108
Endurance horses and connection, 34, 55, *56,* 213
Engagement
    and collected gaits, 75-76, *76,* 226
    and half-pass, 121-123, *122-124*
    of hindquarters, 137, 146, 148
    increasing, *144,* 144-145, *146-147*
    lateral movements for, 86
    maintaining, 149-150, *151*
    for medium and extended gaits, 137, *144,* 144-150, *146-
    147, 151*
    "of-the-new-outside-hind-leg," 170-174, *171-173,* 191
    preventing loss of, 121-123, *122-124*
    See also Self-carriage
"Engaging" spot (leg position), 98, *98*
"Enveloping" horse's barrel, 108
Eros, *36*
Evasions. *See specific movements, hints for;* Troubleshooting
First Level, 66-67, *206, 209,* 209, 215, *215*
Flatwork. *See* Lateral movements
Flexion
    counter-flexion, 102, 165-167, *166, 168-169,* 226
    defined, 226
    lateral (poll), 10
    longitudinal, 10
    "overflexed," *32*
    school figures for, 36
Flying change of lead
    aids for, 161, 164-165, 174-175
    changing late, 165-174, *166, 168-174*
    collecting half-halts for, 160
    counter-flexion for, 102, 165-167, *166, 168-169,* 226
    and deep frames, 163, *163,* 164
    described, 158, 227
    "engagement-of-the-new-outside-hind-leg" exercises,
    170-174, *171-173,* 191
    faulty change, improving, 165-175, *166, 168-175*
    and half-pass, 170, *171*
    and haunches-in, 159, 170, *171*
    and haunches-out, 172-173, *173*
    hints for, 162-175, *163, 166, 168-173, 175*
    overview, 155-158, *156-158*
    preparatory half-halts for, 171-172, 174
    preparatory work for, *159-160,* 159-161
    and self-carriage, 159-160, *159-160*
    and shoulder fore, 159, 173-175, *175*
    and shoulder-in, 174

simple change of lead, 155, 159
straightness, maintaining, 175, *175*
teaching, 161-162
"tempi changes," 158
tension, dealing with, 162-164, *163*
for Third Level, 213
"throughness" exercises, 165-170, *166, 168-171*
and transitions, 159-160, 164, 174-175
and uphill balance, 160
visualization for, 160, *160,* 172, *172*
See also Counter-canter
"Forward and sideways." *See* Lateral movements
Forward movement
defined, 4, 227
"in front of the leg," 5, 17, 82-83, 227
thinking of, 4, 5
See also Straightness
Foss, Amy, *8-9, 14-17, 74, 104-105*
Fourth Level, *206,* 213
"Four tracks," 89
Frames. *See* Deep frames
"Front to back" riding, 6, 58, 60, *60,* 227
Front toe, flipping up, *63*
"Frozen" back, 28-30, *29*
Gaits. *See* Collected gaits; Medium and extended gaits
Galen, *59, 93-94, 107, 113, 127-130, 184-185*
Gathered together. *See* Self-carriage
Goldstern, *178*
"Go with" horse's motion, 119
Gray, Lendon, 3
"Guarding" effect of outside rein, 166, 167
"Half" (driving aids), 10
"Half-go," 3, 5, 18
See also Half-halt
Half-halt
aids for, 5-7, *6,* 9-10, 195, 227
"blend" into upward transition, 145, 151-152
collecting, 25, 75-77, *76, 78-80,* 160, 226
connecting, 25, 37-39, 75, 77, 193, 226
and connection, 10-13, *12-13*
described, 3-4, *4,* 227
"different," 25-26
hints for, *18,* 18-25, *20-21, 23-25*
increasing and outside hand, 22-25, *23-25,* 227
inside rein, how much to use, 7-9, *8-9*
and leg-yielding, 19-22, *20-21*
and lengthenings, *18,* 18-19
as marriage of aids, 9-10
mistakes, common, *14-17,* 15-18
and neck of horse, 19, 20, 22, 38
preparatory, 25, 171-172, 174, 196
preparing to give, 4-14, *5-9, 11-13*
prerequisites for, 4-5
and relaxation, 7, 18
reversed, 25-26, 181, *182,* 228
teaching the horse, 10, 14
timeline, 7
and transitions, 10, 25, 195
visualization for, 6, *6*
during warm-ups, 202
See also Connection

Half-pass
aids for, 117-118, 227
bend, maintaining, 120-121, *121*
described, 115, *115-117,* 227
engagement, preventing loss of, 121-123, *122-124*
and flying change of lead, 170, *171*
and haunches-in, 120-121, *121*
hints for, 118-125, *119, 121-125*
impulsion, maintaining, 118-119
and leg-yielding, 120
places and patterns for, 115-116, *118*
and shoulder-fore, 118, 121
and shoulder-in, 121
and shoulders, influence on, 125-126
tempo, maintaining, 119-120
for Third Level, 213
"too-little-sideways" correction, 123-125, *125*
"too-much-sideways" correction, 122
visualization for, 118, *119,* 124-125, *125*
"Halt" (outside rein), 10
Halts, full, 152
"Hand-riding," 38, 39
Hart, Becky, 213
Haunches-in
aids for, 108-109, 227
angle, maintaining, 111
bend, maintaining, 109-111, *111*
and cantering, 112, *112,* 191-192
and crooked horses, 106, *107*
described, 90, *91,* 106-107, *106-107,* 227
and flying change of lead, 159, 170, *171*
and half-pass, 120-121, *121*
hindquarters, controlling, 111, *111*
hints for, 109-111, *110*
and leg-yielding, 108, 110
rhythm and tempo, maintaining, 109
for Second Level, 211
and shoulder-in, 111, *111*
for straightening and strengthening, 183-187, *184-187*
and turn on the haunches, 131, 134-135
visualization for, 110, *110*
Haunches-out, 90, 113, *113,* 227
"Head-and-neck-in," 100, *100,* 102
"Head-set" riding, 6, 58, 61
Head-to-the-wall leg-yielding, *90*
Hickey, Chris, *116-117, 122-124, 140-141, 156-158, 182*
Hindquarters
as "bridge" connecting to front end, 86, 225
and collected gaits, 75-76, *76*
engagement of, 137, 146, 148
as "engine," 6, 27, *28*
and haunches-in, 111, *111*
and self-carriage, 58
Hopper, *56*
Horizontal balance, 30-33, *30-33,* 60, 66, 227
Horses
attention of, 3, 28
conformation and self-carriage, 67
and connection, 28, *29*
and disciplines, 34, 36, *36,* 55, *56-57,* 158, 213
one-sidedness of, 101-102, 180-181
topline and connection, 39, *39*

"Hot off the leg," 83, 159, 164, 227
Hunters and connection, 34, 158
Huntington Farm (Vermont), *64*
Imagery. *See* Visualizations
Impulsion. *See* Thrust
Increasing half-halt, 22-25, *23-25*, 227
"In front of the leg," 5, 17, 82-83, 227
Inside, 86, *113*, 228
Joffrey, *173, 188*
Jumpers and connection, 36, *36*, 55, *56*, 158, 213
Kousteau, *101, 146-147, 188*
Kursinski, Anne, *36*, 213
Lateral movements
    arenas for, 88
    and bending, 86-89, *87-88*
    "inside," 86, *113*, 228
    for obedience to aids, 85
    "outside," 86, *113*, 228
    paces for, 88, 89, 115
    and precision, 88
    for self-carriage, 36, 205
    tracks, 89-91, *89-91*, 106, *107*
    for warming-up, 85
    See also Deep frames; Half-pass; Haunches-in;
    Haunches-out; Leg-yielding; Shoulder-fore; Shoulder-in;
    Shoulder-out; Turn on the haunches; Turn on the fore-
    hand
Leads (canter). *See* Flying change of lead; Simple change of
    lead
Left behind the movement, 119, 132
Leg-yielding
    "four tracks," 89
    and half-halt, 19-22, *20-21*
    and half-pass, 120
    and haunches-in, 108, 110
    head-to-the-wall position, *90*
    and shoulder-in, *87*, 93, 97, *99*
    for warming-up, 22, 86, 203, *203*
    when cantering, 192
Lengthenings
    for collected gaits, 81, 228
    and connection, 40, 228
    and half-halt, *18*, 18-19
    for Second Level, 210
    and shoulder-in, *96*
    during work sessions, 203-204
Lighter in the hands. *See* Self-carriage
"Little bit more," 204
"Loading of the hind legs." *See* Self-carriage
Longitudinal bending. *See* Deep frames
McCutcheon, Scott, *57*
Mastermind, *29, 47-48, 68-69, 163, 166, 168-169, 186*
"Match" driving aids and outside hand, 17
Medium and extended gaits
    aids for, *144*, 228
    on the bit, 151-152, 228
    blend half-halt into upward transition, 145, 151-152
    canter, 142-143, *142-143*, 150, *151*, 211, *211*
    collection, transition downward to, 152-153
    described, 135-137, *136-137*, 228
    diagonal legs, keeping parallel, 148-149, *148-149*

engagement, increasing, *144*, 144-145, *146-147*
engagement, maintaining, 149-150, *151*
extension, developing bigger, 146, 148
hints for, *144*, 144-153, *146-149*, *151*
and lengthenings, comparison, 135-137, *136-137*
and shoulder-fore, 153
and shoulder-in, 145, 150
and transitions, 145, 151-153
trot, 139-141, *140-141*, *144*, 148-149, *148-149*, 211
uphill balance, 137, 149-150
visualization for, 137, *137*, 145, *146*, 149, *149*
walk, 137-139, *139*
Medium Level (UK), *206*, *212*, 212-213, 215, *215*
Monique, *20-21*
"Moving from the hind legs into the hands." *See* Connection
Moxie, *30, 32, 91*
Novice Level (UK), 66-67, *206*, 209, *209*, 215, *215*
"Obsessing," 163
"Off the bit," *29*, 36-37
Olympic Bonfire, 180
One-sidedness, 101-102, 180-181
"On the bit." *See* Connection
"Open" hind leg, 46, *46-48*
Outside, 86, *113*, 228
"Out the back door" (hind legs), 152
"Overflexed," *32*
"Over the back." *See* Connection
"Packaged," 134
    See also Connection; Self-carriage
"Passage-y" trot, 81
Piaffe and self-carriage, *57*
"Play days," 190, 203
Pleasure horses and connection, 34
Podhajsky, Alois, 27
Poll flexing (laterally), 10
Poulsen, Ruth, *29, 47-48, 68-69, 163, 166, 168-169, 179, 186*
Preliminary Level (UK), 66, *206-208*, 208
Preparatory half-halt, 25, 171-172, 174, 196
"Promising more in front than delivering behind," 149
Putting the horse on the bit, *209*, 209-210, 228
Quarter Horses and self-carriage, 67
Rebalancing, 4, *5*, 10, *11*
    See also Connection; Half-halt
Rein aids
    "chew the reins out of the hands," 40, *41*, 49
    "guarding" effect of outside rein, 166, *167*
    inside rein, how much to use, 7-9, *8-9*
    "take the reins out of the hands," 208, *208*, 211
    uneven in the rein, 180-181, *182*
    See also Aids
Rein backs (backing up), 83
Reining horses and self-carriage, 55, *57*, 213
Reis, Dennis, 213
Renvers. *See* Haunches-out
Reversed half-halt, 25-26, 181, *182*, 228
Rhythm
    defined, 4, 228
    for haunches-in, maintaining, 109
    maintaining, 77, 80-81
    for turn on the haunches, maintaining, 131, *131*

Riding
back to front, 5-6, 38
crooked, 181, 183
front to back, 6, 58, 60, *60*, 227
"hand-riding," 38, 39
"head-set" riding, 6, 58, 61
school figures accurately, 202-203, 216-217
and work sessions, 203, *203*
Rockwell, Gary, 164
"Round outline, shape, or frame." *See* Connection
"Rubber band effect," 203
Rupert, 214
"Safe" walk, 88, 108, 112, 229
School figures
for collected gaits, 81
for flexibility and suppleness, 36
riding accurately, 202-203, 216-217
Schooling sessions. *See* Work sessions
Seat
driving, 77
"stilled," 82, 130, 192, 229
and tempo, controlling with, 119-120
See also Aids
Second Level, 67, *206, 210-211,* 210-212
Self-carriage
appearance of, *60,* 60-61, *62-64*
and center of gravity, *58,* 58-59
and conformation of horse, 67
and connection, comparison, *59,* 59-60
described, 55-57, *56-57,* 229
feeling of, 61, *65,* 65-66
and flying change of lead, 159-160, *159-160*
and hindquarters, 58
and horizontal balance, 32, *33, 60,* 66
piaffe and, *57*
prerequisites for, 66
for Second Level, 211, *211*
shoulder-in for, 103-104
timetable for, 67-69, *68-69*
and transitions, 61, 65, 205
turn on the haunches for, 134
"uphill" look of, 61, *62,* 103
visualization for, 65
during warm-ups, 59-60
when to ask for, *66,* 66-67
during work sessions, 204-205
See also Connection; Lateral movements; Medium and extended gaits
Shifting the center of gravity. *See* Self-carriage
Shoulder-fore
described, 90, *90, 91,* 229
and flying change of lead, 159, 173-175, *175*
and half-pass, 118, 121
for medium and extended gaits, 153
and shoulder-in, comparison, 92, 96
and turn on the haunches, 133
Shoulder-in
aids for, 95-96, *95-96, 97*
angle, maintaining, 100, *100*
for balance and extensions, 187
bend, maintaining, *97-99, 98-99*

for cantering, 192
and counter-flexing, 102
described, *87-88,* 90, *90,* 93-94, *93-94,* 229
and flying change of lead, 174
and half-pass, 121
and haunches-in, 111, *111*
hints for, 96-104, *98-101*
and leg-yielding, *87,* 93, 97, *99*
and lengthenings, 96
for medium and extended gaits, 145, 150
and rein aids, 96, *97*
for Second Level, 211
for self-carriage, 103-104
and shoulder-fore, comparison, 92, 96
shoulders, controlling, *100-101,* 100-103
for straightening and strengthening, 92
tempo, maintaining, 96-97
and transitions, downward, 103-104
uses of, 92, *92*
visualization for, 96, 97-98, *98,* 100, *100,* 103
at walk, 96-97
Shoulder-out, 104-105, *104-105,* 191, 229
"Shoulders up," 103
Simple change of lead, 81, 155, 159, 211, 229
"Single track," 89, 90, 230
"Sitting down behind," 76, *76*
Soft (weak) side of horse, 101-102, 180-181
Spanish Riding School of Vienna, 27
Special Effects, *8-9, 14-17, 74, 87, 90, 91, 104-105*
"Speeding up the tempo" with seat, 120
"Stepping down" into the stirrup, 118, 132
"Stepping into the hands," 65
"Stepping through the hand," 18
Stiff (strong) side of horse, 102, 180-181
"Still" the seat, 82, 130, 192, 229
Straightness
axis-straight, 167, 181, 182, 187, 225
described, 4, 6, *90,* 229
during flying change of lead, 175, *175*
haunches-in for, 183-187, *184-187*
shoulder-in for, 92
See also Lateral movements
Strengthening, 92, 183-187, *184-187*
Stretching. *See* Warm-ups
"Sucking back," 109
Suppling
counter-suppling, 165-167, *166, 168-169,* 226
defined, 229
school figures for, 36
shoulder-in for, 92
See also Lateral movements; Transitions
"Swimmy" trot, 81
"Take the reins out of the hands," 208, *208,* 211
Tempo
for half-pass, maintaining for, 119-120
for haunches-in, maintaining, 109
maintaining, 77, 80-81, 229
seat, controlling with, 119-120
for shoulder-in, maintaining, 96-97
"Thin air," 146
"Thinking" forward, 4, 5

Third Level, *206, 212,* 212-213, 215, *215*
"Three" tracks, 106, *107*
"Throughness," *209,* 209-210, 229-230
    See also Connection
Thrust, 146, 209, *209*
    See also Forward movement
"Tracking to the left, right," 89
Tracks, 89-91, *89-91,* 106, *107*
"Tracks up," 89
Training Level, 66, *206-208,* 208
Transitions
    blending aids and, 145, 151-152
    for canter, 190-193
    collected gaits and, 81-83
    and flying change of lead, 159-160, 164, 174-175
    half-halt and, 10, 25, 195
    for medium and extended gaits, 145, 151-153
    preparatory half-halts and, 196
    self-carriage and, 61, 65, 205
    shoulder-in and, 103-104
    "transition on the bit," 195
    troubleshooting, *194-195,* 194-197
"Trap" hind leg, 97-98, *98,* 133
Travers. *See* Haunches-in
Trot
    collected, 71, *71, 73, 140,* 211
    disconnected, 81
    for lateral movements, 88, 89
    medium and extended, 139-141, *140-141, 144,* 148-149, *148-149,* 211
    for Third Level, 213
    "tracks up," 89
Troubleshooting
    balance (blending aids), 193-198, *194-195*
    balance and extensions (shoulder-in), 187
    and the basics, 177-178, *178*
    bend changes, 197-198
    canter transitions, faulty, 190-193
    collected and extended gaits, 187-190, *188-190*
    crookedness, 180-190, *182, 184-190*
    with deep frames, *179,* 179-180
    rider created crookedness, 181, 183
    straightening and strengthening (haunches-in), 183-187, *184-187*
    tension and tightness, *179,* 179-180
    transitions, *194-195,* 194-197
    uneven in the rein, 180-181, *182*
"Tuesdayish," 203, *203*
Turn on the forehand, 86
Turn on the haunches
    aids for, 128-130
    bend, maintaining, 132-133
    described, 126-127, *126-130,* 230
    and haunches-in, 131, 134-135
    hind legs, controlling, 133-134
    hints for, *131,* 131-134
    rhythm, maintaining, 131, *131*
    for Second Level, 211
    for self-carriage, 134
    and shoulder-fore, 133
    size of turn, adjusting, 132

tension, reducing, 131, *131*
visualization for, 126, *126,* 131, *131*
and walk pirouette, 126-127
"Two tracks," 89, 90, *90-91,* 230
Überstreichen
    one-handed, 44, *44-45, 211,* 211-212, 230
    two-handed, 213, 230
Uphill
    balance, 137, 149-150, 160, 230
    look of, *31,* 61, *62,* 103
"Up" in front. *See* Self-carriage
Upward transitions
    "blend" half-halt into, 145, 151-152
    and flying change of lead, 159
van Grunsven, Anky, 180
Visualizations
    for collected gaits, 82
    for flying change of lead, 160, *160,* 172, *172*
    for half-pass, 118, *119,* 124-125, *125*
    for halt-halt, 6, *6*
    for haunches-in, 110, *110*
    for medium and extended gaits, 137, *137,* 145, *146,* 149, *149*
    for self-carriage, 65
    for shoulder-in, *96,* 97-98, *98,* 100, *100,* 103
    for turn on the haunches, 126, *126,* 131, *131*
    for work sessions, 203, *203*
"Wake-up" call, 119
Walk
    collected, 71, *71-72, 138*
    for lateral movements, 88
    medium and extended, 137-139, *139*
    pirouette, 126-127
    "safe," 88, 108, 112, 229
Warm-ups
    and lateral movements, 85
    and leg-yielding, 22, 86, 203, *203*
    and self-carriage, 59-60
    during work sessions, 199, 201-204, *203*
"Weight-lift," 183, *188,* 189-190, *190*
Weiss, Kelly, *101, 146-147, 189*
Western horses and self-carriage, *57,* 155, 158
Work sessions
    arenas, large (standard), 217-222, *217-222*
    and connection, 201
    cool-downs, 200, 214, *214*
    and deep frame, 201, 214
    and half-halts, 202, 205
    and leg-yielding, 203, *203*
    lengthenings and shortenings, 203-204
    middle of, 199-200, 204-213, *206-212*
    overview, 199-200, *201*
    progressive levels of dressage, 205-213, *206-212*
    samples, 215, *215-216*
    school figures, riding accurately, 202-203, 216-217
    and self-carriage, 204-205
    visualization for, 203, *203*
    warm-ups, 199, 201-204, *203*
Zapatero, 145

Illustration Credits

PHOTOGRAPHS

All photographs are taken by Rhett B. Savoie unless otherwise noted.

DRAWINGS

Susan E. Harris:
Pages: 5; 11; 33; 39; 46; 50; 57; 58 (top); 60; 65; 71; 88; 92; 94; 95; 96; 99; 100 (bottom); 106; 107; 110 (bottom); 111, 113, 115, 121; 126 (top); 136; 144; 148; 163; 185.

Patricia Peyman Naegeli:
Pages: 4; 6; 18; 25; 28; 58 (bottom); 66; 76; 89; 90; 96; 97; 98; 100 (top); 110 (top); 112; 118; 119; 125; 126 (bottom); 131; 137; 146; 149; 159; 160; 170; 171; 172; 175; 187; 190; 200; 203; 214.